I0795987

IMAGES
of America

NORTH PLAINFIELD

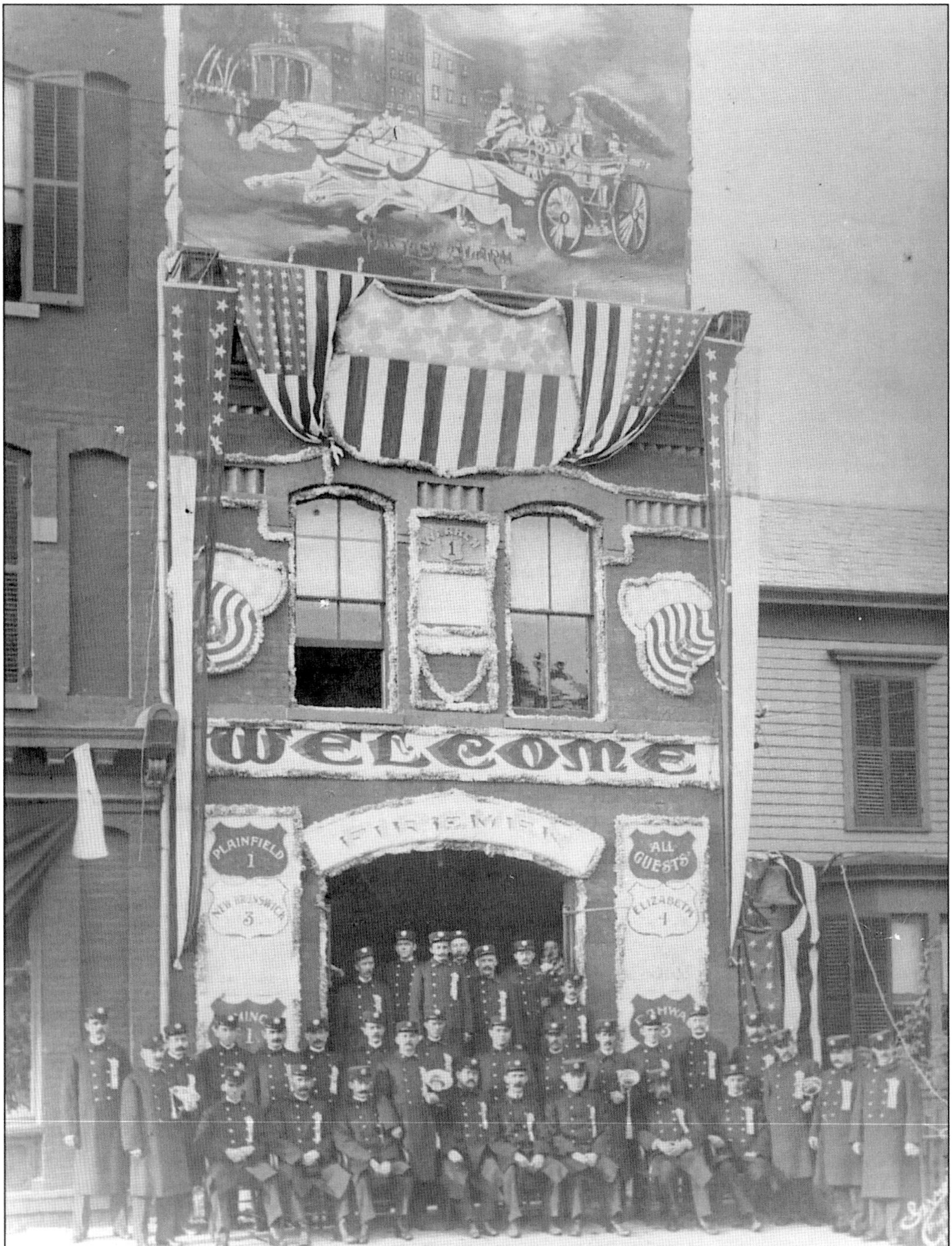

The Warren Engine Company members are ready for a parade. The firehouse of the Warren Engine Company was built in 1869 on Somerset Street. All the firemen were volunteers. They took pride in their red shirts, their helmets, and their speed in getting to the scene of a fire. Until 1904, the men of the Warren Engine Company answered the fire alarms in the borough.

IMAGES
of America

NORTH PLAINFIELD

Mario Caruso, Bruce Ryno,
and Joann Kohler

ARCADIA
PUBLISHING

ISBN 978-0-7385-0005-8

Published by Arcadia Publishing
Charleston, South Carolina

Printed in the United States of America

Library of Congress Catalog Card Number: 2007924639

For all general information contact Arcadia Publishing at:
Telephone 843-853-2070
Fax 843-853-0044
E-mail sales@arcadiapublishing.com
For customer service and orders:
Toll-Free 1-888-313-2665

Visit us on the Internet at www.arcadiapublishing.com

Dedicated to Marion Milne and Harold Jeffrey

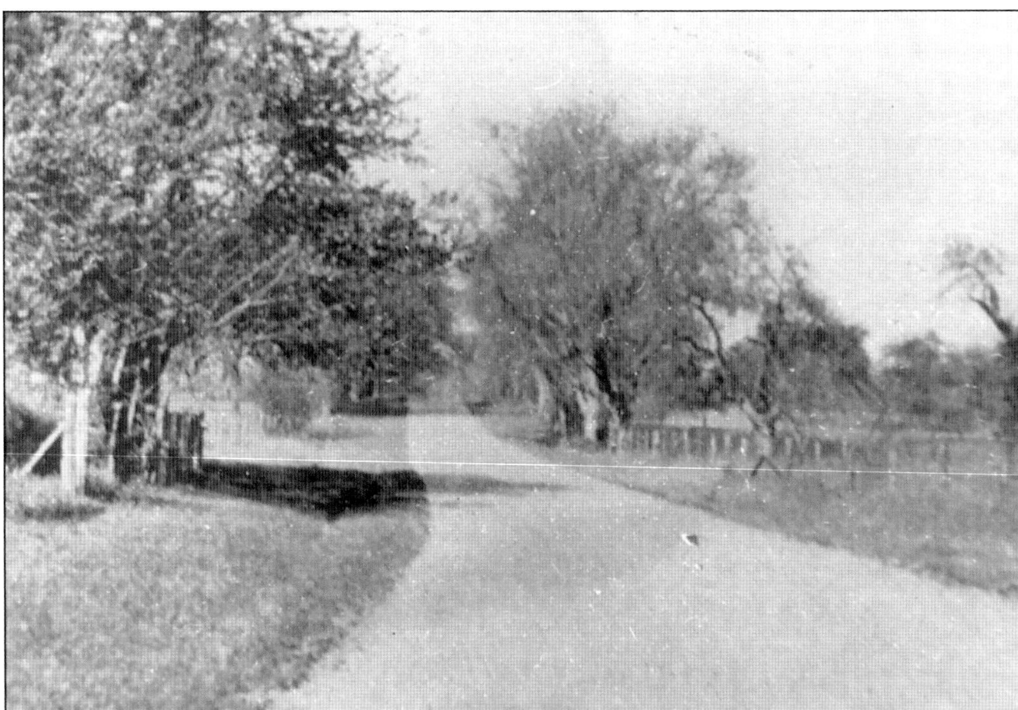

This lonely country road seemed so quiet and peaceful when this picture was taken pre-1920. Cows could be seen grazing in the pasture along this stretch of Greenbrook Road.

Contents

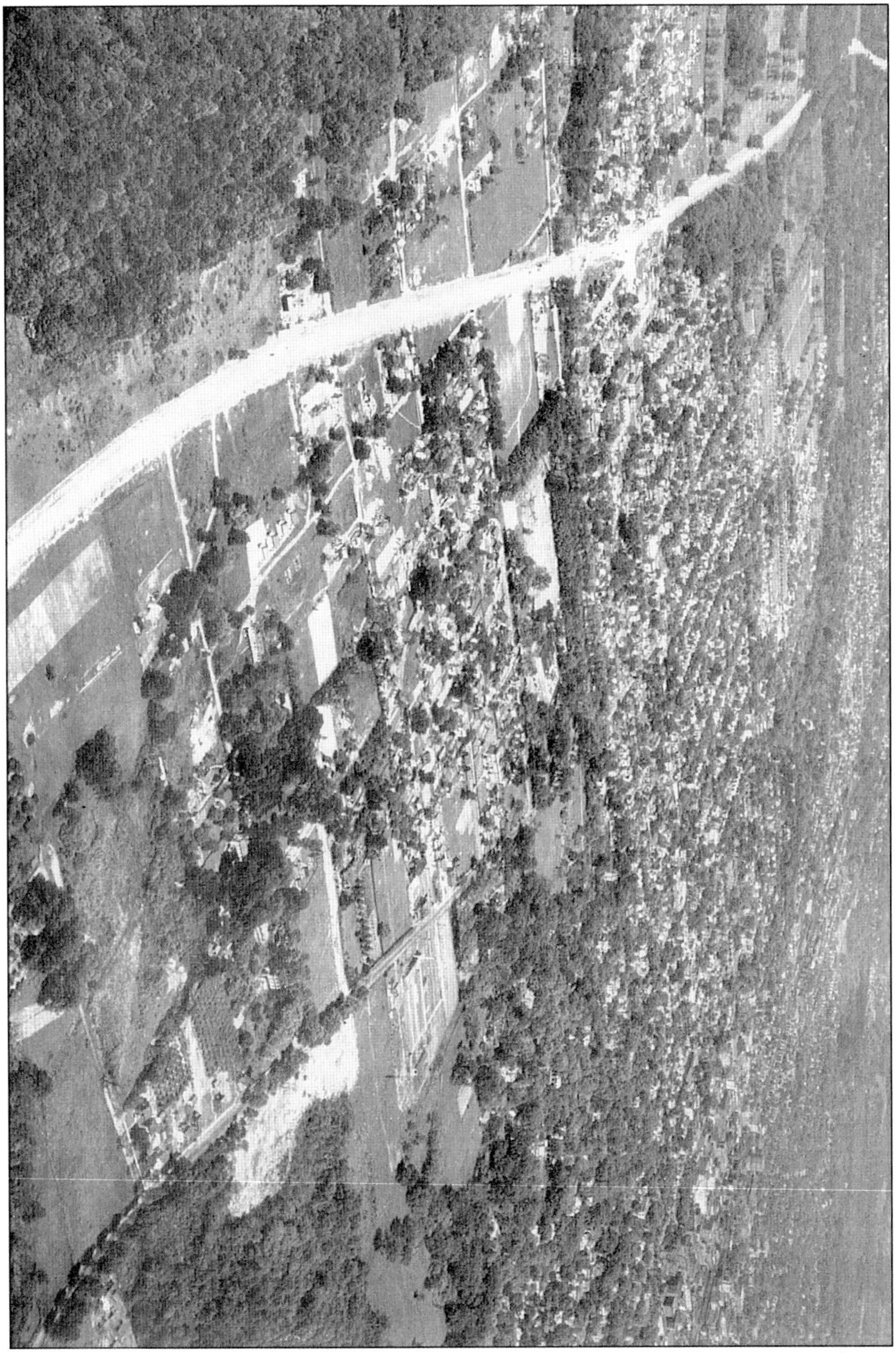

This 1930 aerial view of North Plainfield shows Route 29 passing through this rural area that has considerably fewer homes and businesses.

INTRODUCTION

Nestled in the northeast corner of Somerset County lies the small borough of North Plainfield. It is bordered on the northwest by the first ridge of the Watchung Mountains; the Green Brook provides a natural boundary between Union and Somerset Counties on the south and east. Rock Avenue, on the west, divides the towns of North Plainfield and Green Brook.

The first settlers could be found coming to the Plainfield area in the latter part of the 17th century. Primarily a farming community, the growth of this borough was stimulated by the many mills and quarries built along the brooks. During the Revolutionary War, there were several operating mills in the North Plainfield area. The earliest mill was started *c.* 1755; by 1782, it moved to Somerset Street on what is now the boundary of North Plainfield and Plainfield.

Originally, Somerset County operated as a single township. In 1769, by Royal charter, Bernard Township was formed out of the northern precinct of the county. On March 5, 1806, Warren was created as a separate township, composed of the present-day North Plainfield, Warren, Green Brook, and Watchung.

On April 2, 1872, an act of the New Jersey Legislature was passed which divided North Plainfield Township from the Township of Warren. This new township included the towns of North Plainfield, Watchung, and Green Brook. North Plainfield was set off from the township in the year 1885 when a vote was taken to change the local government from a township to a borough. Watchung followed in 1926 and Green Brook in 1932.

With the coming of the Jersey Central Railroad in the 1850s, the population of North Plainfield started to change. Jumping from 75 people in 1832 to 4,000 in 1885, the railroad brought many New York commuters to locate in the borough and take advantage of the beautiful country environment. Today, approximately 19,000 people make this "Proud Community" their home.

ACKNOWLEDGMENTS

We wish to express our sincere appreciation to all those in the community who have generously shared their memories, photographs, maps, and knowledge of North Plainfield, which made possible the writing of this book. Any errors or omissions are entirely unintentional. Thank you to: Ed Apgar, Janice Allen, the Harold Blackford Collection, the Blue Hills Historical Society, the Borough of North Plainfield, the Church of the Holy Cross, the Paul Collier Collection, Roger Carroll, Frank Caruso, Louis Caruso, Mario Caruso, Pat Ciarlariello, Bea Clark, Camille Corona, Howard Dietzman, Echo Sentinel, Shirley Ferri, Lois Force, Richard Gain, George Hammond, James Harper, Carolyn Hummel Jansen, the Harold Jeffrey Collection, Bill Jennings, Joann Kohler, Eleanor Leiss, Vince Lewis, Joan Long, Anne Luley, Sr. Virginia McGarry, Ben Marchio, Janice Fox McKee, Pio DeMatteo, Al Meissner, the Marion Milne Collection, Sue Taylor Monroe, Mount Saint Mary's, North Plainfield Exempt Firemen, the North Plainfield Fire Department, the North Plainfield High School Alumni Association, the North Plainfield Public Library, the North Plainfield Police Department, Steve Novak Jr., Nancy Piwowar, the Plainfield Public Library, Paul Rabidau, Janet Rasmussen, Angelo Rosato, Anthony Rosato, Bruce Ryno, Sr. Mary Theresa McCarthy, Jim Satterlee, Alan Snyder, Herb Snyder, St. Joseph's Church, Stine family, the *Courier-News*, the Thorn Photo Collection, the Vermeule Community Center, John Vitelli, Fran Vitelli, the Watchung Public Library, the Wish family, Jack Wilson, and Bernice Zimmerman. A special thank you to the Washington Park Historical Society and Fred Sheeler.

One

BEGINNINGS

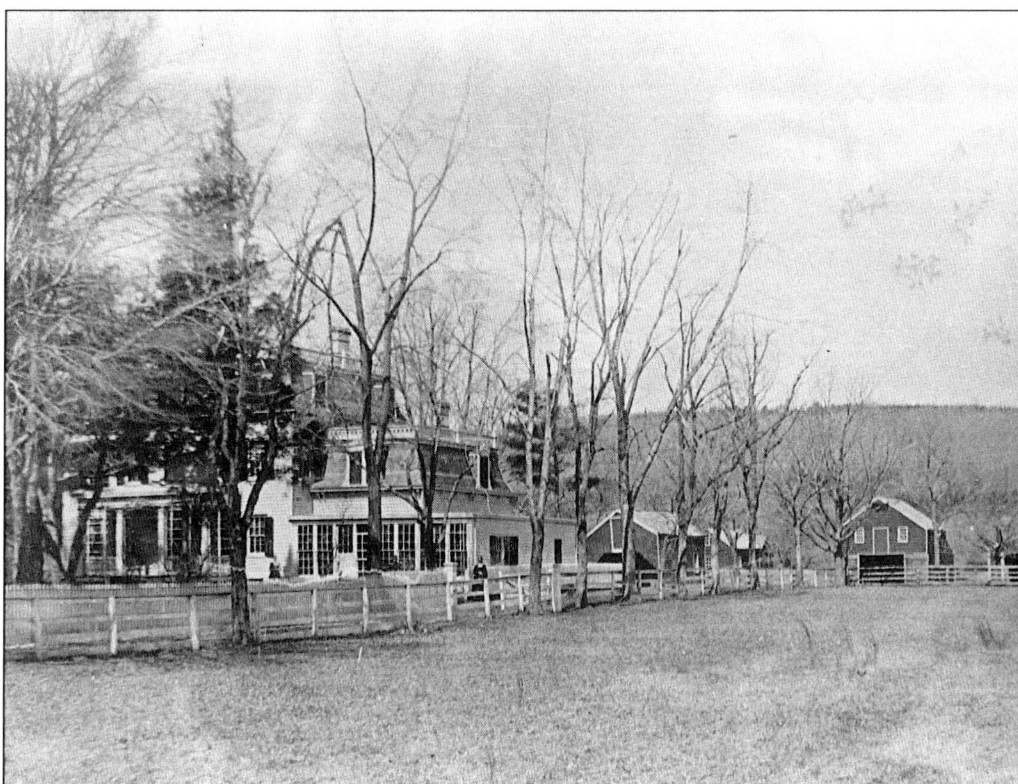

The Brunson Farm, shown above, stood on part of the 1,200 acres owned by Cornelius Vermeule Sr. The original Dutch farmhouse of the Vermeule family, built in 1736 by Cornelius and Frederick Vermeule, was located near the intersection of Clinton Avenue and Greenbrook Road, along the path to the "rock." They named this land "The Blue Hills Plantation." Records indicate the old homestead burned and was later torn down to build the new house.

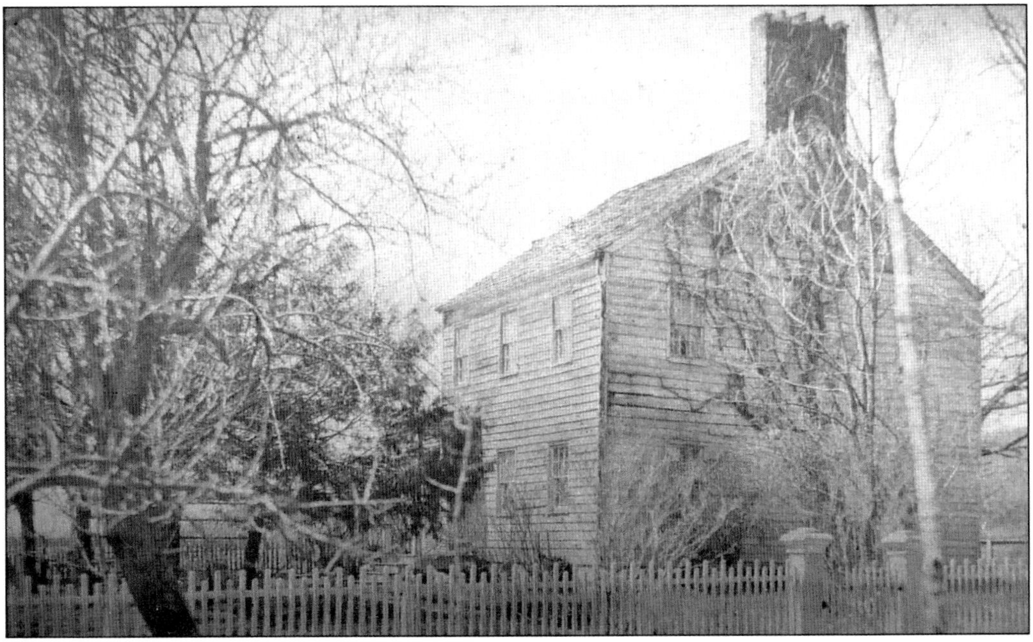

Cornelius Cadmus purchased 1,200 acres of land from King George of England in 1734 and built the original Cadmus house. The house stood on Crosson Place near Greenbrook Road. Cadmus was the brother-in-law to Cornelius Vermeule.

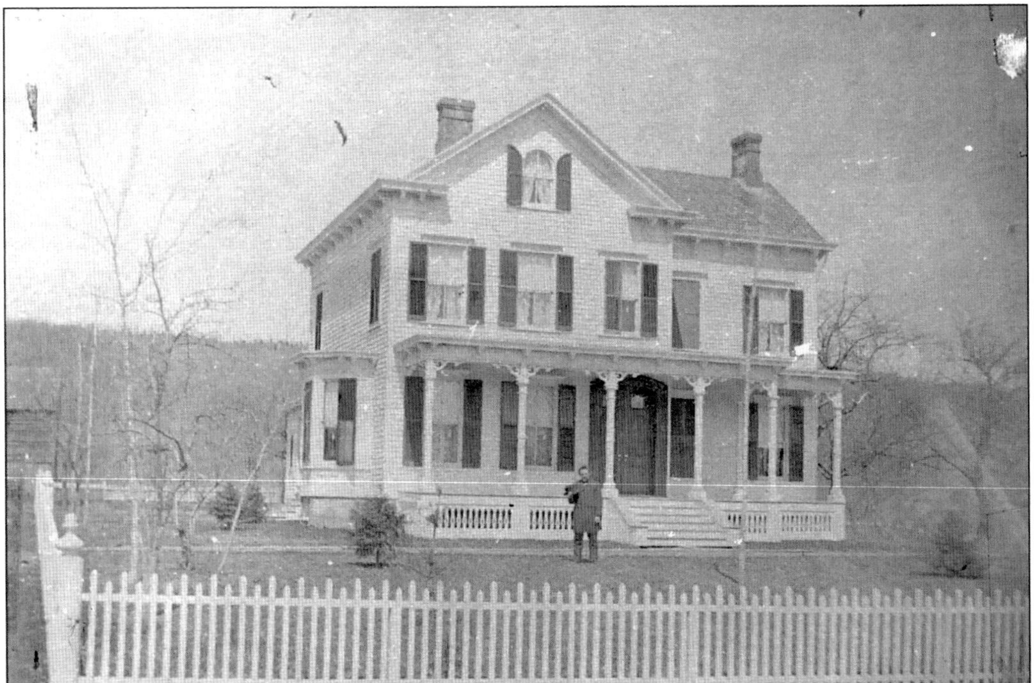

The home of Rutgers V. Cadmus, son of Cornelius Cadmus, was built in 1878 on the same tract of land originally owned by the pioneer Cadmus family. The house remains much the same as when it was built; few changes were made through the years.

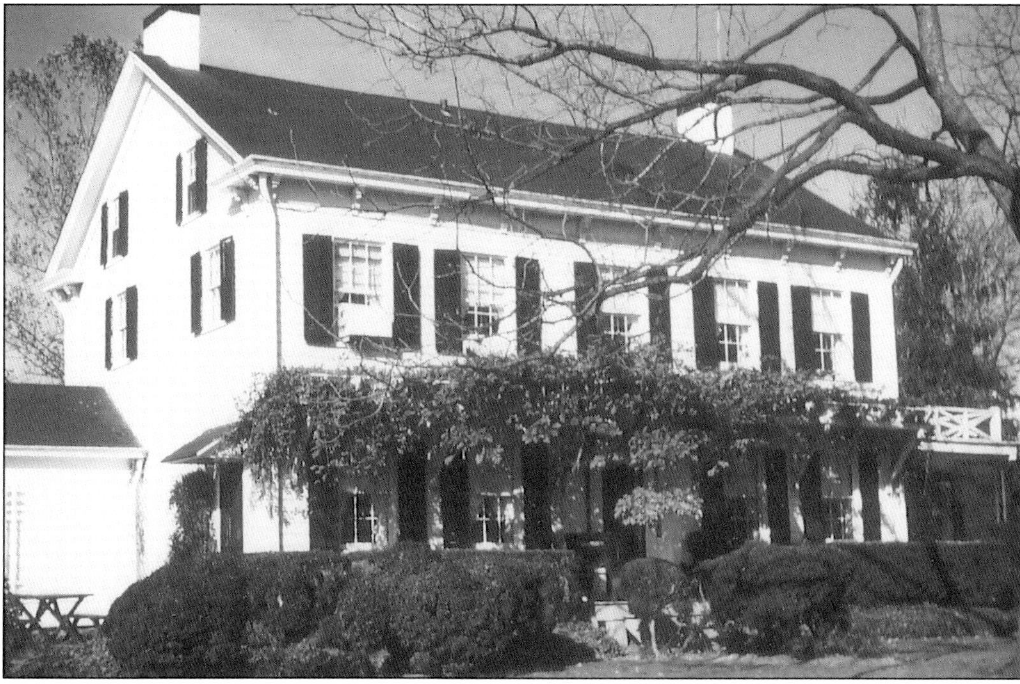

The Eder Vermeule house, built *c.* 1777 for the second son of Cornelius Vermeule Sr., is located at 113 Myrtle Avenue. It stands well back from the street and the front facing the old millpond. Today, the well-preserved house remains in nearly the same state as when it was constructed over 200 years ago.

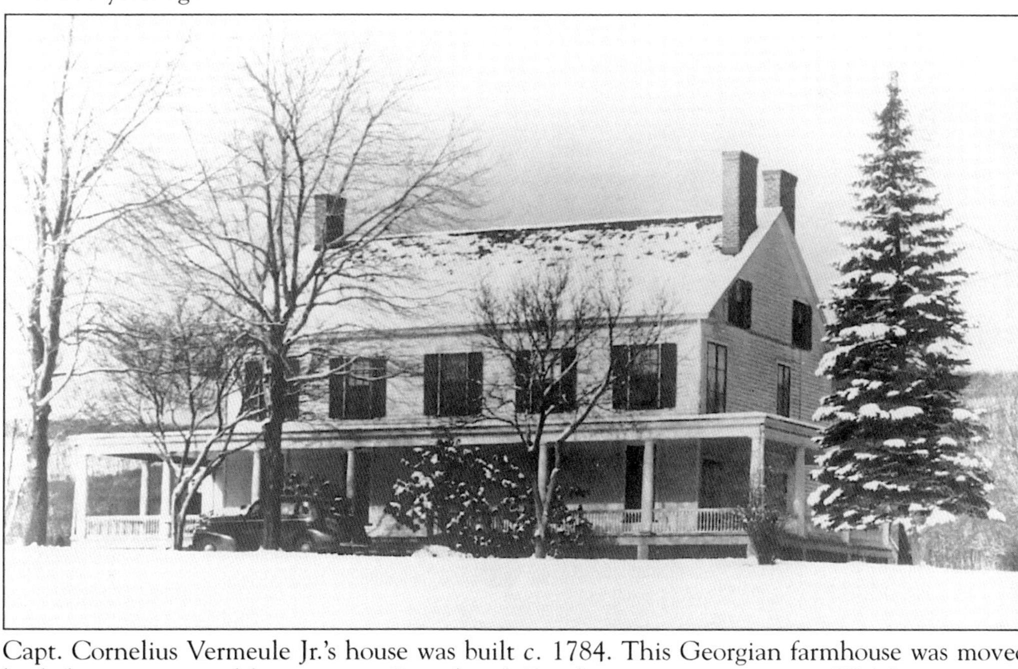

Capt. Cornelius Vermeule Jr.'s house was built *c.* 1784. This Georgian farmhouse was moved back from its original location on Greenbrook Road to its present site at 457 Mountainview Drive in 1910. Cornelius Vermeule died March 14, 1784, while a home was being built for his youngest son and namesake.

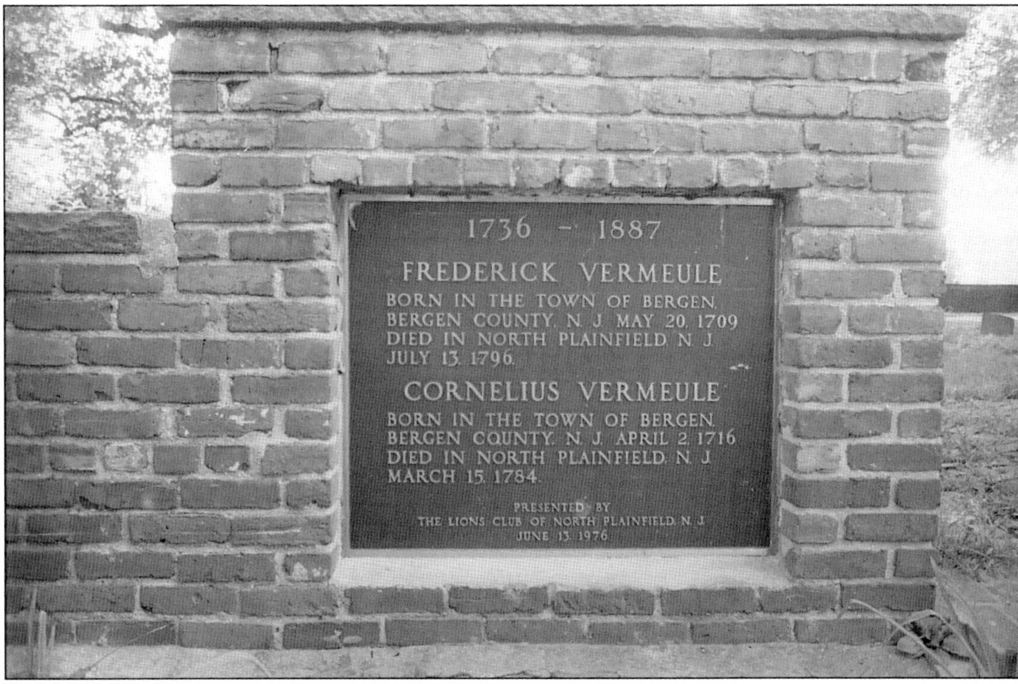

The Vermeule Cemetery was located on a wooded knoll within sight of the original Vermeule home. Just off Carter Place, behind a restored brick wall, lies the remains of this early pioneer family whose sons fought in the Revolutionary War.

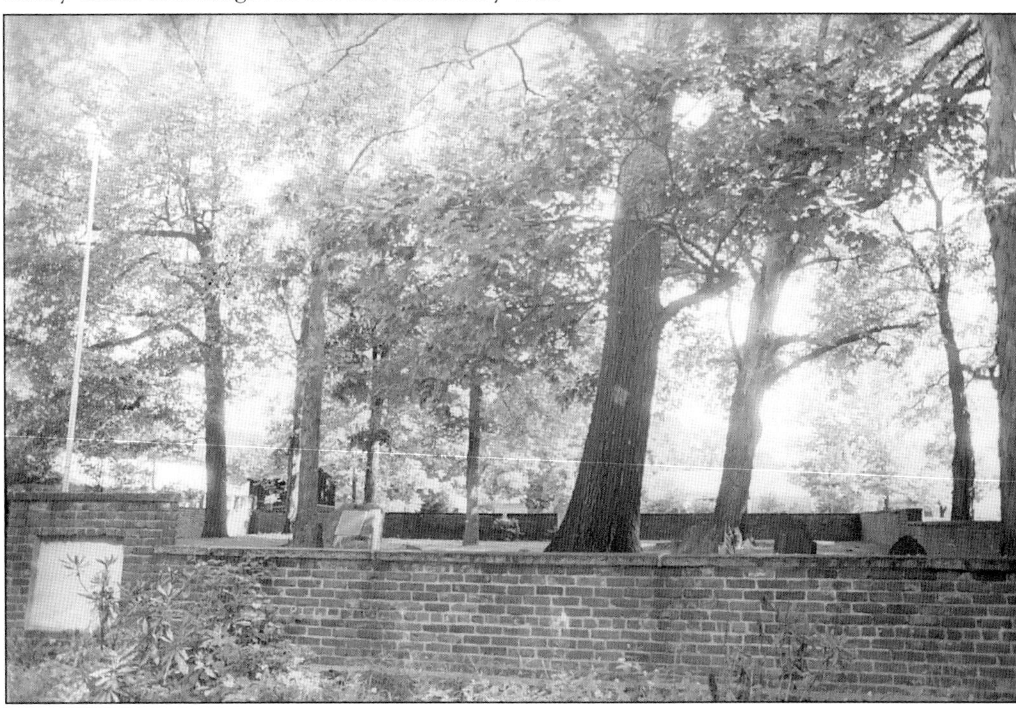

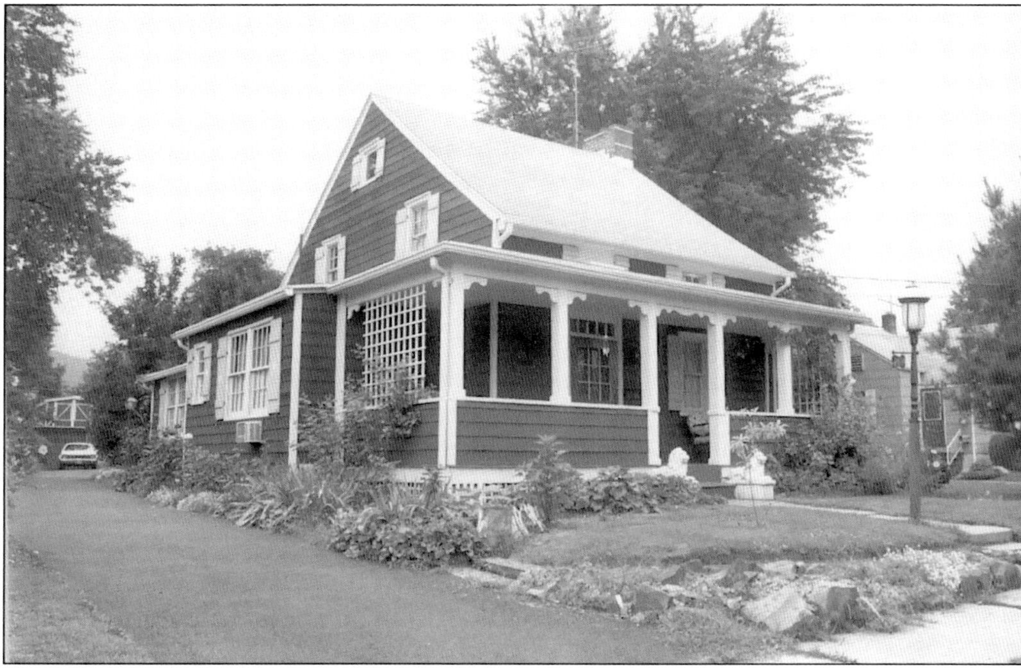

Located on the original Vermeule farm at 704 Greenbrook Road, one can find a little one-and-a-half story farmhouse, which was constructed *c.* 1740. This home consisted of two downstairs rooms with an attached summer kitchen and four small rooms above.

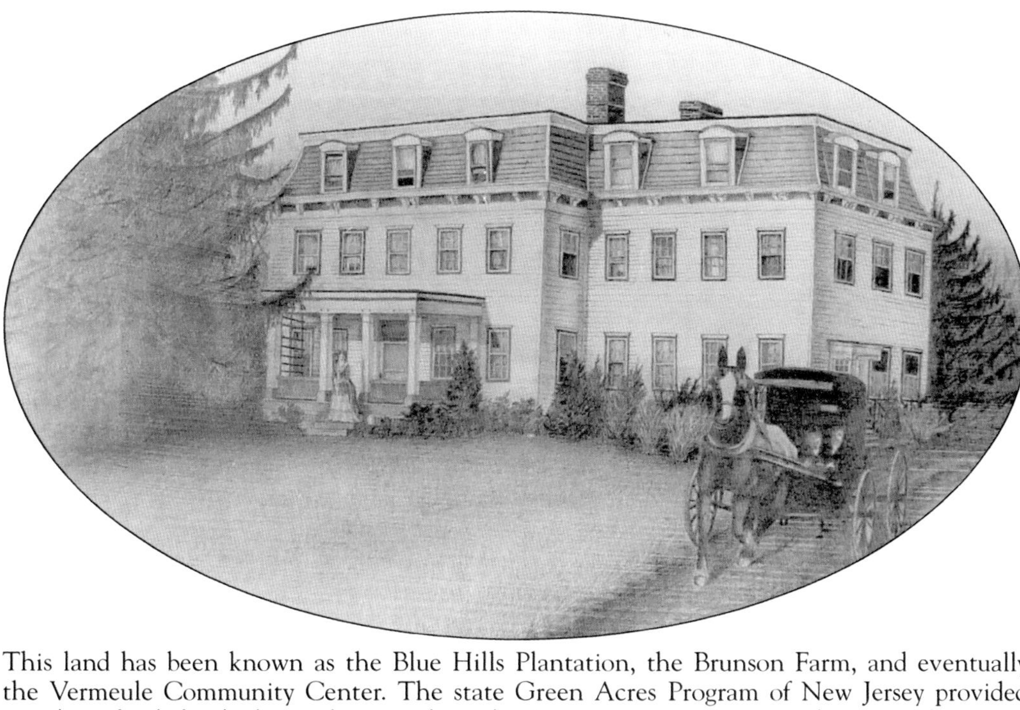

This land has been known as the Blue Hills Plantation, the Brunson Farm, and eventually the Vermeule Community Center. The state Green Acres Program of New Jersey provided matching funds for the borough to purchase this 7.9-acre area in 1974. At that time, the center included the mansion, the Vermeule Cemetery, the barn building, three small cottages, an antique smokehouse, and two other meeting rooms.

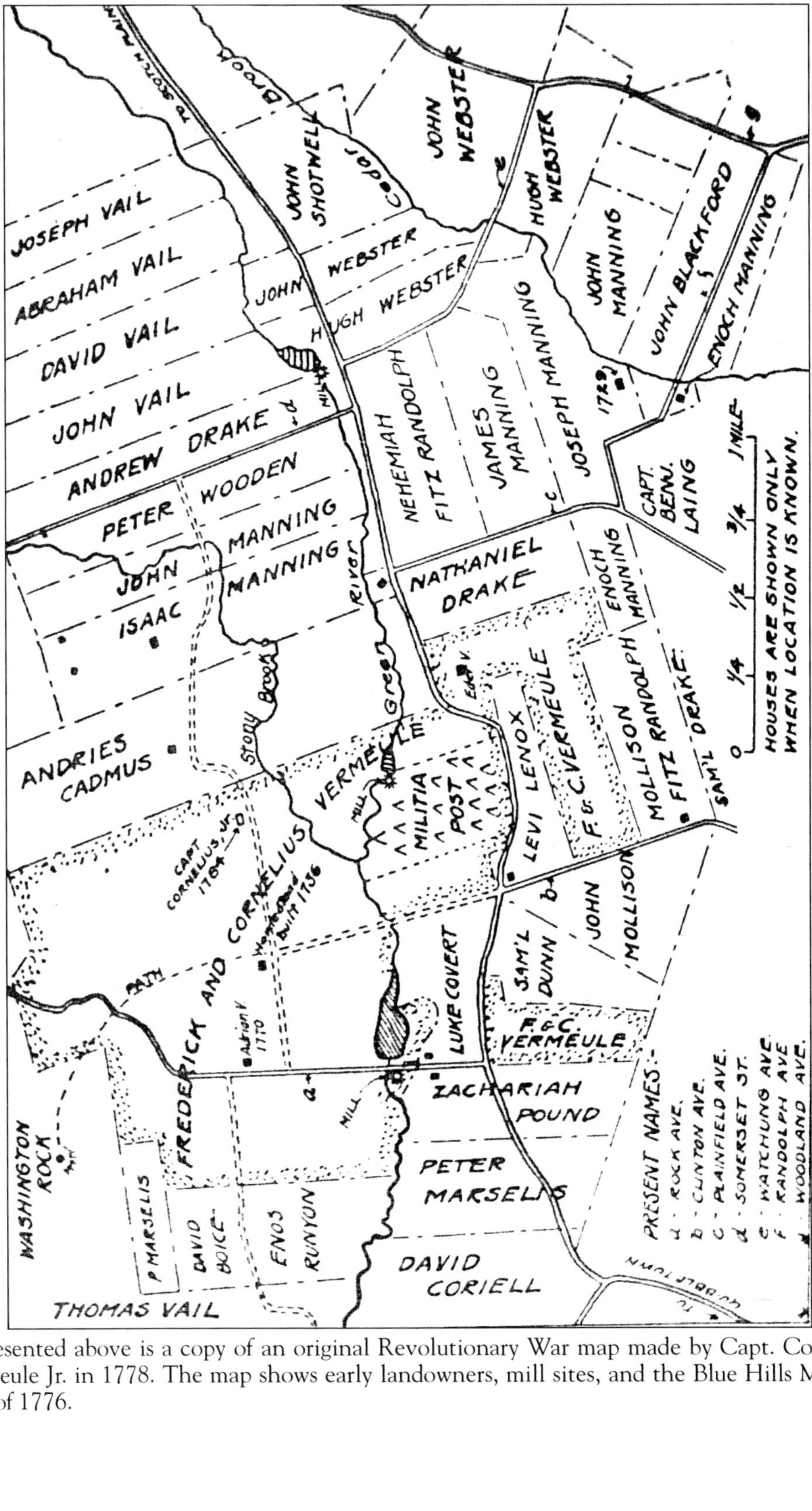

Represented above is a copy of an original Revolutionary War map made by Capt. Cornelius Vermeule Jr. in 1778. The map shows early landowners, mill sites, and the Blue Hills Military Post of 1776.

Two

North Plainfield Township

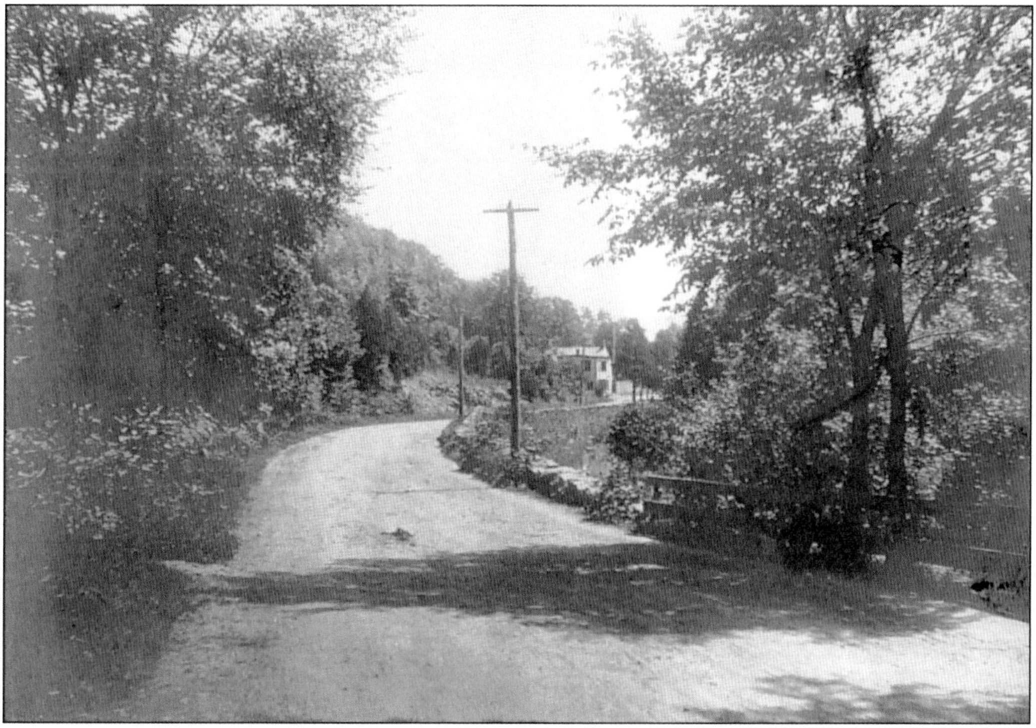

On April 2, 1872, a new township was formed from Warren Township. It was called North Plainfield Township. This new township included what are now Green Brook, Watchung, and North Plainfield. The picture above shows Somerset Street, *c.* 1900, looking south from Watchung. The Lenni-Lenape Indians were said to have used this road as they headed for the Atlantic Ocean to fish and collect shells for wampum.

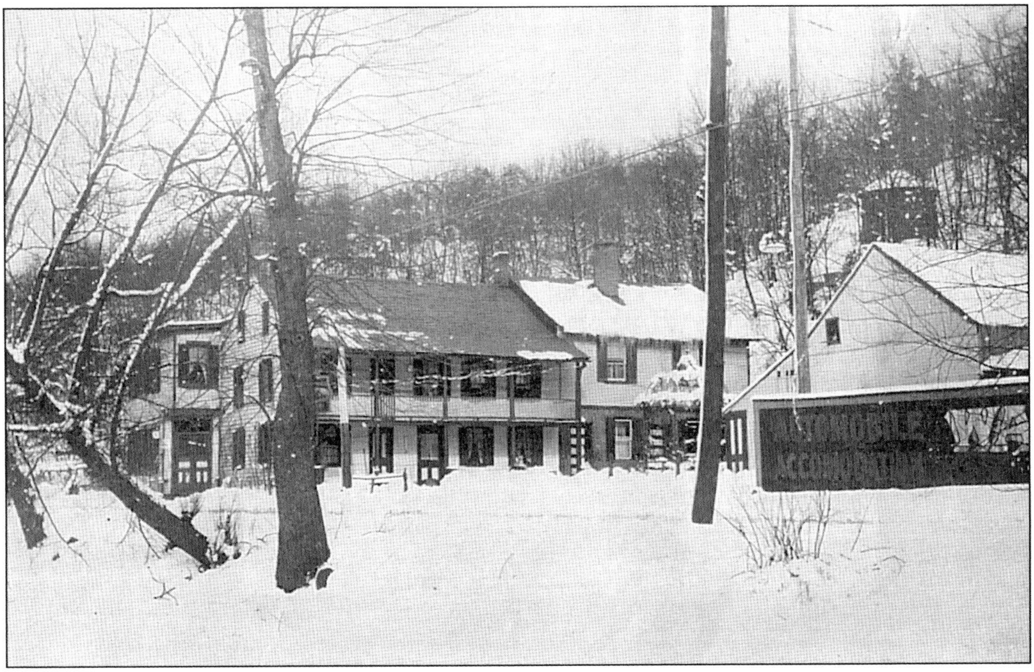

Located on Somerset Street in the "Notch" on the border of North Plainfield and Watchung, sat the Washington House. The earliest recorded owner was Joseph Jennings in 1727. In 1806, it was David Stewart's Tavern where many town meetings were held.

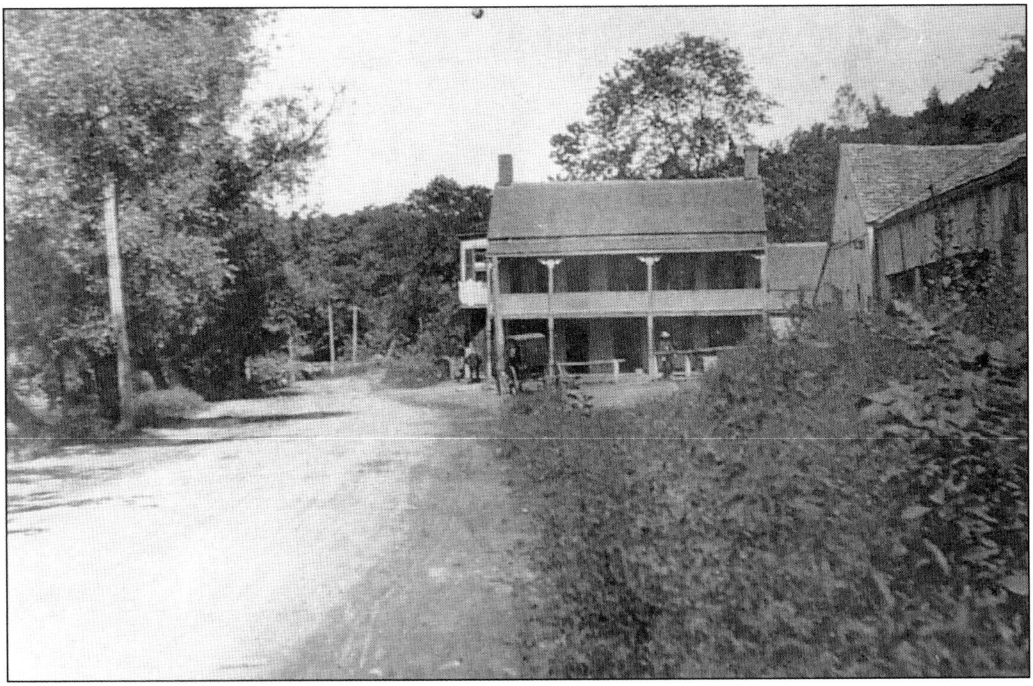

In 1861, George Demler purchased the Washington House and, for 33 years, it was known as the Demler's Hotel. Ownership changed many times over the next few years. In 1963, this famous local landmark came to an end when a fire destroyed the 236-year-old building.

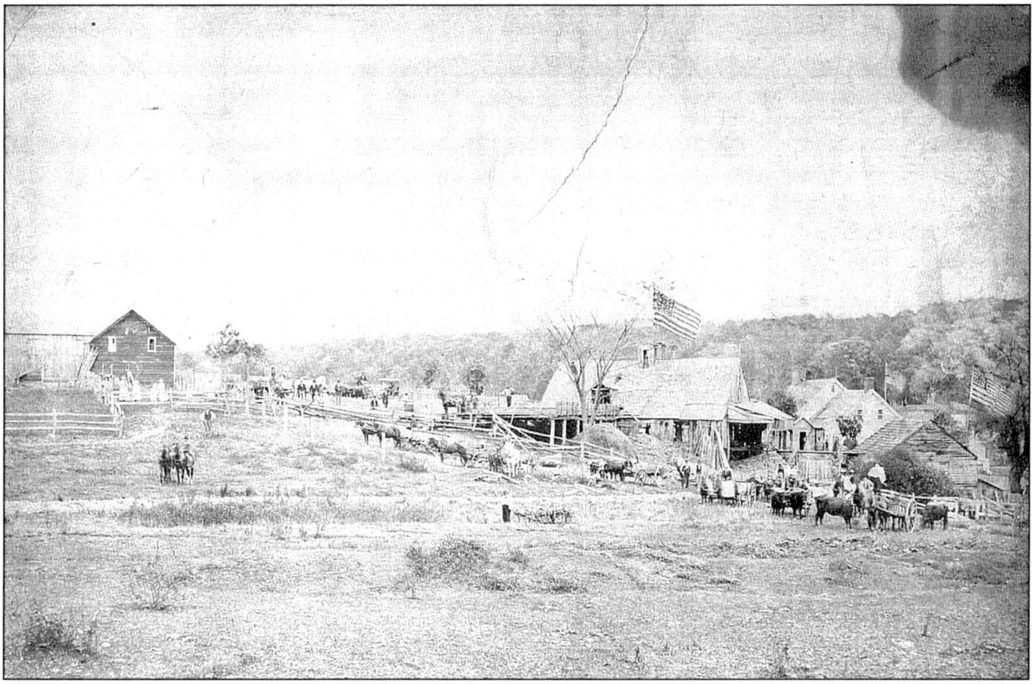

The early farm of the Spencer family was located in the center of Watchung, on what is now the circle. The early farmhouse sat where the medical building now stands. These pictures show the farm, *c.* 1880s, when Somerset Street was still a dirt road. The bridge has been washed out by the brook. In the distance, one can see the barn and the apple cider mill.

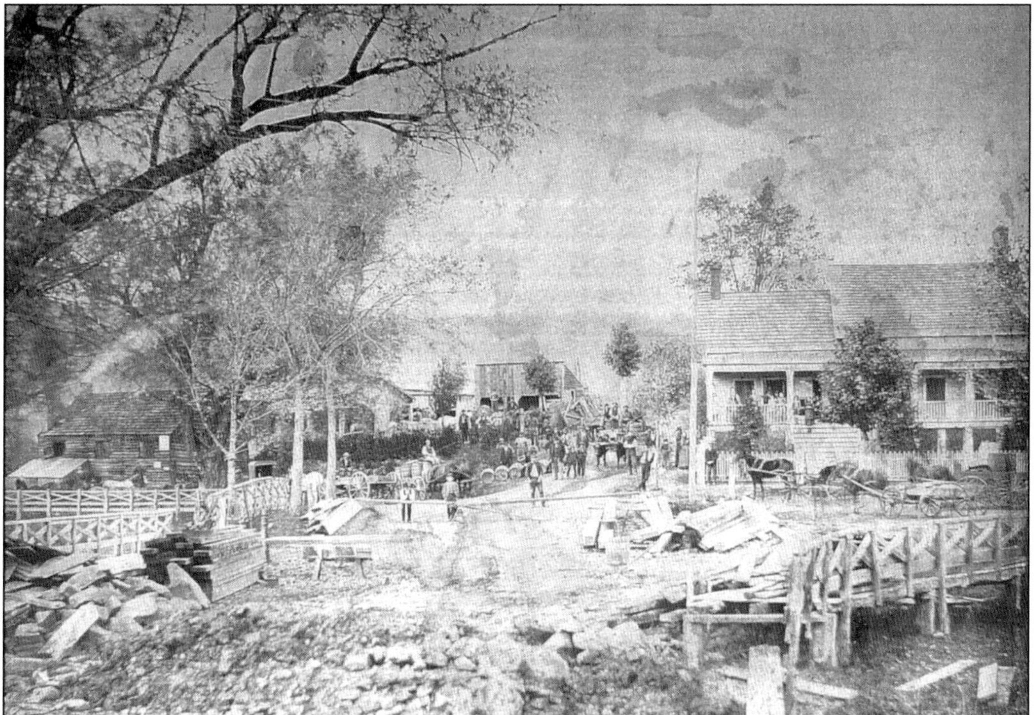

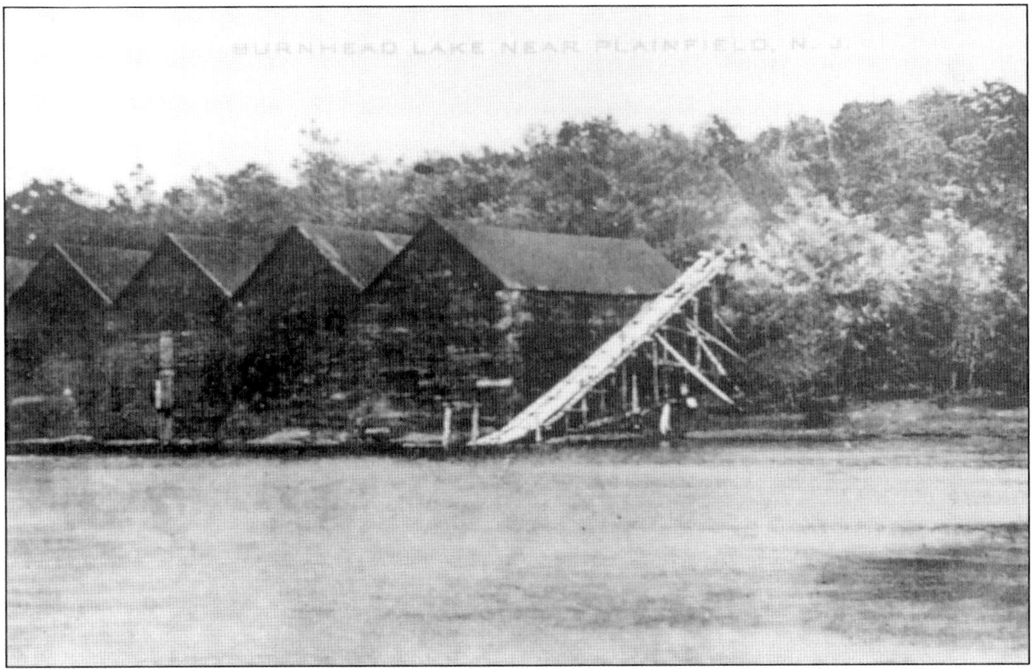

The icehouses on Watchung Lake stood three stories tall and were located at the foot of the dam. This business had an average daily sale of about 2 tons of ice when the houses burned to the ground in 1933.

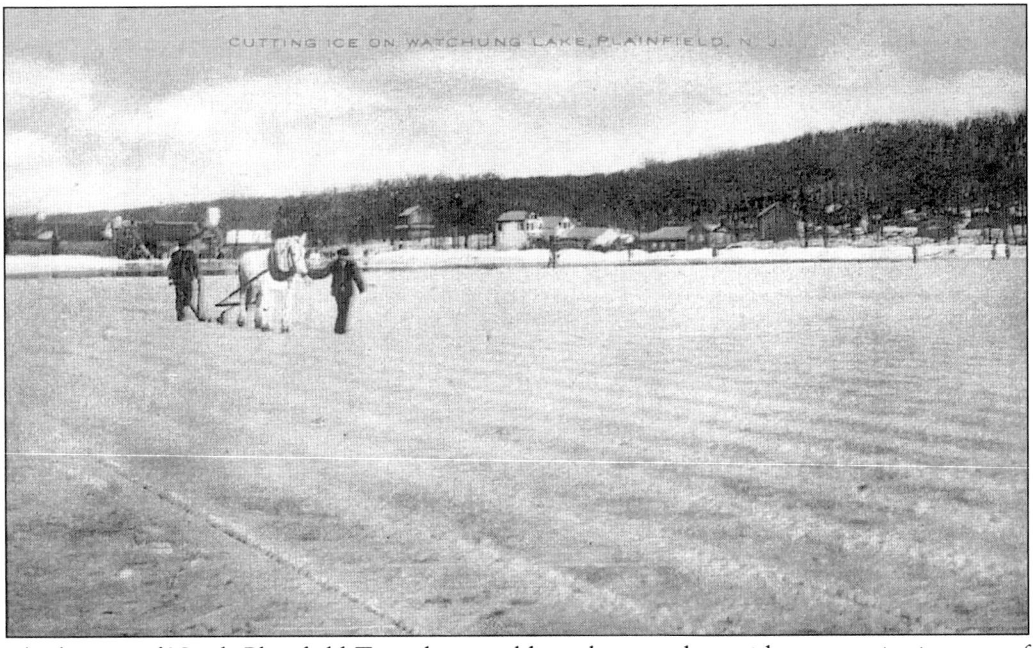

The history of North Plainfield Township would not be complete without mentioning one of its earliest industries—the harvesting of ice. The Natural Ice Company was founded by Mr. J. Wilson, c. 1880. The small lake was located across the street from the Wilson Memorial Church. The cutting of ice continued on this pond until the Watchung Lake across the street was enlarged and the Plainfield Ice and Supply Company was established.

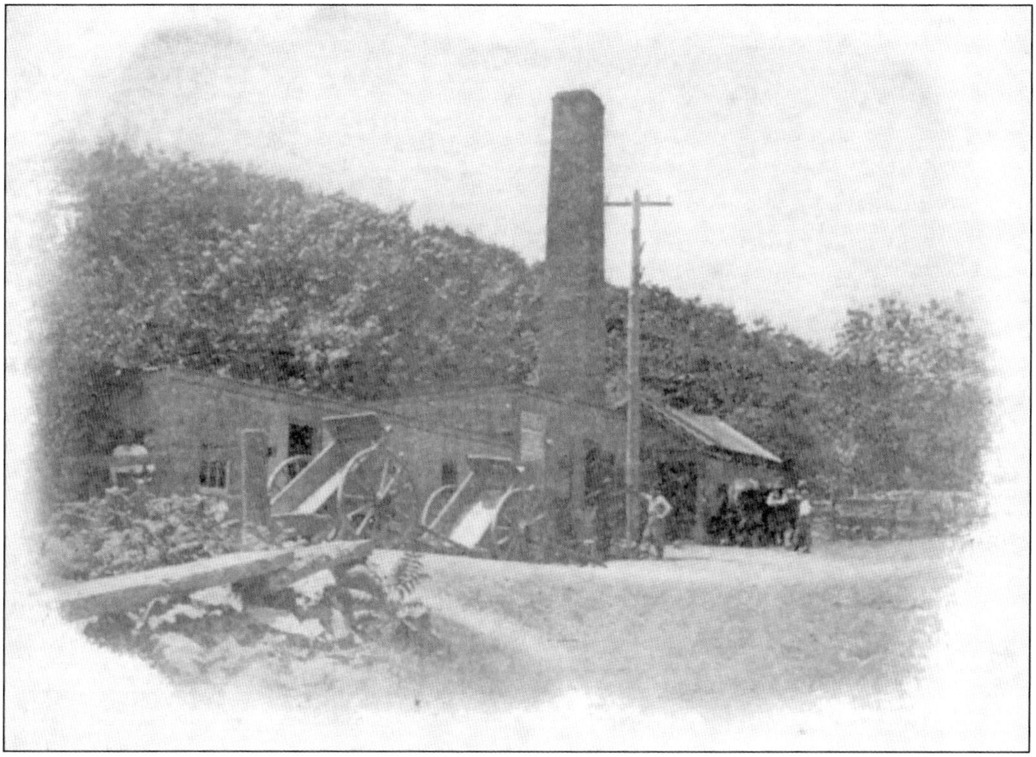

The largest quarry in North Plainfield Township was known as Wilson's quarry. Located on Somerset Street, it was founded in 1885 by J.Y Wilson and was known as the Somerset Trap Rock Company. Mr. Wilson was the first to crush trap rock, which was blasted from the mountainside. The nearby Wetumpka Falls in the Stony Brook provided the waterpower for the machinery. Early deliveries were made by horse and wagon. The quarry closed in the 1930s.

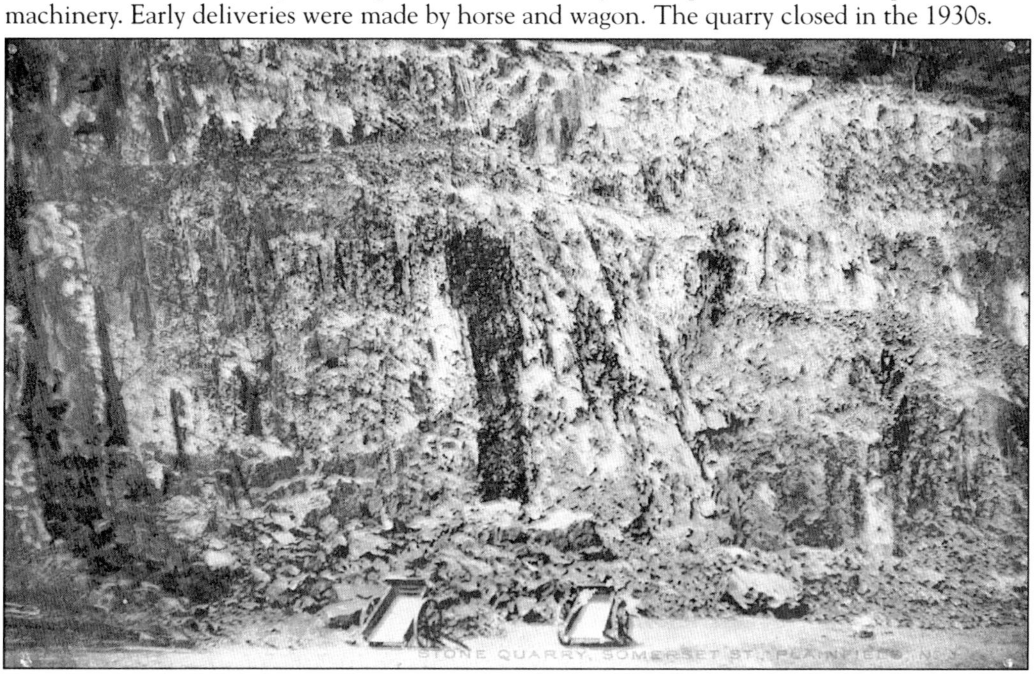

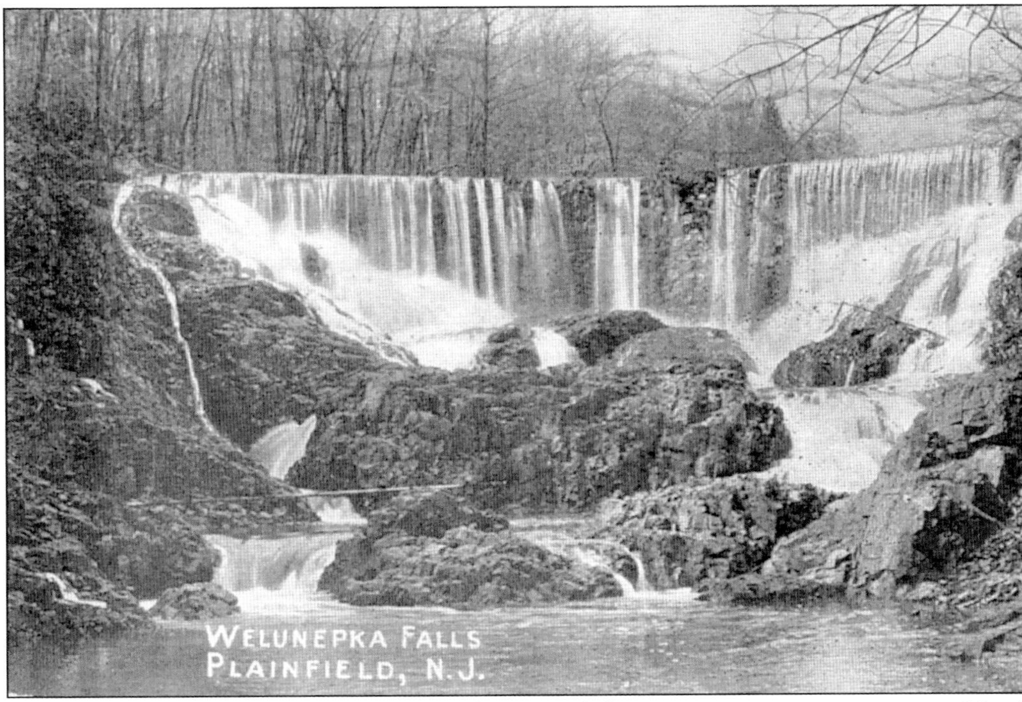

The site known as Wetumpka Falls provides one of the most picturesque settings in North Plainfield Township; it is located near the "notch," between the present North Plainfield and Watchung. This scenic spot, located on the Stony Brook, was a favorite stopping place for picnics and long summer walks. The falls were built in order to make power for the Wilson Stone Crusher. The name Wetumpka comes from the Native American legend of Watchung.

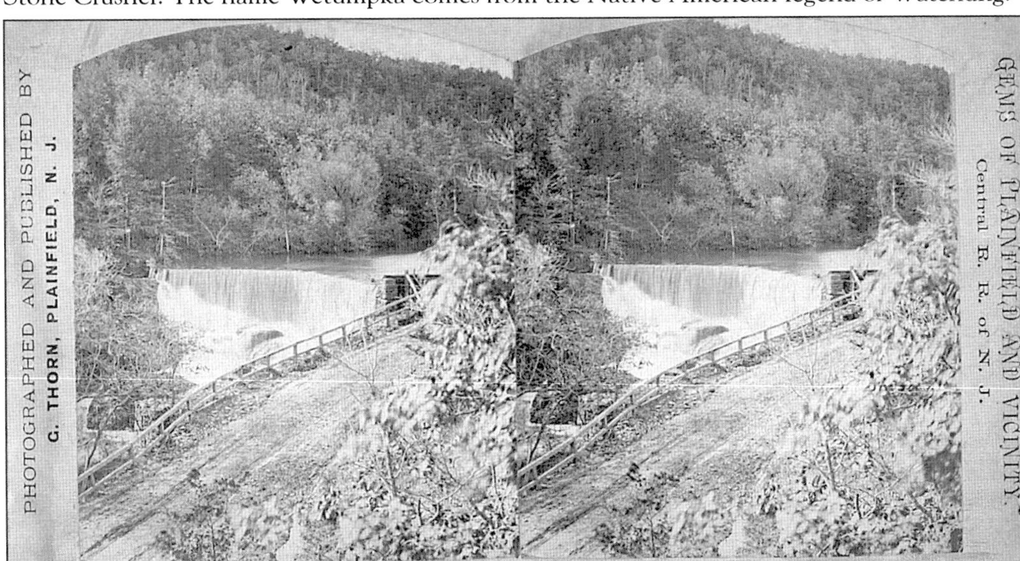

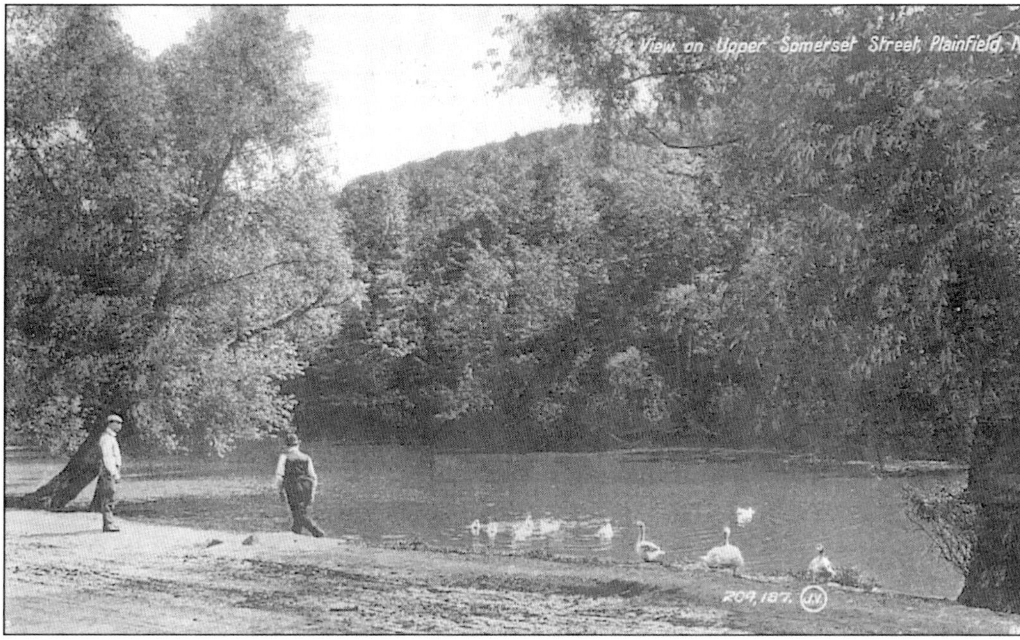

This early-1900s view of North Plainfield Township shows Upper Somerset Street.

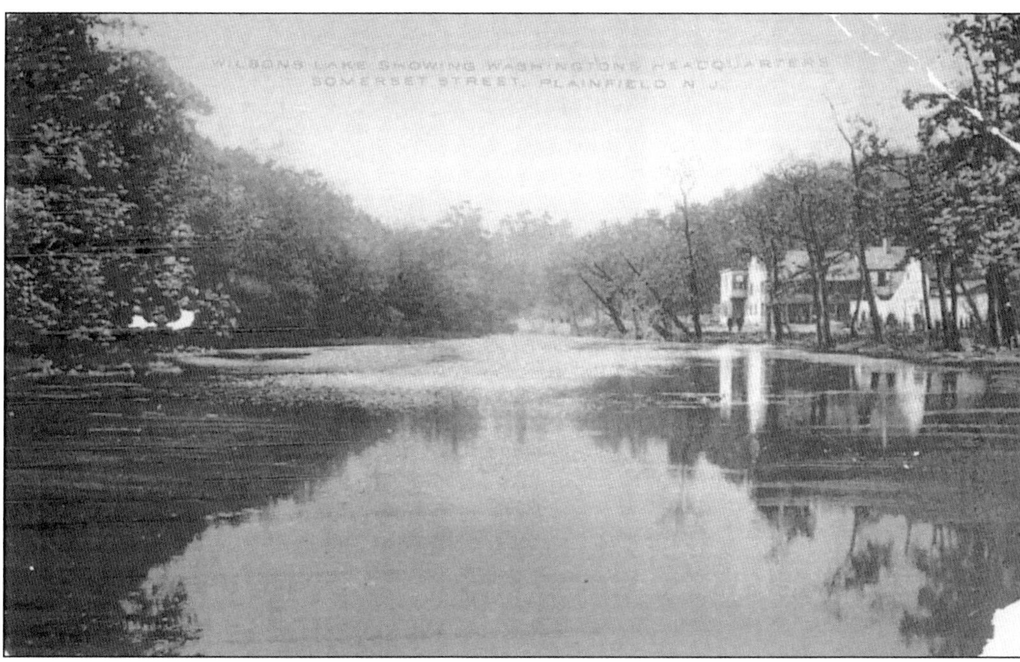

Wilson Lake is located just south of the Wetumpka Falls, near today's Houston Lumber. The Washington House on Somerset Street can be seen overlooking the lake. The falls provided waterpower for the Wilson's stone quarry that was located on the Stony Brook in the "notch."

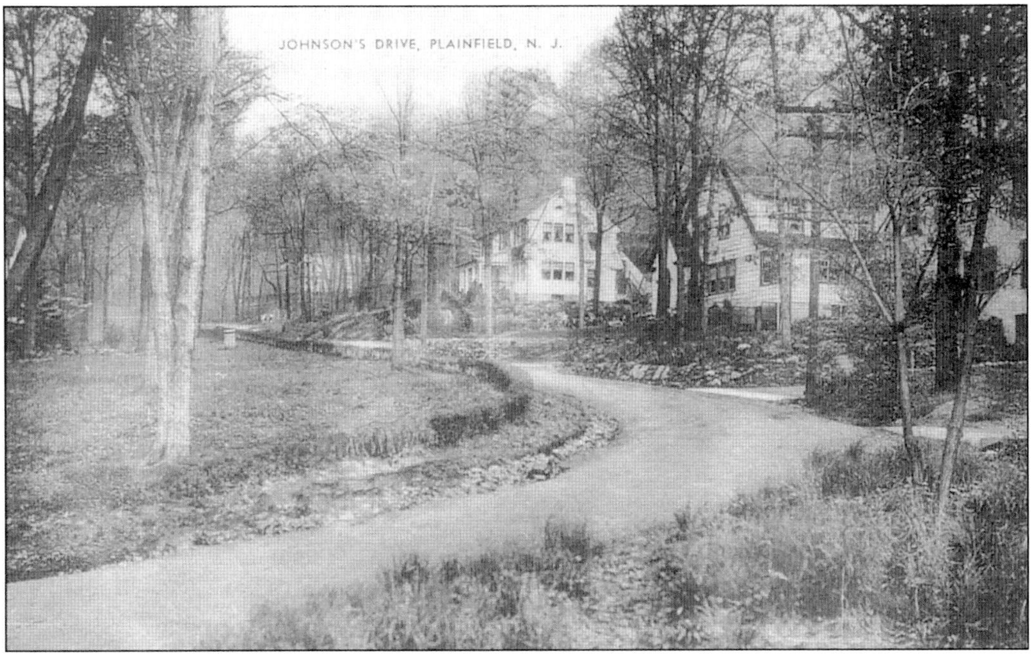

Johnson's Drive was one of the first macadamized roads in the State of New Jersey. The road cost $25,000 to build and was 3 1/2 miles long. Built by John Taylor Johnson, the road was 600 feet above sea level and commands one of the most magnificent views in the state. Local horsemen raced their trotters the full length. Car races were also popular at the time.

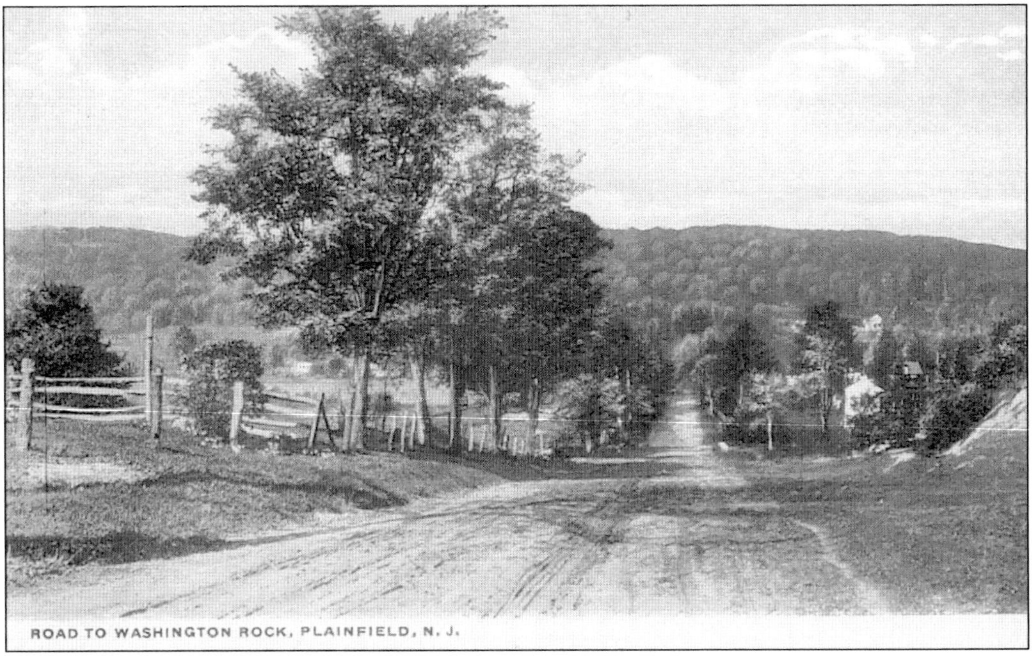

This picturesque road from the early part of the 19th century led to Washington Rock, which was located in the middle of North Plainfield Township. This favorite lookout is now a part of Greenbrook.

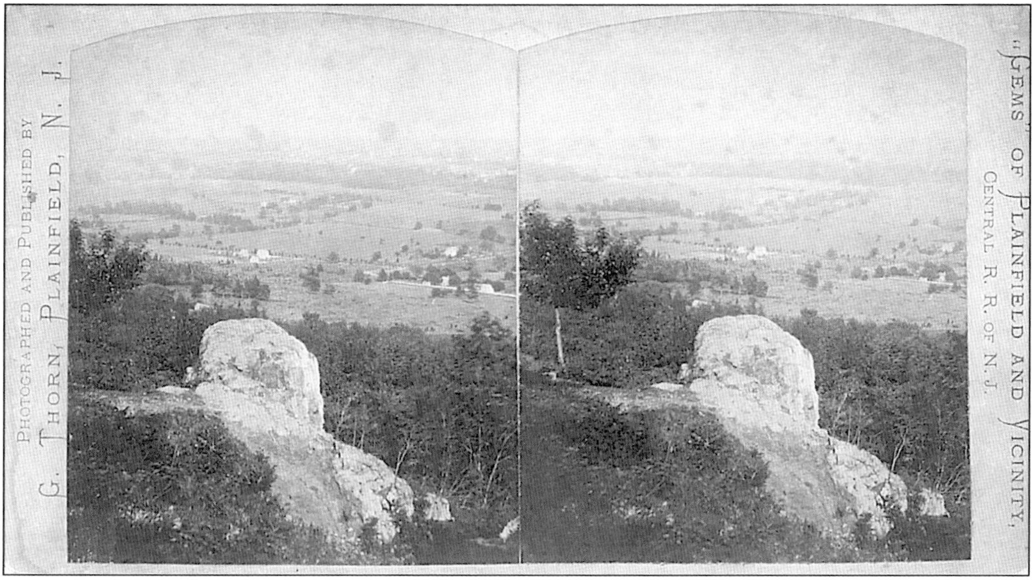

Washington Rock, as portrayed in this photograph, is about 25 feet in height and 30-40 feet in circumference. It projects boldly from the mountainside, affording an ideal lookout where one can command the wide view below for a span of 60 or more miles. It is said that during May and June of 1777 during the Revolutionary War, George Washington would closely scan the scene below with a spyglass in hand.

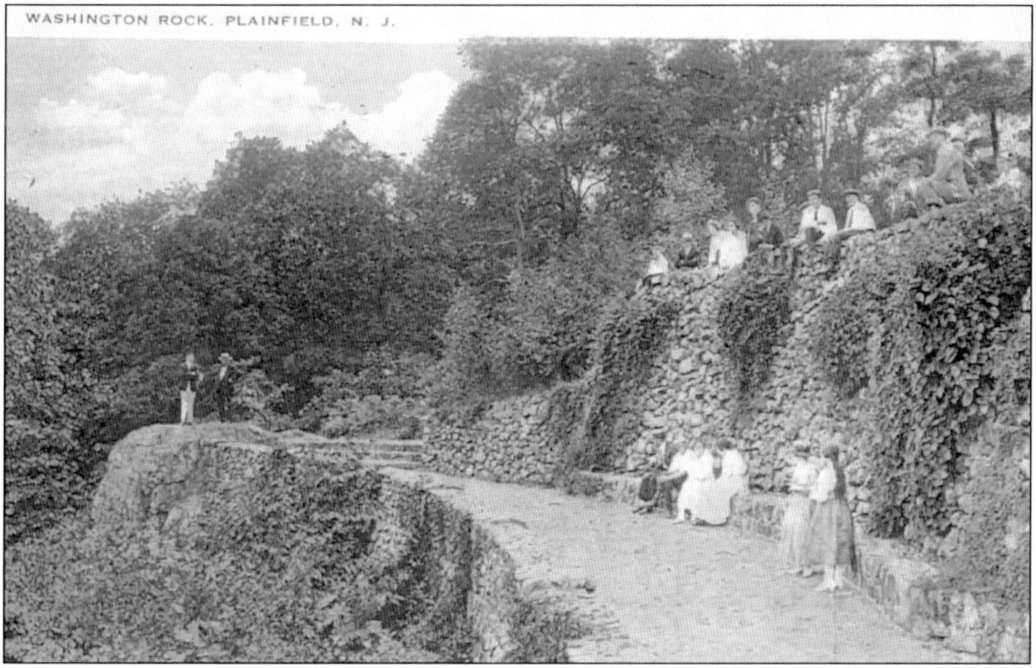

Washington Rock became a popular summer resort in the mid-1800s. People flocked to this picturesque and grand tourist location that was situated on the brow of the First Watchung Mountain, 3 miles west of Plainfield and approximately 600 feet above the plain. In the distance could be seen New York, Newark, Elizabeth, Rahway, and many other cities. All in all, it was said to be one of the finest landscapes in the United States.

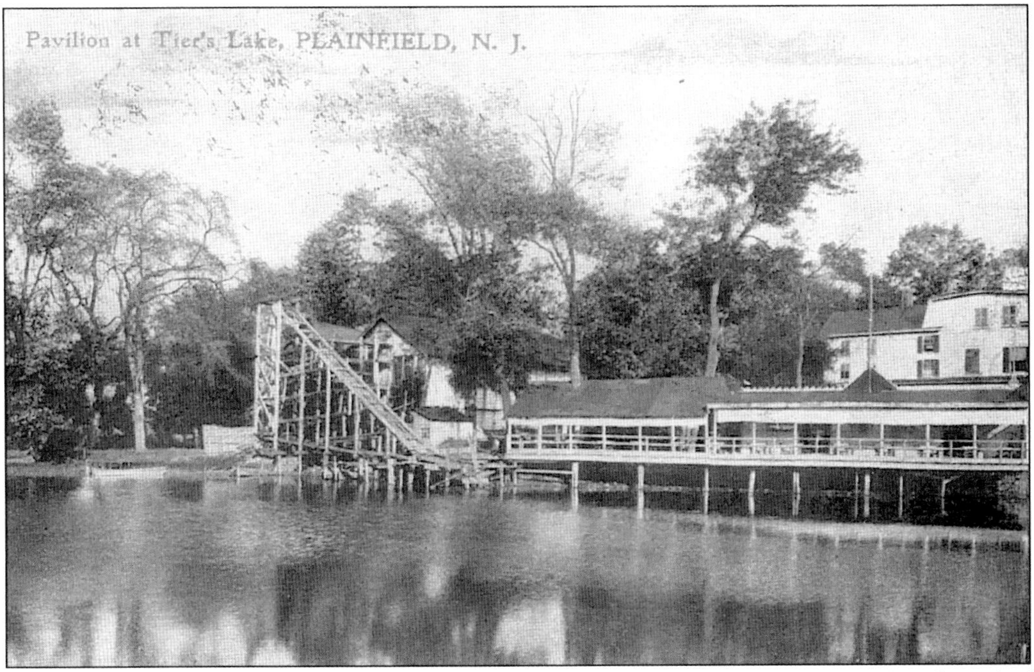

Tiers pond, located on the border of North Plainfield and Plainfield, was the old millpond of John Vail and William Webster. John Tier purchased the property, built a pavilion, and turned it into a popular amusement park with boating, concerts, fireworks on Fourth of July, ice skating, and homemade ice cream. In the winter, Mr. Tier harvested ice and stored it in icehouses along the brook for delivery during the winter.

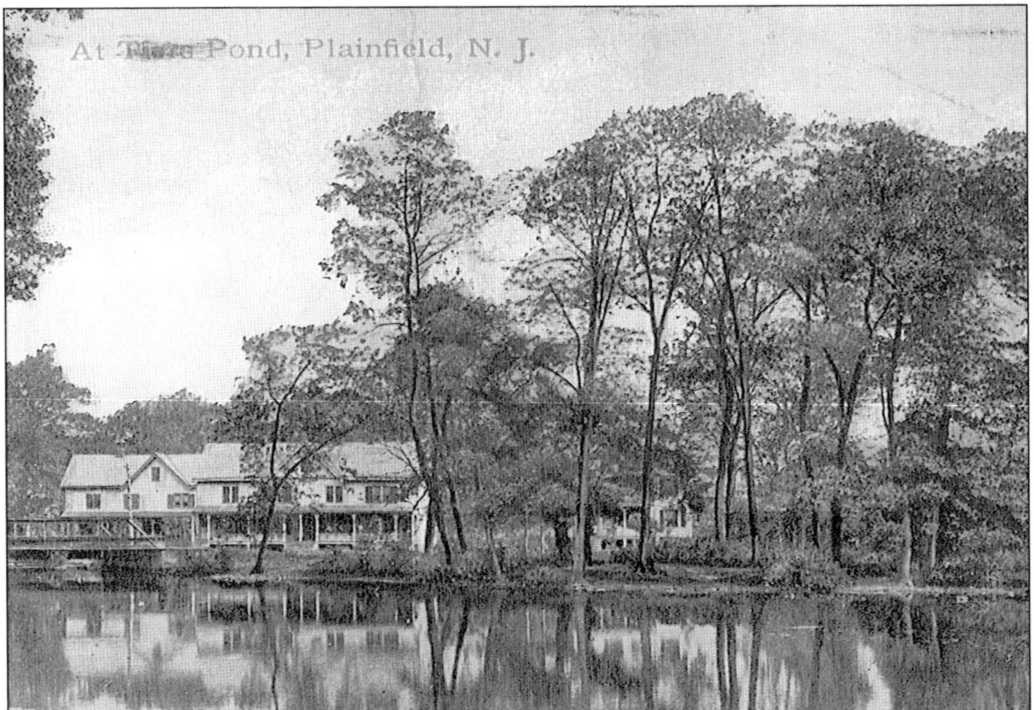

Located along Somerset Street and the Green Brook, French's Mill was the hub of activity over 100 years ago. Built *c.* 1755 by John Webster, the mill was located on the Green Brook. In 1782, the mill was moved to Somerset Street. In 1853, Phineas French purchased the mill and built a new main building onto the existing structure. Farmers traveled miles to bring wagon loads of grain to the mill to be ground into flour. In 1905, a fire destroyed a large portion of the building.

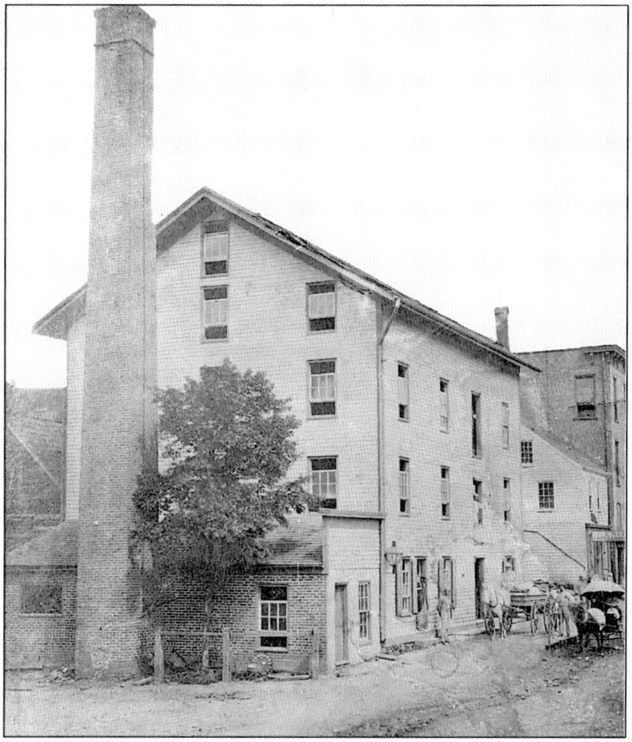

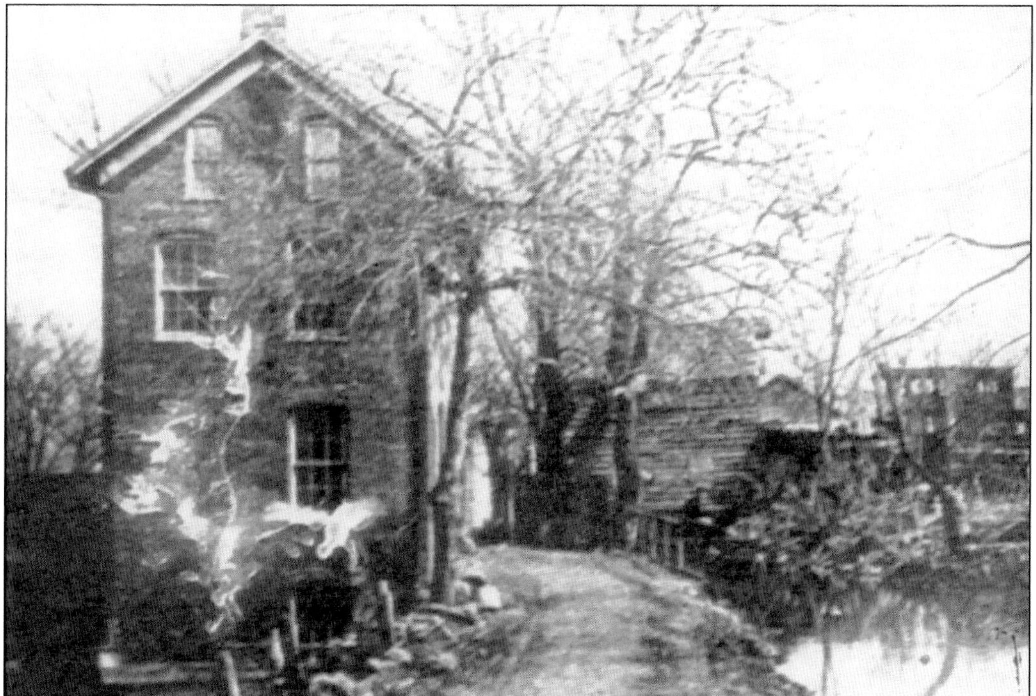

This structure was part of the original Phineas French mill, located on Somerset Street. The building also served as a hat factory and upholstery shop of J. William Klein.

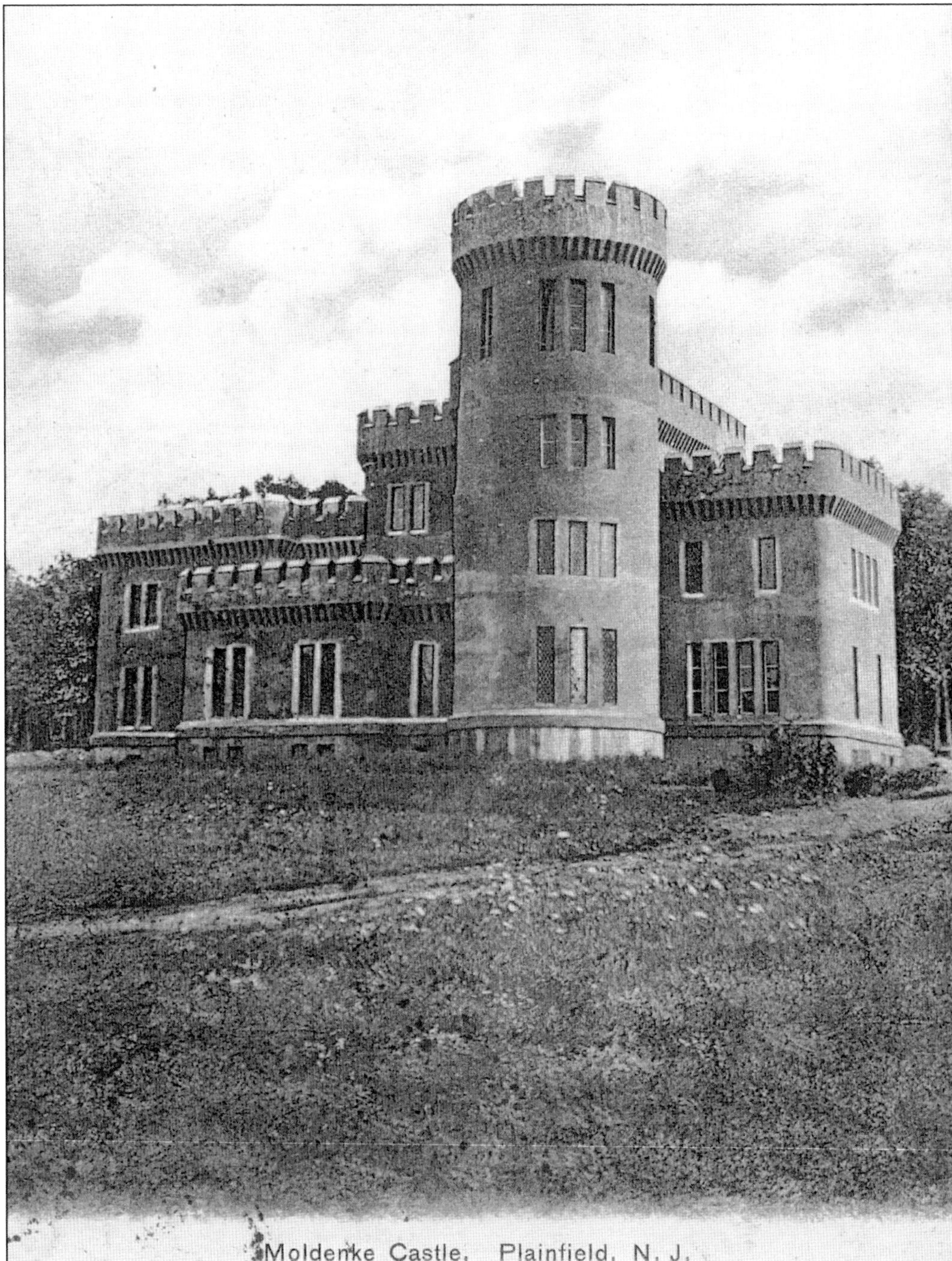

Moldenke Castle was built in 1899 by Dr. Richard Moldenke. He named it "Castle Elsinore" after a castle on the Rhine where his mother was born. Dr. Moldenke was a world-renown consulting metallurgist for cast iron. The castle had 35 rooms; the basement had 10-foot ceilings and contained a machine ship, a foundry, and a laboratory. In later years, the castle was left to ruin; it was eventually destroyed by fire in February 1969.

Three

SOMERSET STREET

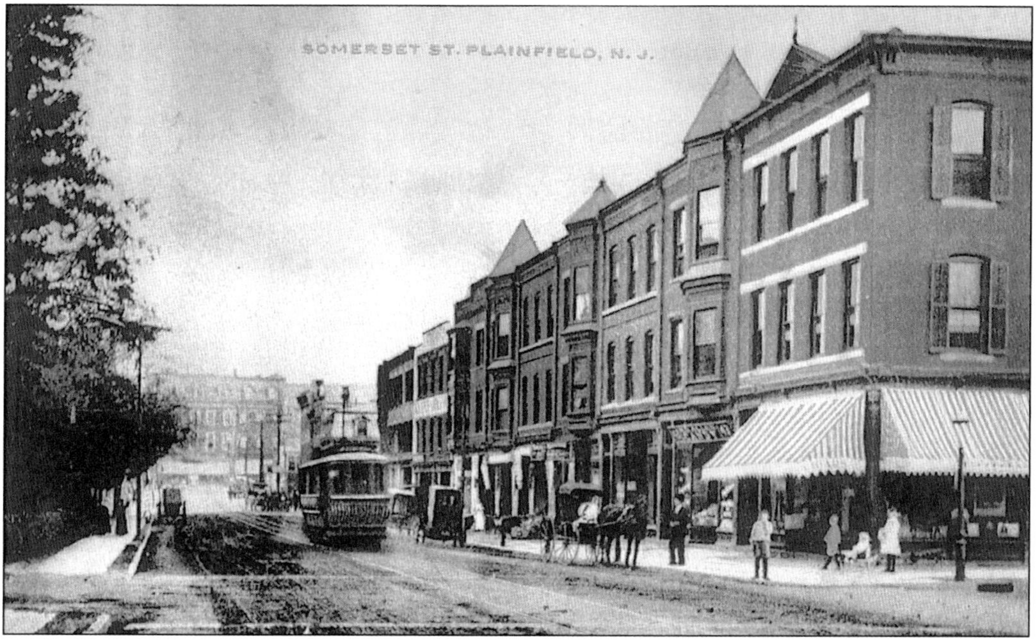

Somerset Street was once a Native American trail leading from the Watchung Mountains to the local waterways, which were much deeper 300 years ago. The Native American trail later became a rough wagon road, the main line of travel for the early settlers to bring their grain to be ground at the mills along the Green Brook. Stagecoaches traveling down the old York Road (now Front Street from Elizabeth) stopped to water their horses at the village pump that stood at the corner of what is now Front and Somerset Streets.

By 1876, the street had to be paved because wagons and carriages kept getting bogged down in mud during the rainy season. In 1891, a single line of trolley tracks was laid as part of the Fourth Street Line. As a result of heavy traffic, Somerset Street was widened several more times until the old trolley tracks were removed in 1926; Somerset Street then became paved with concrete and asphalt. Many old landmarks disappeared with the laying of the new pavement, but it was considered an important step forward in the progress of the borough.

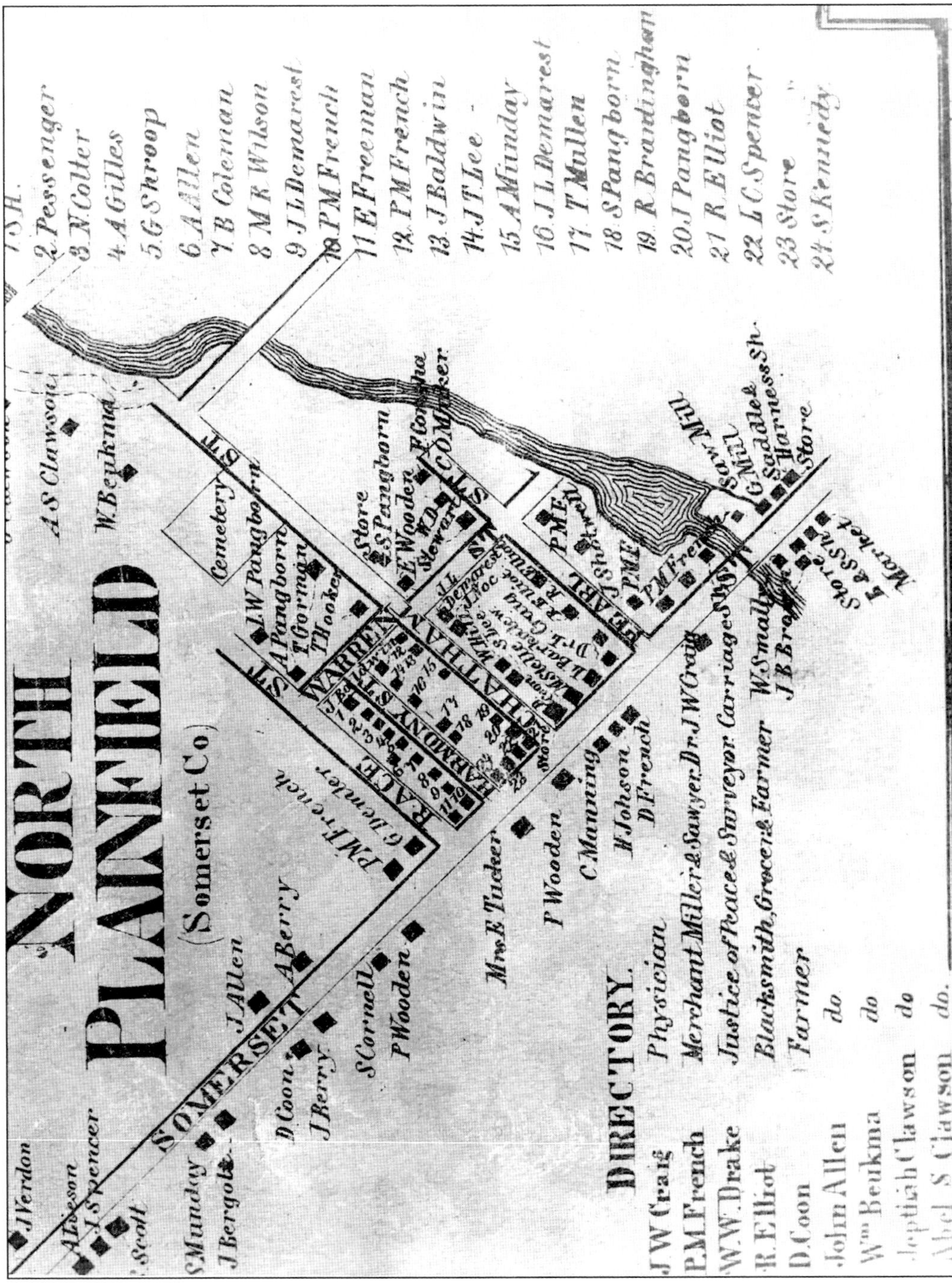

This early map and directory are of Somerset Street, North Plainfield.

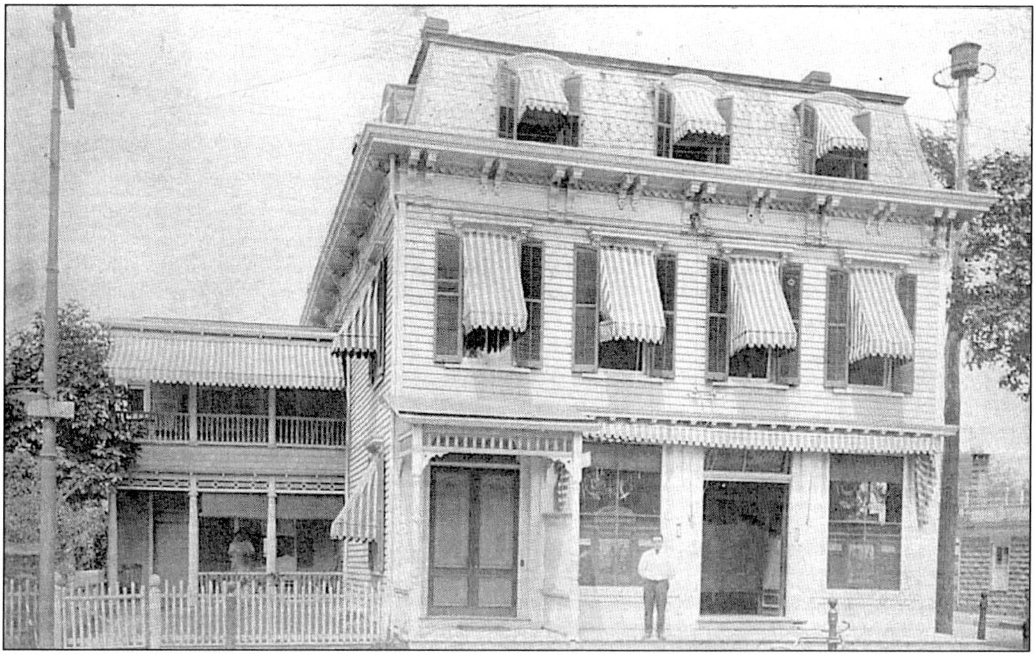

One of the most popular hotels in the two Plainfields was the Hotel Chatham located at 70–72 Somerset Street. It was established by Joseph K. Blatz and later taken over by his son. The hotel had one of the best cafes in the city with a stock of fine wine, liqueurs, beers, and cigars kept on hand. The hotel also had ten sleeping rooms and private apartments for the family.

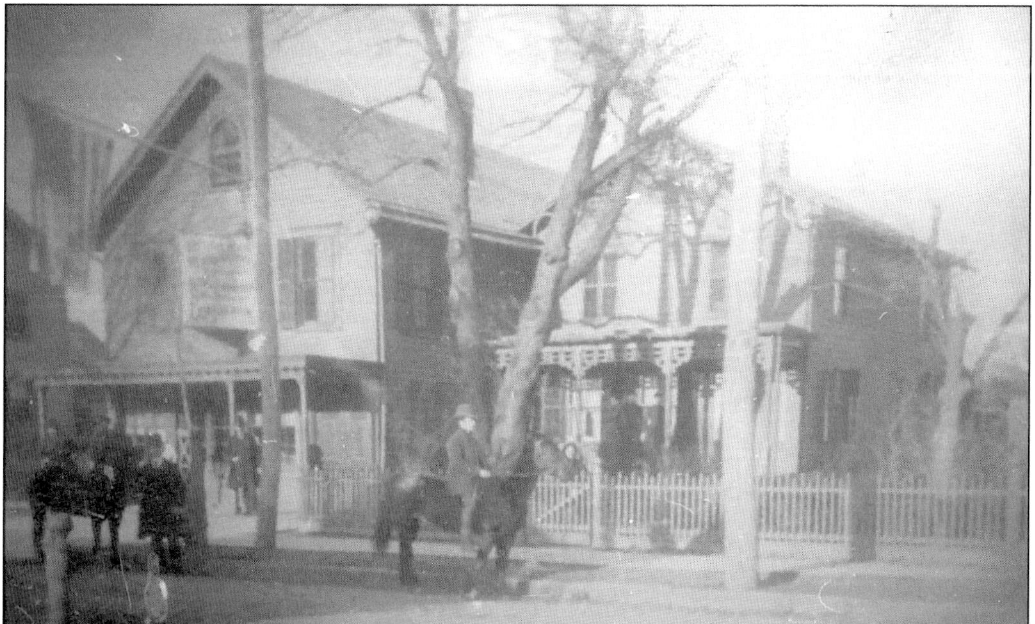

Spencer's grocery store was built on the east side of Somerset Street in 1850. The Spencer family lived in the house on the right. A second story was added to the grocery store and it became known as Spencer Hall. Political meetings were held there; the mayor and borough council held their first meeting there in 1885.

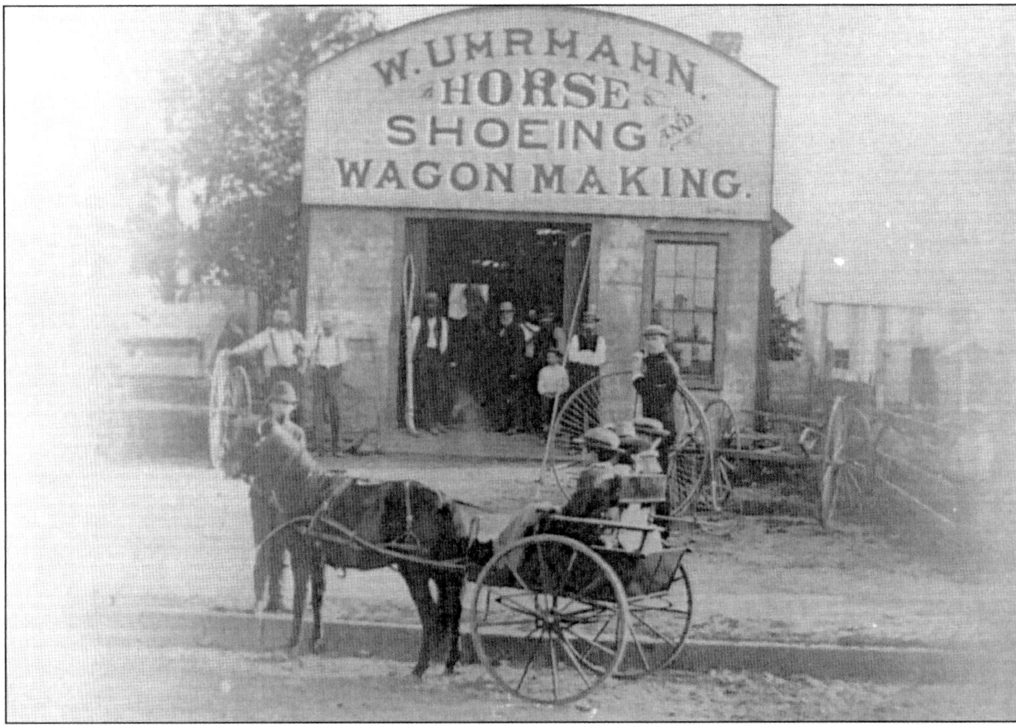

The W. Uhrhahn Horse Shoeing and Wagon making establishment was located on Regent Street near Somerset Street. The 1918 directory lists William and Madeline, their daughter Ida as a telephone operator, and their son Henry as a chauffeur.

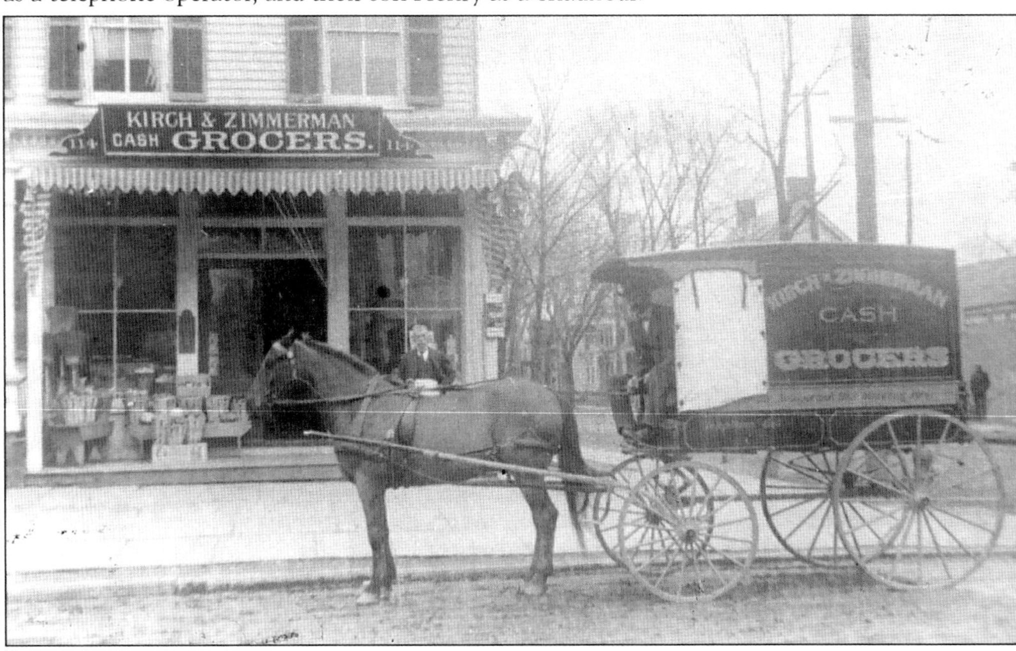

Kirch and Zimmerman Grocers was located at the corner of Somerset Street and Manning Avenue. Note the cash sign on the building and the delivery wagon. Other grocery stores allowed housewives to run tabs for short periods of time.

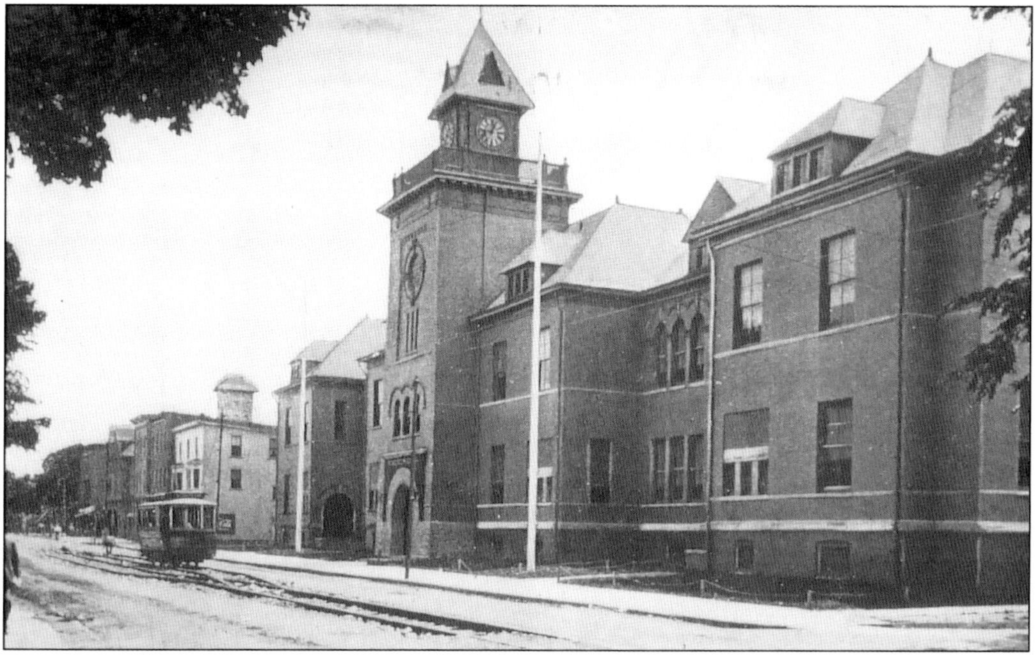

In 1893, a trolley line was built from West Front and Somerset Streets to Johnson Drive in North Plainfield. The fare was 5¢. In the summer, riding an open trolley car at a daring clip of about 20 miles per hour to Sunday afternoon picnics was a favorite outing of many young couples. By 1925, buses had replaced the trolley in North Plainfield.

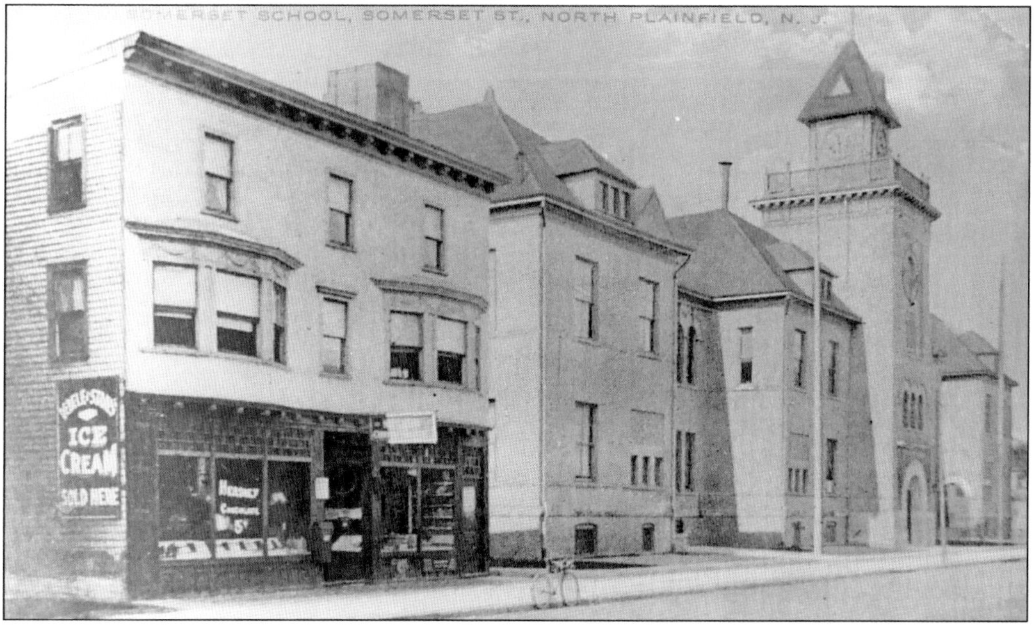

The confectionery and ice cream store of Debele and Stahl, manufacturers and dealers in ice cream and candies, was located at 111–113 Somerset Street. William Debele started the establishment about the turn of the century; Julius Stahl joined a few years later. People of the city and the suburbs knew that Debele and Stahl dealt in the purest and best goods, which were made under their personal supervision.

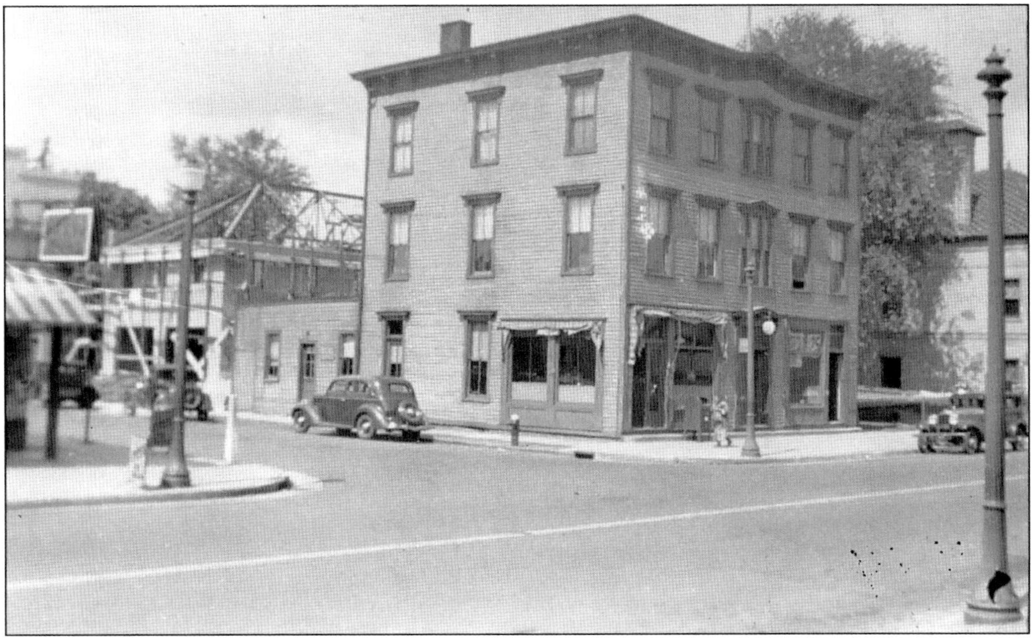

Located at the corner of Somerset Street and Lincoln Place was the Somerset Hotel. For many years it was one of the most popular hotels in North Plainfield. The food was the best money could buy and the rooms were light, airy, clean, and comfortable. The Borough Hall is now located on this site.

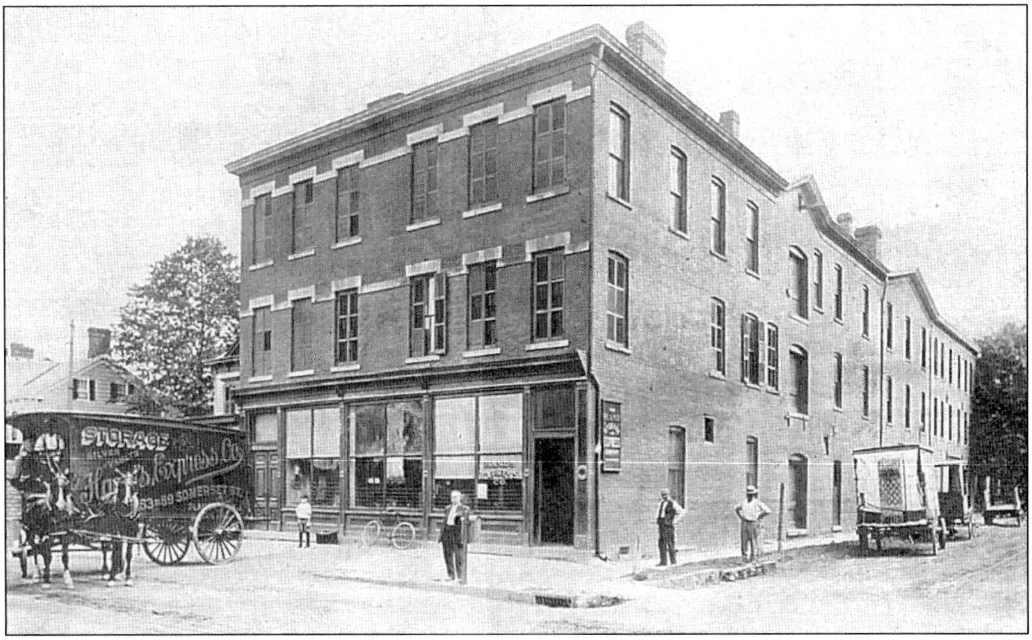

The building at Somerset Street and Somerset Place was once occupied by C. Frank French for his flour, hay, grain, and straw store. It later became the home of Hand's Storage and Express Co., one of the area's largest and most successful businesses. The three-story storage warehouse fronted on Somerset Street for 180 feet, extended to the rear 300 feet, and was built of brick. It now is the location of Somerset Plumbing.

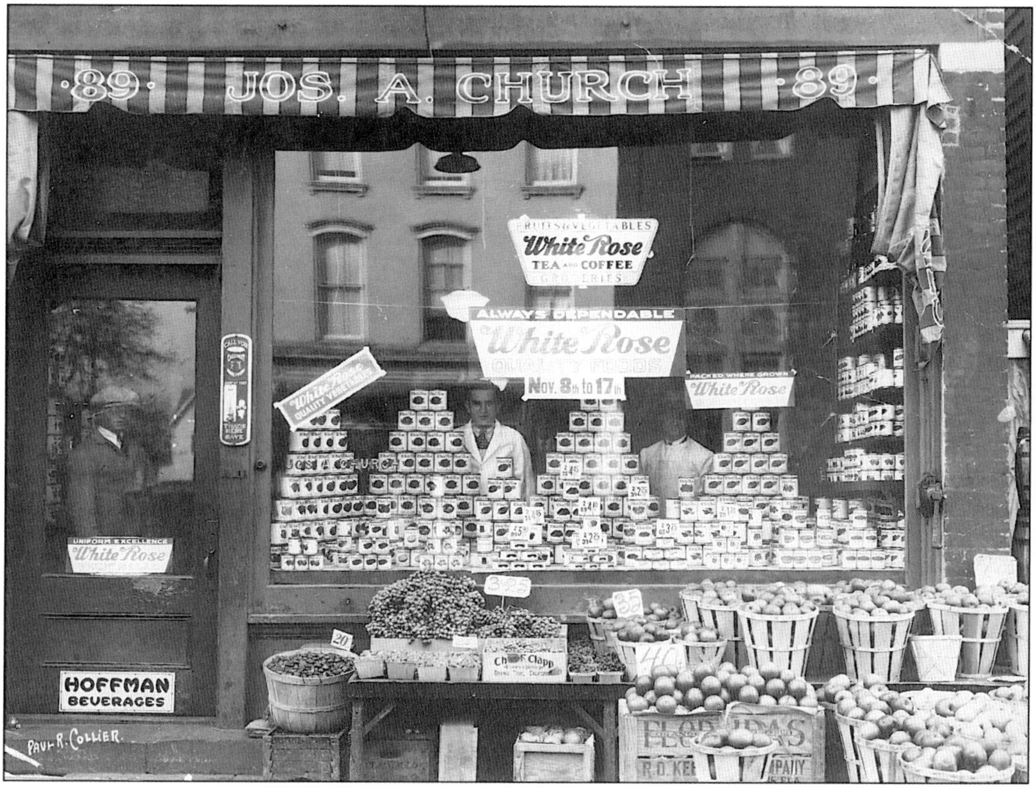

Church's Market was one of the finest grocery stores located on Somerset Street. Food and household goods are stacked to the ceiling in this 1920s photograph. Church's Market closed in the 1980s.

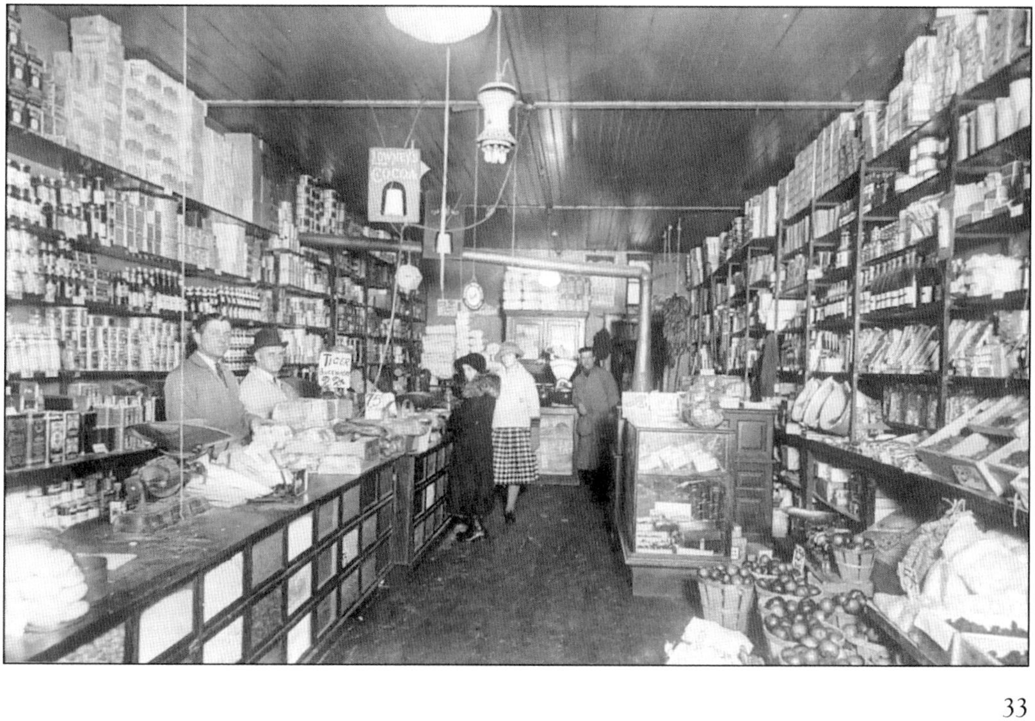

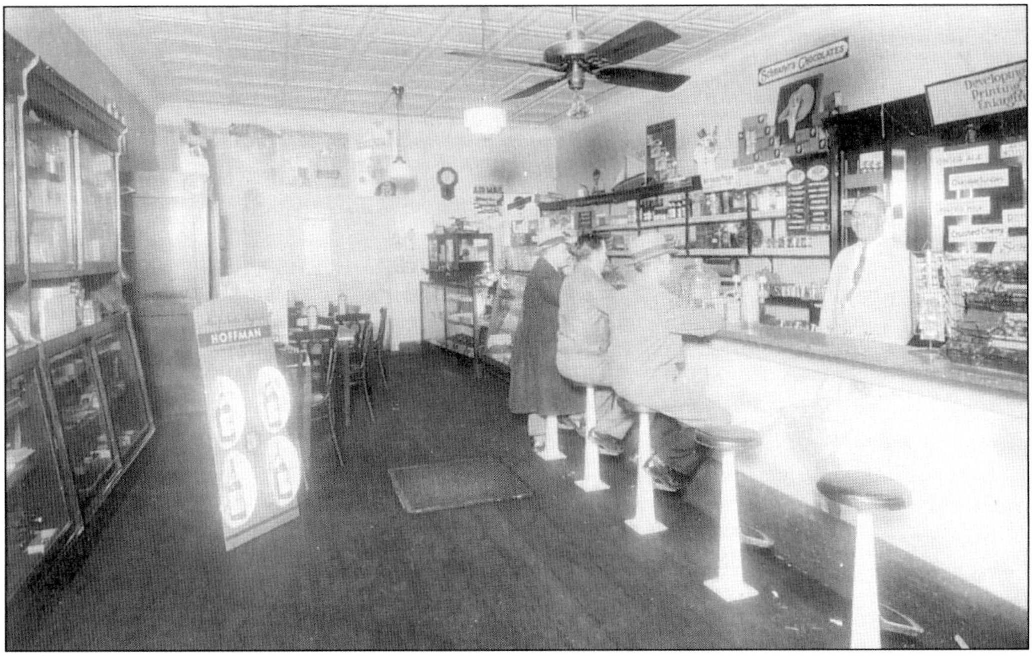

The "Sunny Shoppe" was a popular stopping place for school-age children in the early 1920s and 1930s. Started *c.* 1925, the Sunny Shoppe was purchased in 1931 by David M. Acken. This photograph shows LeRoy S. Force, manager, behind the counter. The Sunny Shoppe was also a sub-station of the Plainfield Post Office, held a circulating library, a film developing service, and sold candy, ice cream, and soda.

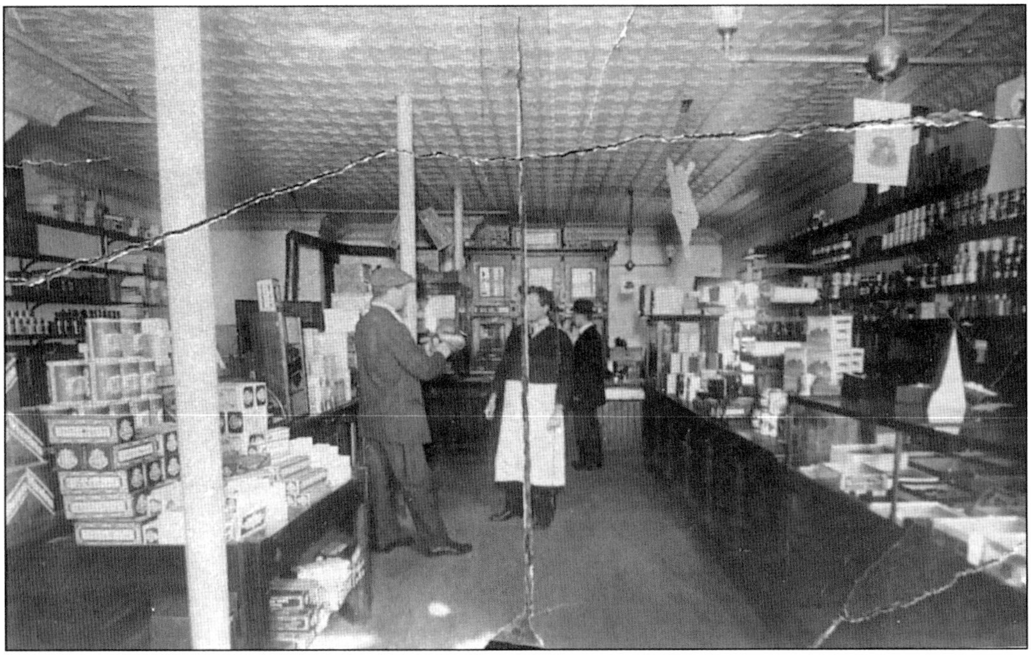

Small grocery stores were located throughout the borough in the early 1900s. This store is believed to be at the corner of Somerset Street and Summit Avenue. For many years, the store was used as a pharmacy.

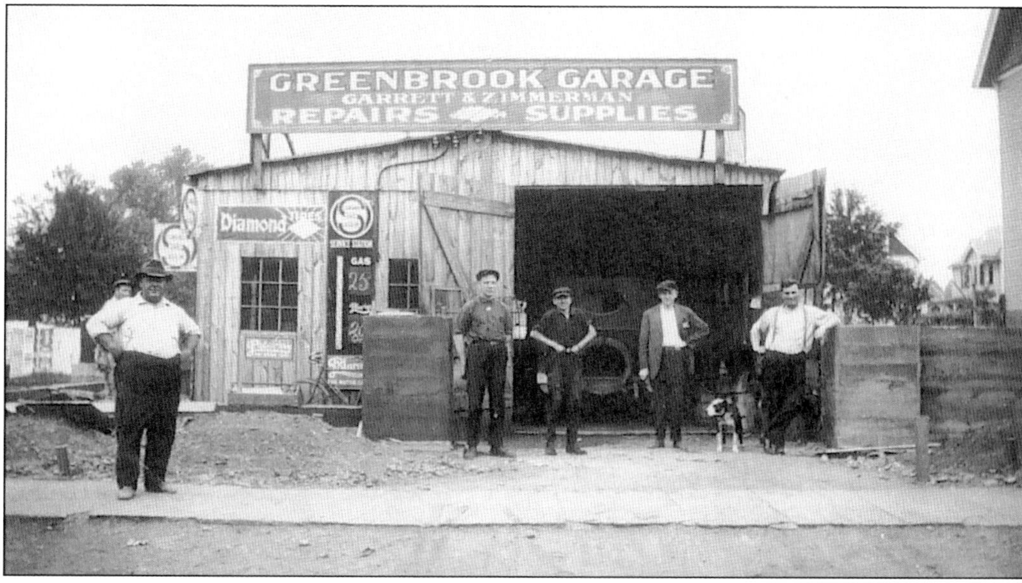

The corner of Greenbrook Road and Somerset Street was the site of Zimmerman's Garage. The old garage was torn down before or during the early 1920s. In the photograph above, Arthur L. Zimmerman is the middle figure wearing the black pants and black shirt.

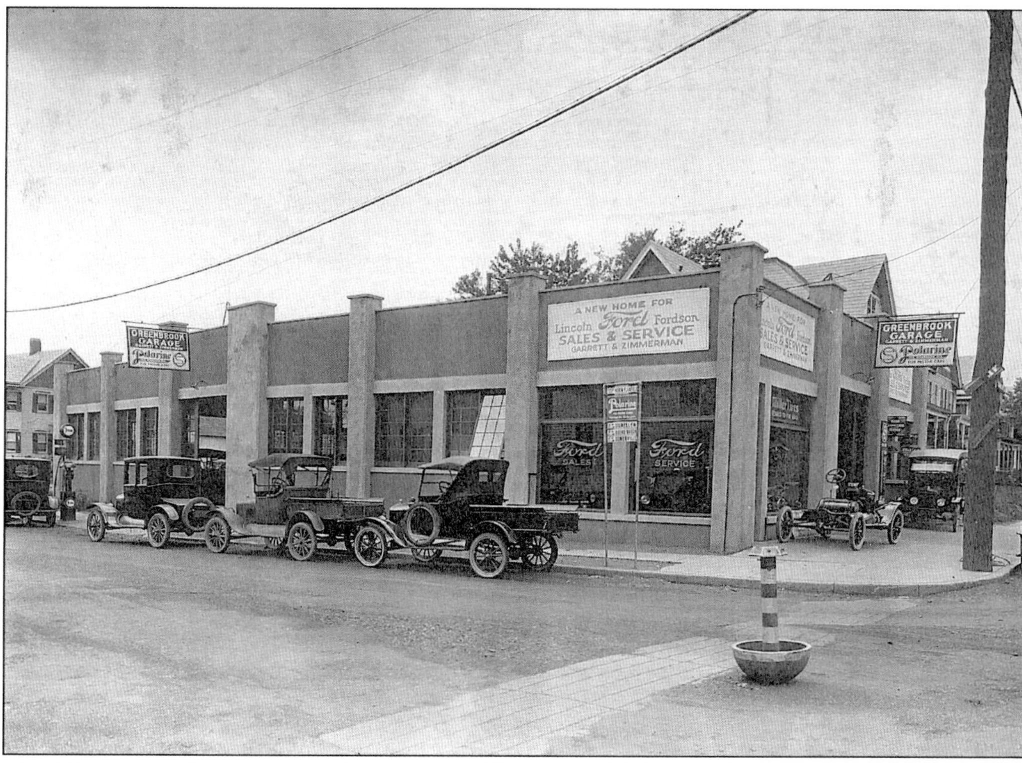

The Zimmerman's new garage, built pre-1925, was established as "The Ford Agency" and was managed by Mr. Zimmerman. In 1925, Mr. Zimmerman drove his family to Daytona Beach, Florida, in a Model-T or A.

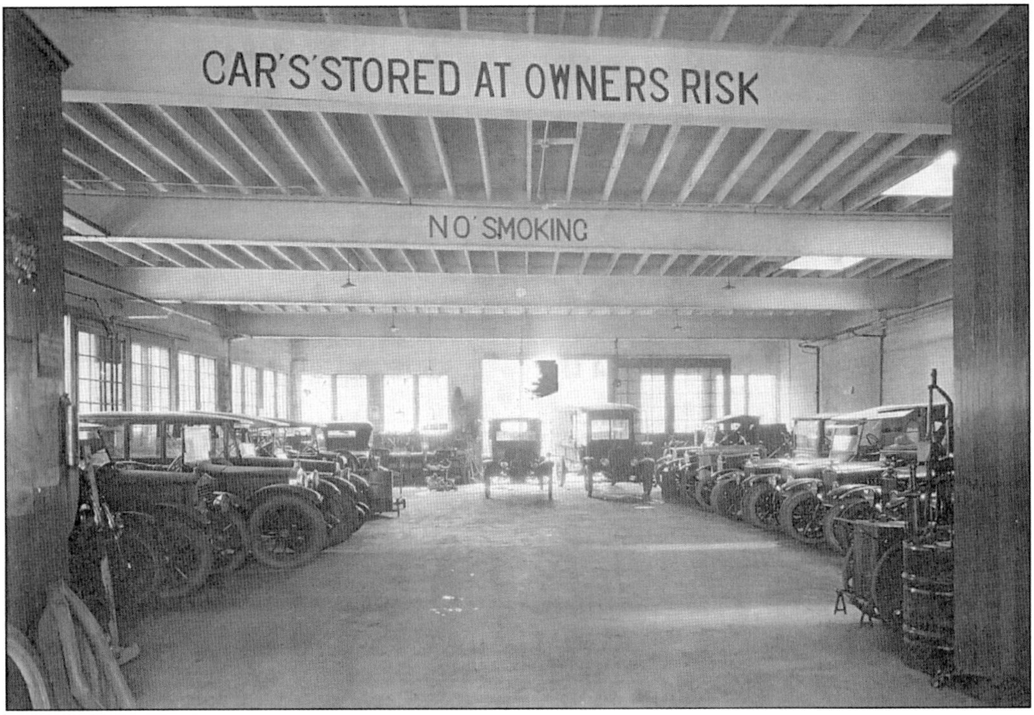

Foot power, bicycles, horses and buggies, and streetcars were the methods by which most people got around in the early 1900s. By 1925, buses and automobiles replaced the streetcars and horses. The slogan "A car in every garage" kept the owners of the Ford Agency on Somerset Street busy.

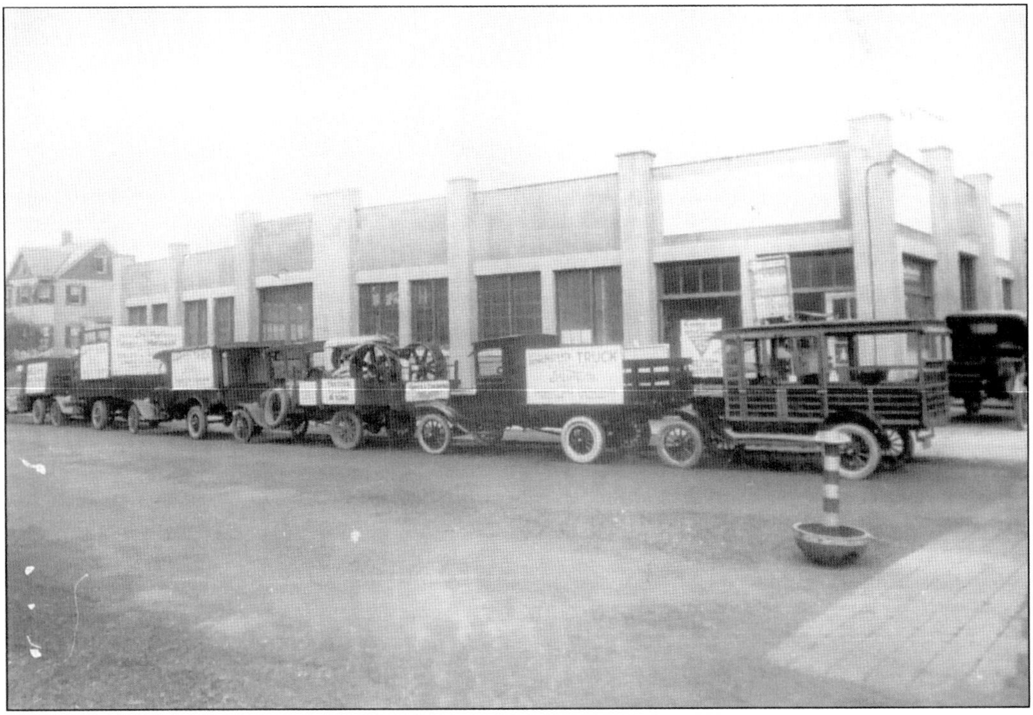

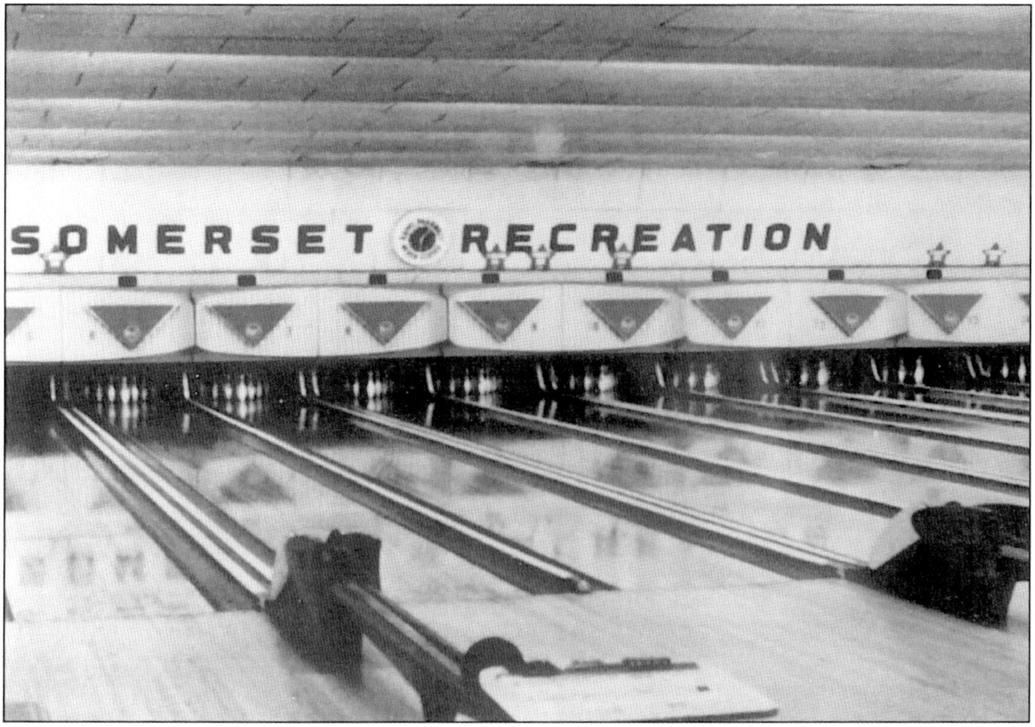

Somerset Recreation was North Plainfield's own bowling alley. Located on Somerset Street at the current site of Quick Check, this popular attraction burned to the ground in the 1980s.

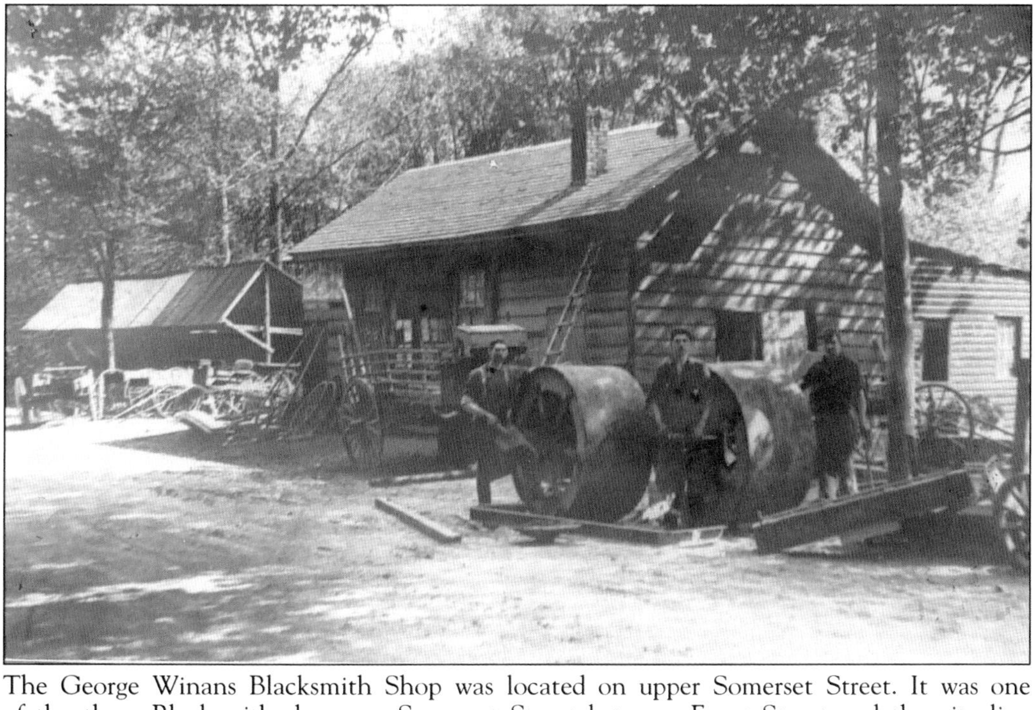

The George Winans Blacksmith Shop was located on upper Somerset Street. It was one of the three Blacksmith shops on Somerset Street between Front Street and the city line of Watchung.

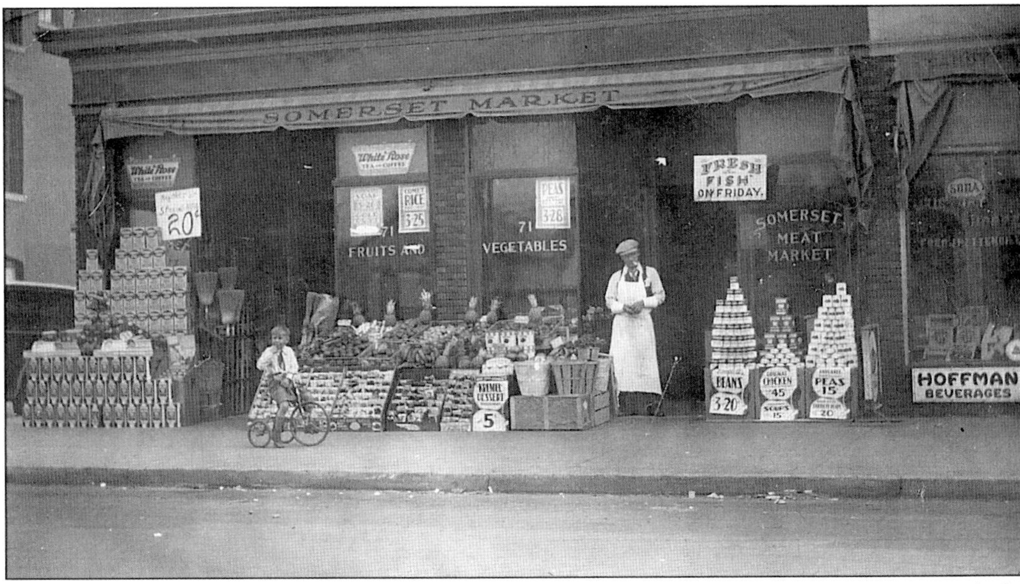

The Somerset Market, located at 183 Somerset Street, was owned and operated by Nicholas Marchio. "My idea is to sell everything for the housewife under one roof," stated Marchio. He also sold his own special brand of macaroni and items from abroad. On the counter could be found candy, cheeses, condiments, and cold cuts. Everything from a clothespin to a frankfurter could be found on display. Pictured are Ben Marchio (on tricycle) and Jack Galuppo (in doorway) in 1929.

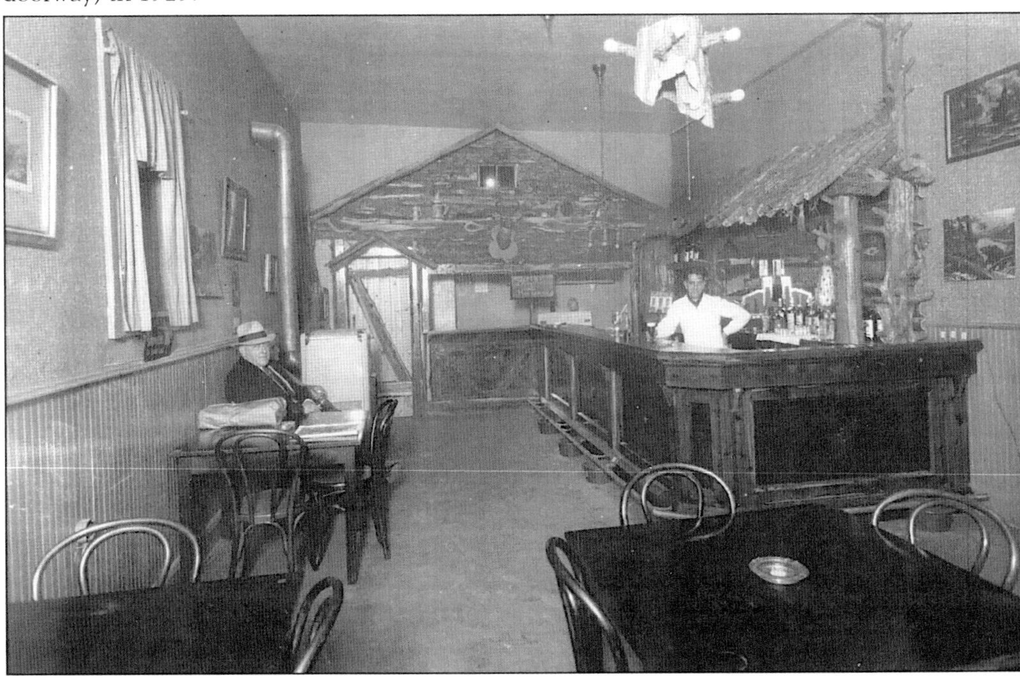

Over the past 100 years, the corner of Harmony and Somerset Streets has seen many different establishments come and go. At one time, this building was home to a bakery; around the turn of the century, it was home to Becker's Hook Shop. Later, as in the picture above, it became the Cedar Bar. Recently, it has been best known as the Harmony Street Restaurant.

Four

SCHOOLS

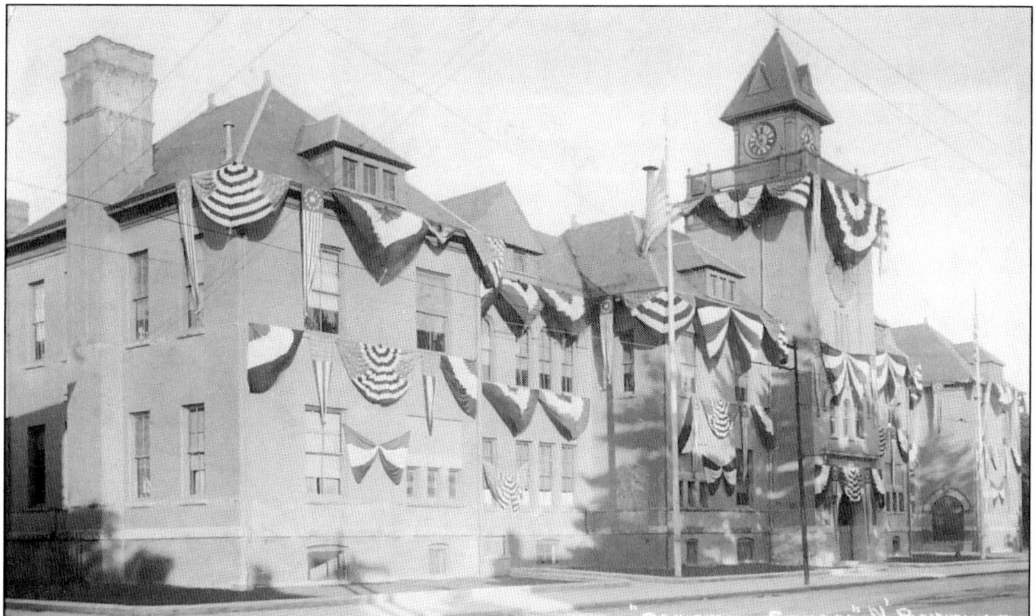

The Somerset School was decorated for the Fourth of July celebration in the early 1900s. Built in 1882, Somerset was the borough's oldest school. It was built as a grammar school at the cost of $25,000 and contained 12 rooms. In 1896, North Plainfield established its first high school on the second floor of the Somerset School building. The school grounds were also the site of a manual training school, which was a gift of Charles W. McCutchen. This building was devoted to the teaching of manual arts to boys and household science to girls. Somerset School was severely damaged by fire in 1950. The clock tower, which stands today, was originally the center of the building.

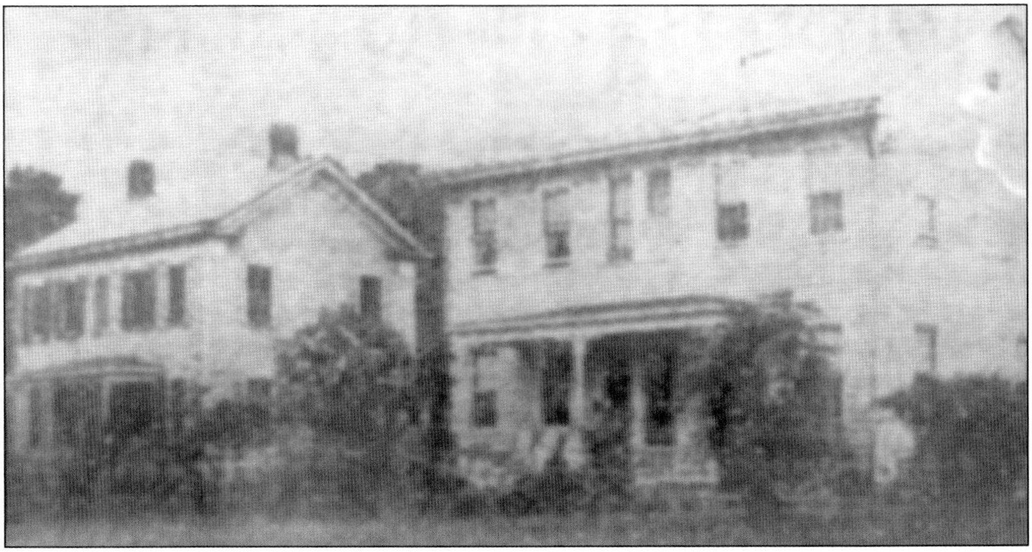

On April 7, 1856, the North Plainfield school district No. 10 was established, and on July 12, 1856, the legal voters met and unanimously voted to raise $2,000 to purchase a lot and build a suitable schoolhouse. On April 6, 1857, a lot on the corner of Harmony, Warren, and Race Streets was selected. The cost of the lot was $300 and the building was than erected for $1,500. It later became known as "Mud Lane" because Harmony Street got so muddy every time it rained.

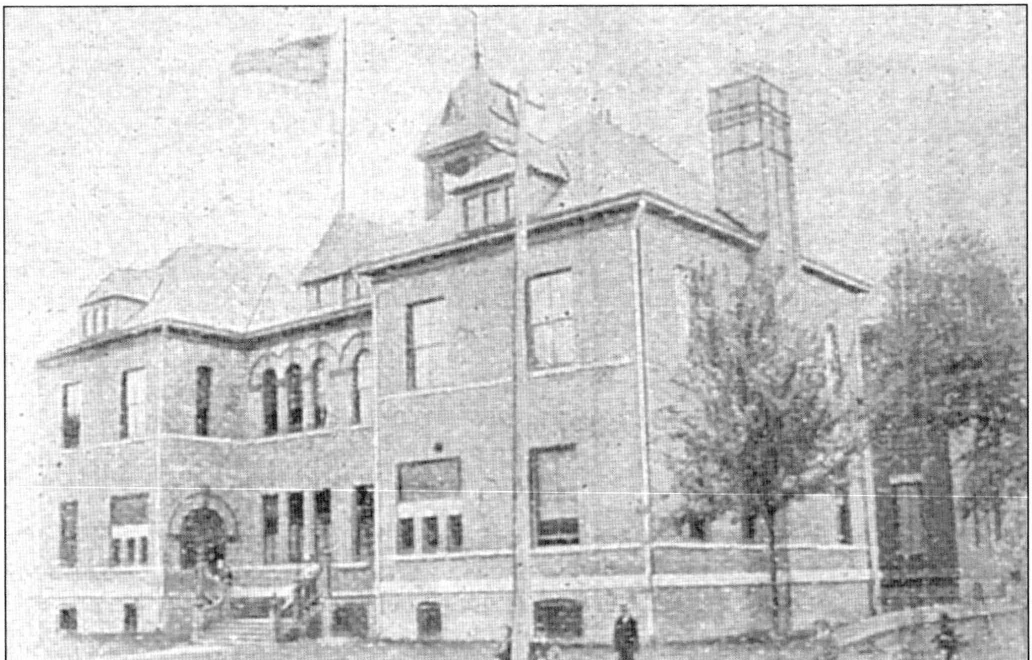

North Plainfield established its first high school in 1896. Classes began on the second floor of the Somerset School building. Four courses of study were available to pupils, including classical, commercial, Latin Scientific, and general. Since the building did not contain a large auditorium, graduations were held at Plainfield until 1900.

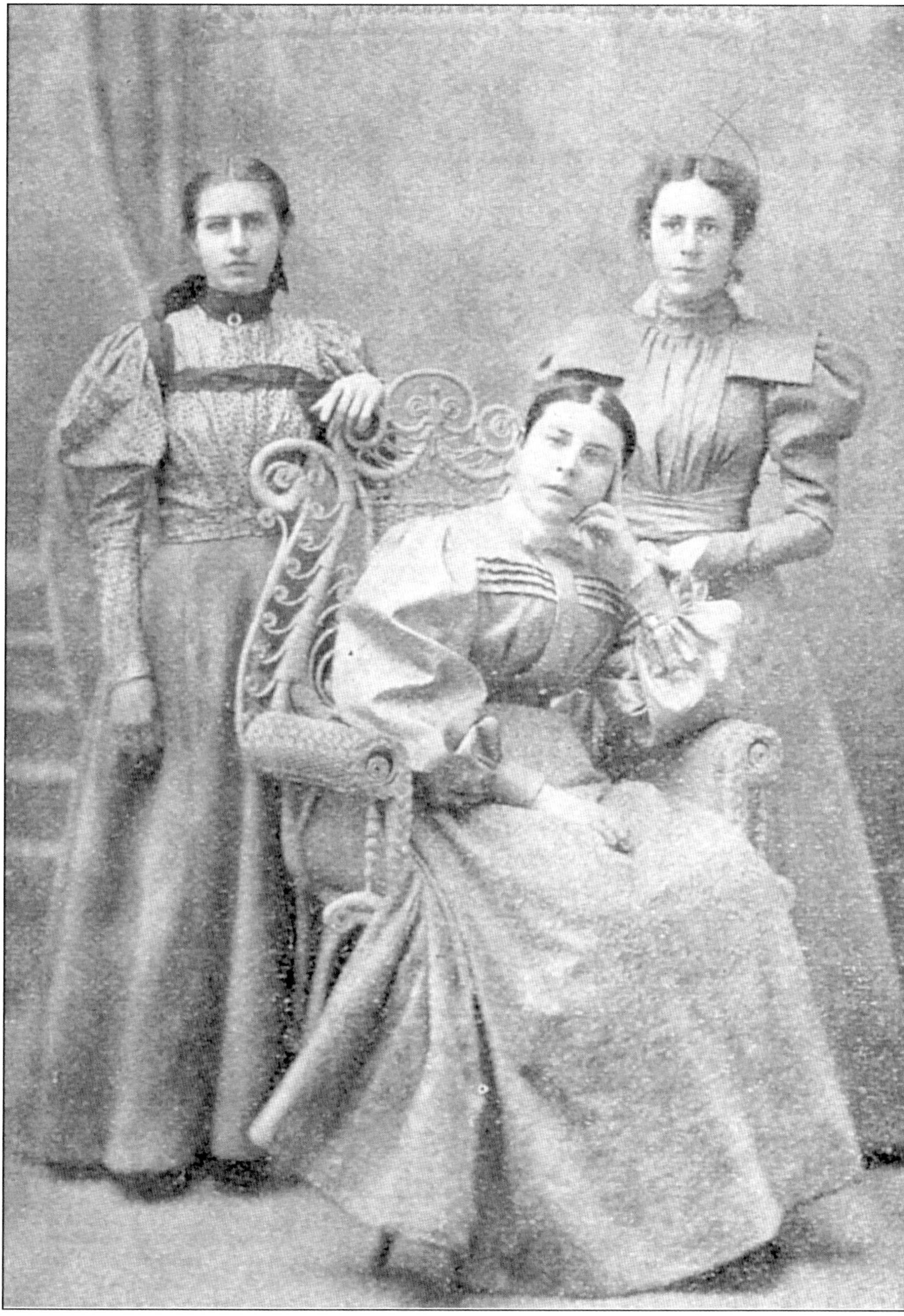

In 1897, North Plainfield's first high school graduates were three women. They were Bessie Thompson Day, Edna Louise French, and Harriet Helen Philips.

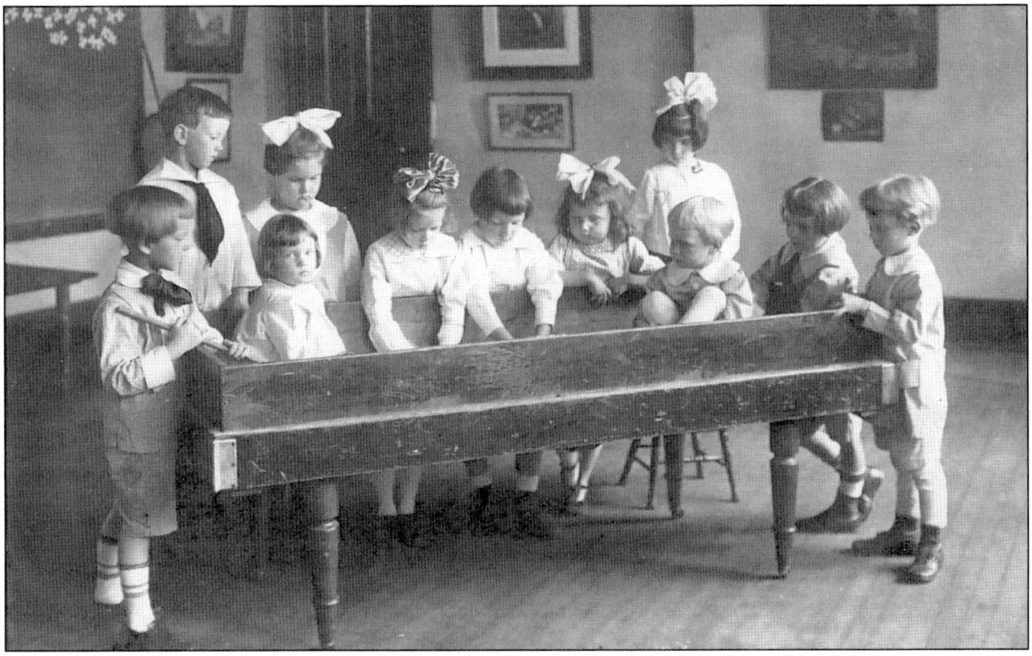

Kindergarten children play in sandbox at Somerset School, *c.* 1917. The teacher was Miss Edna Louise French, a graduate of the class of 1897. The goal was to teach children to be well-rounded, patriotic American citizens.

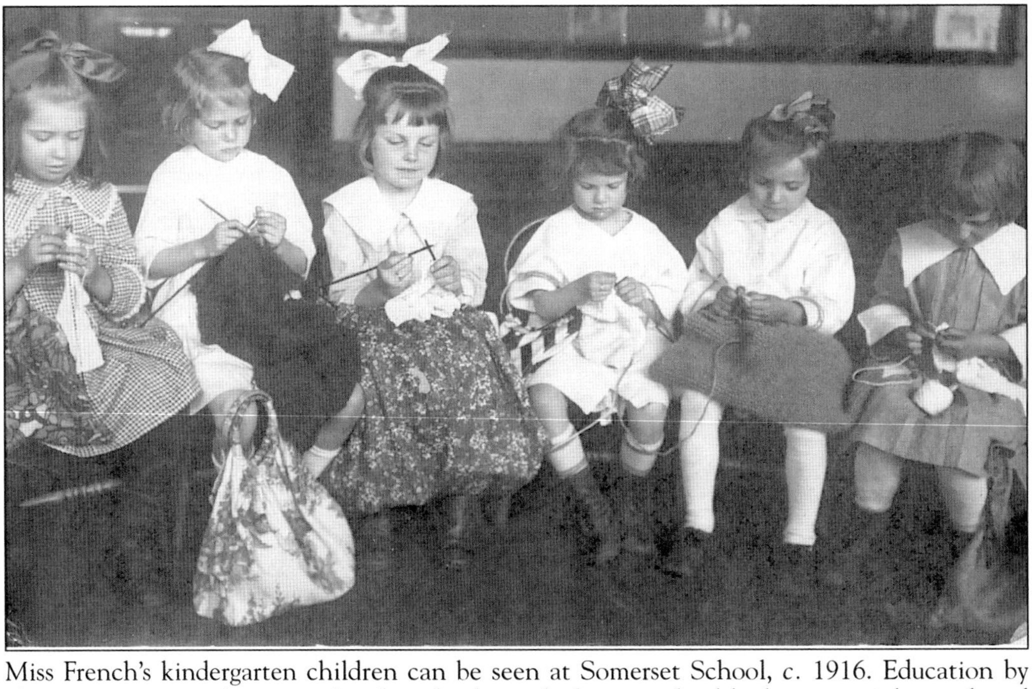

Miss French's kindergarten children can be seen at Somerset School, *c.* 1916. Education by plays, games, songs, dramatics, handiwork, physical education, healthy living, social, moral, and esthetic elements were stressed in kindergarten.

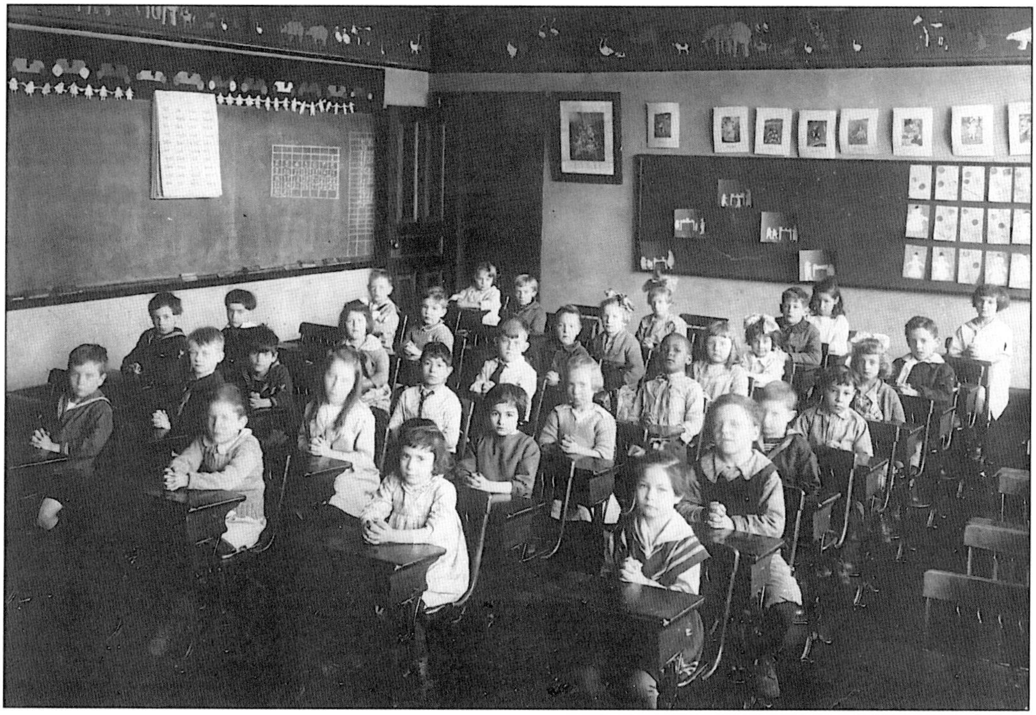

Miss Rogers's first grade class at Somerset School can be seen in the above photograph, c. 1920–1921. First grade curriculum included: Language, Reading, writing, numbers, Nature Study, Vocal Music, Art, and Physical Education.

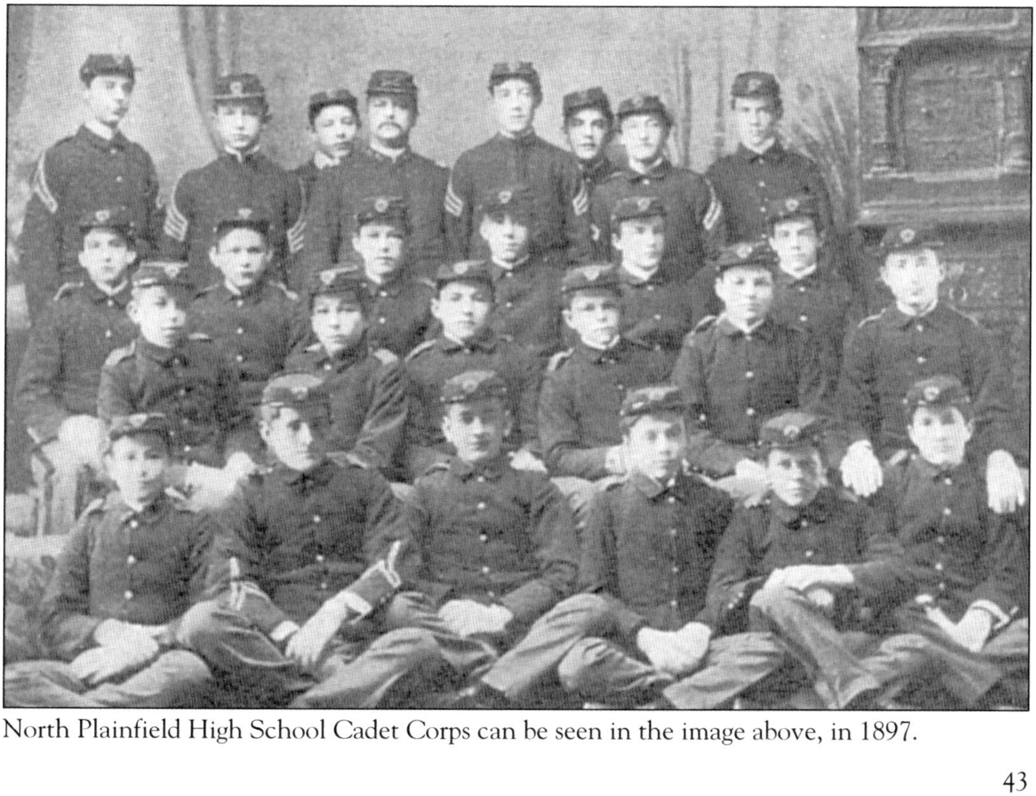

North Plainfield High School Cadet Corps can be seen in the image above, in 1897.

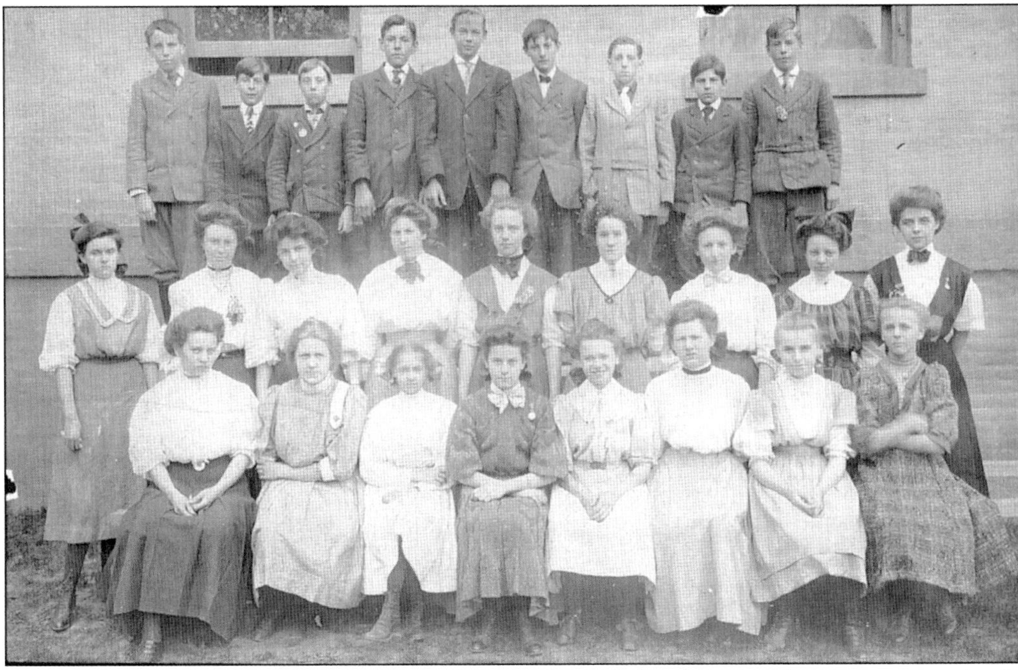

In 1907, this Somerset School elementary class posed for their yearly picture outside the building. Albert Force, standing in the back row, was captain of the high school basketball team in 1918.

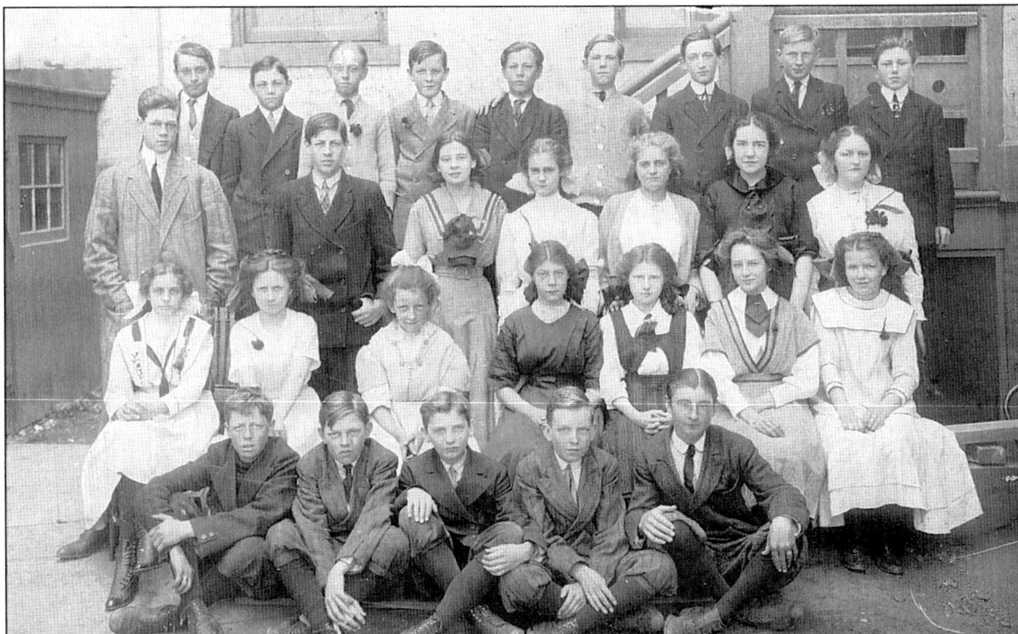

The seventh and eighth grade classes of Somerset School had their picture taken outside the school in 1907.

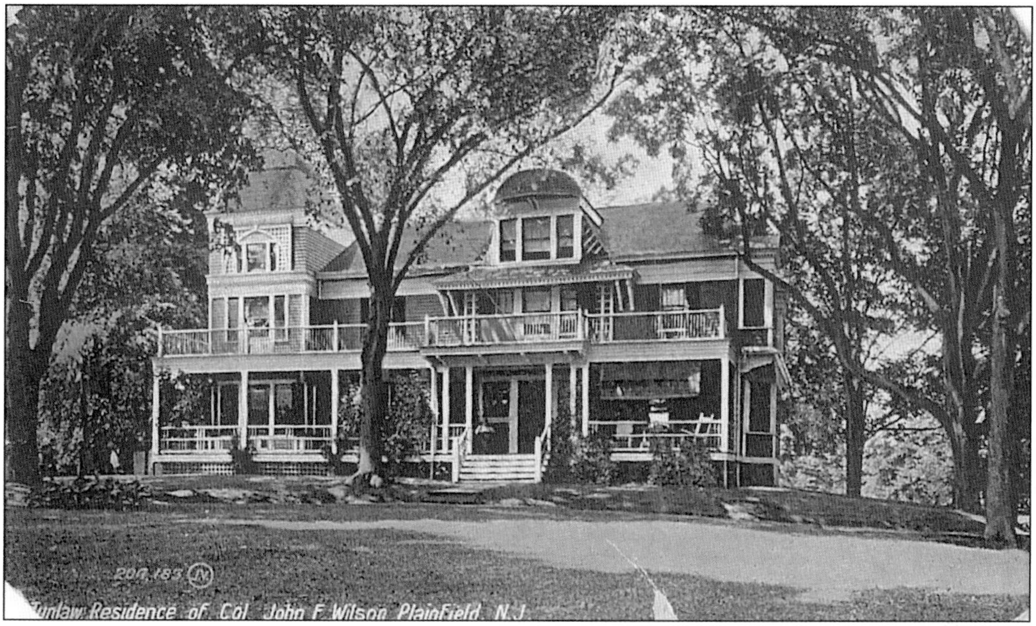

"Tunlaw" was the name of the home of Col. John F. Wilson. Wilson purchased the property from Judge Cary; at that time, it was the only home on Greenbrook Road from Somerset Street to West End Avenue. When Colonel Wilson died, his daughter sold the property to the board of education. The new high school was erected and opened to pupils in September 1925.

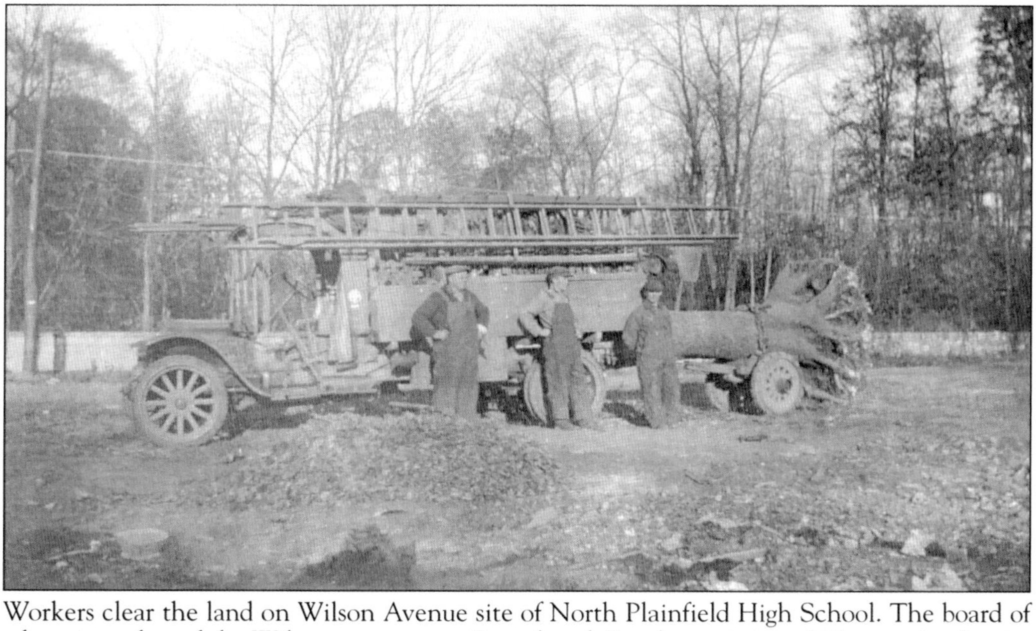

Workers clear the land on Wilson Avenue site of North Plainfield High School. The board of education selected the Wilson property on Greenbrook Road, consisting of 27 acres, for the site of the new school. No other property offered presented as much ground for landscaping and athletic activities as did this tract.

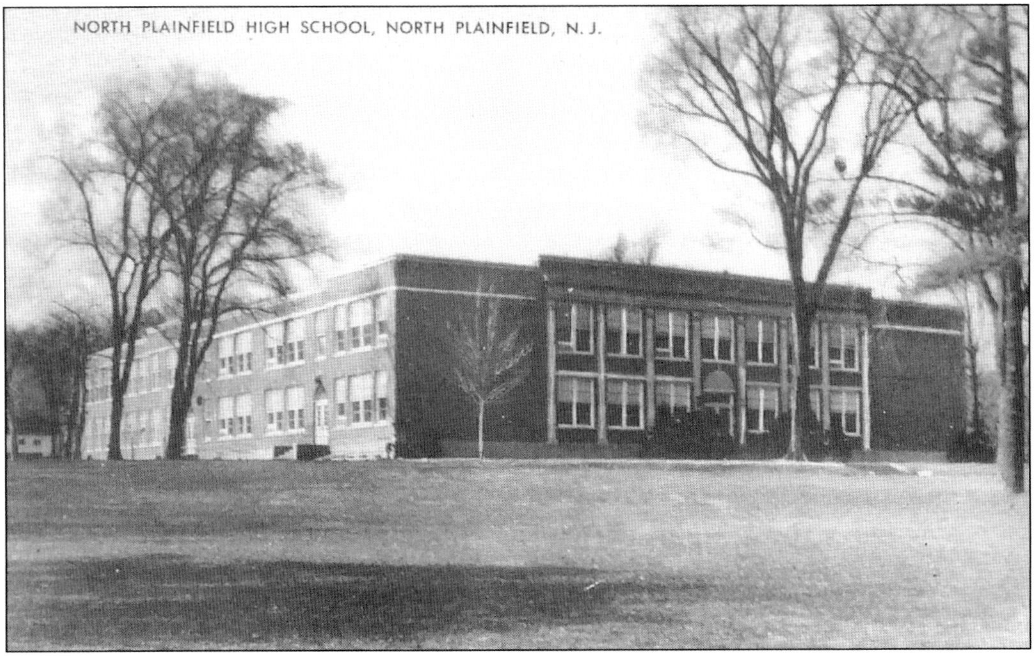

In 1924, a new high school was built at the site of the present middle school and high school on Wilson Avenue and Greenbrook Road. In the early days of the current campus, pupils came from other districts to attend high school on a tuition basis. *Tunlaw*, the school newspaper, takes its name from Colonel Wilson's estate. Tunlaw comes from the word walnut spelled backwards.

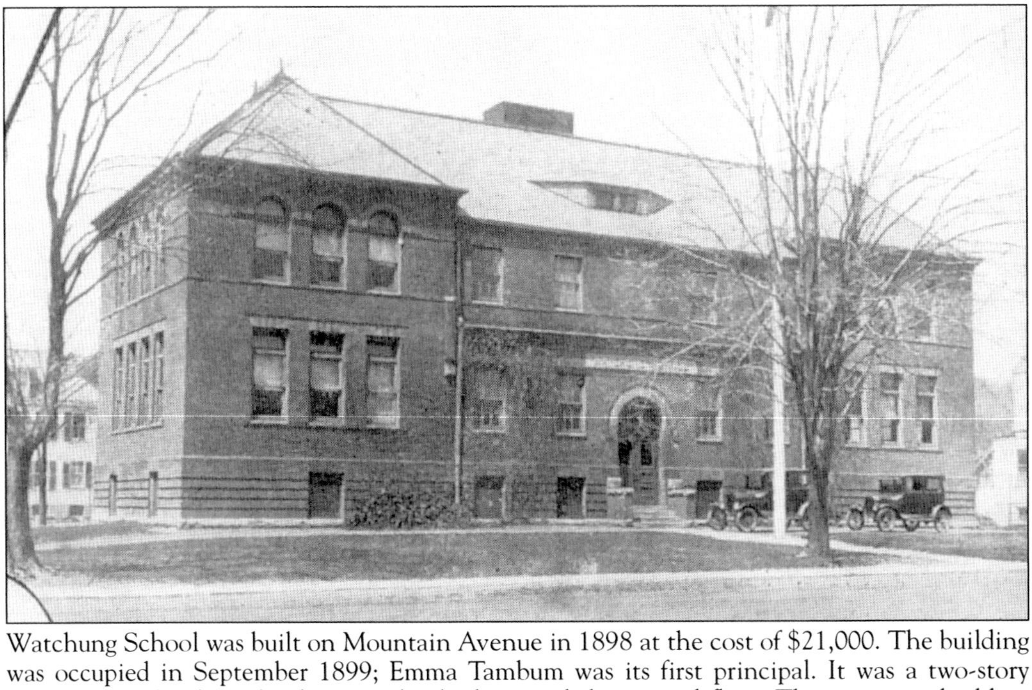

Watchung School was built on Mountain Avenue in 1898 at the cost of $21,000. The building was occupied in September 1899; Emma Tambum was its first principal. It was a two-story elementary school until a fire completely destroyed the second floor. The one story building now officially houses the board of education and its offices.

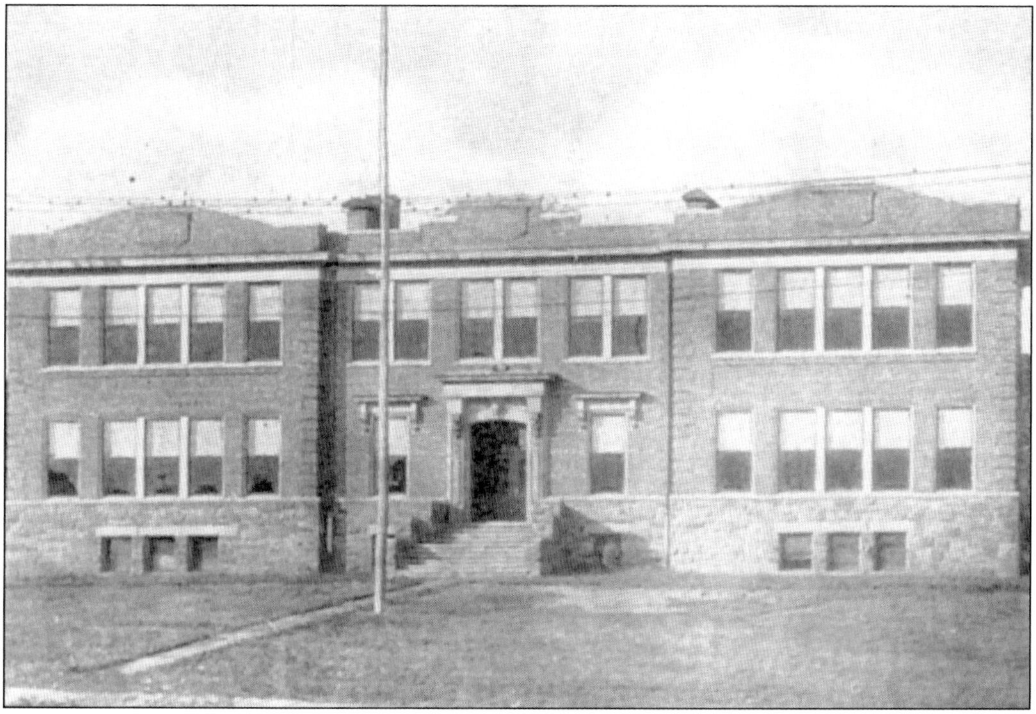

Harrison School was built in 1914 as a primary school at the cost of $30,380. It had the largest playground in the school system and remained the most modern in the area until East End and West End Schools were constructed.

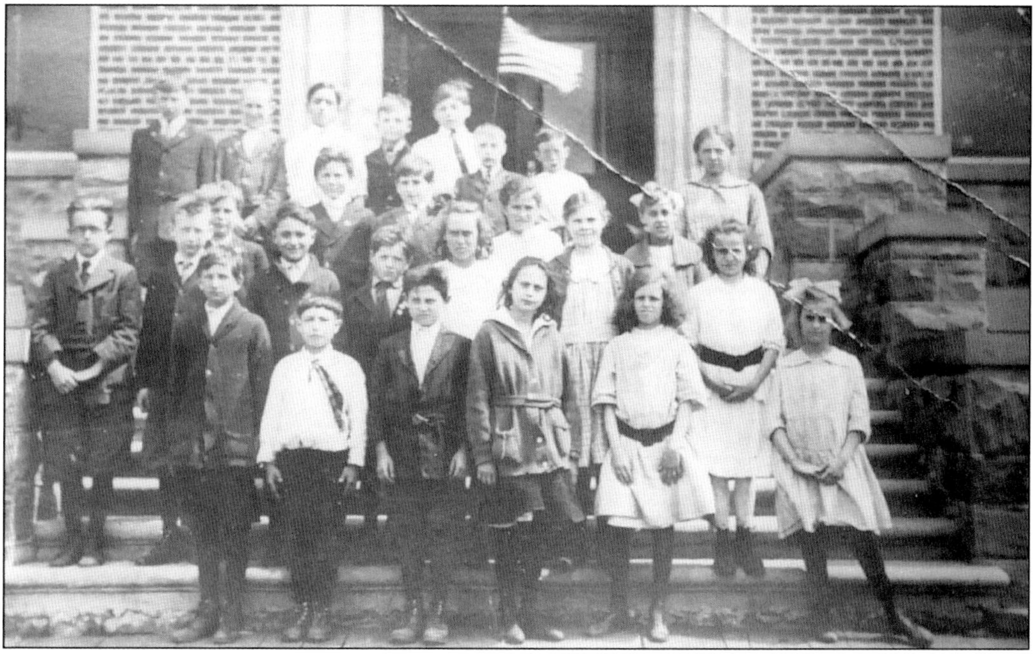

This 1918 photograph of the fifth grade was taken on the front steps of Harrison School, located on Harrison Avenue. This school, according to records of the time, was thoroughly fireproof, easy to exit, sanitary, and well lit.

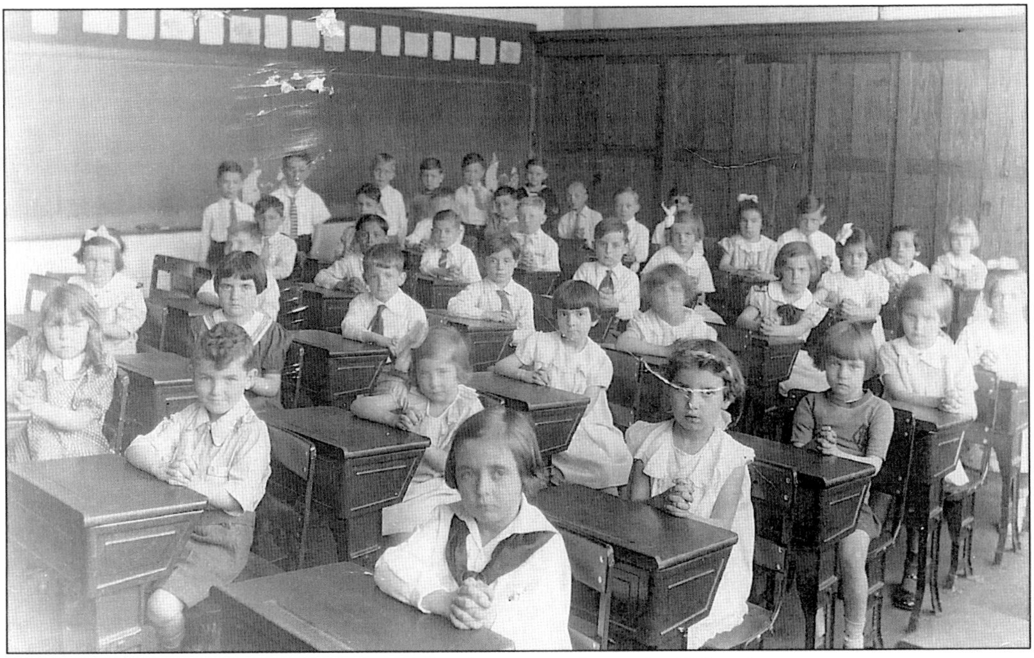

This elementary class of St. Joseph's School sits straight and tall for the camera.

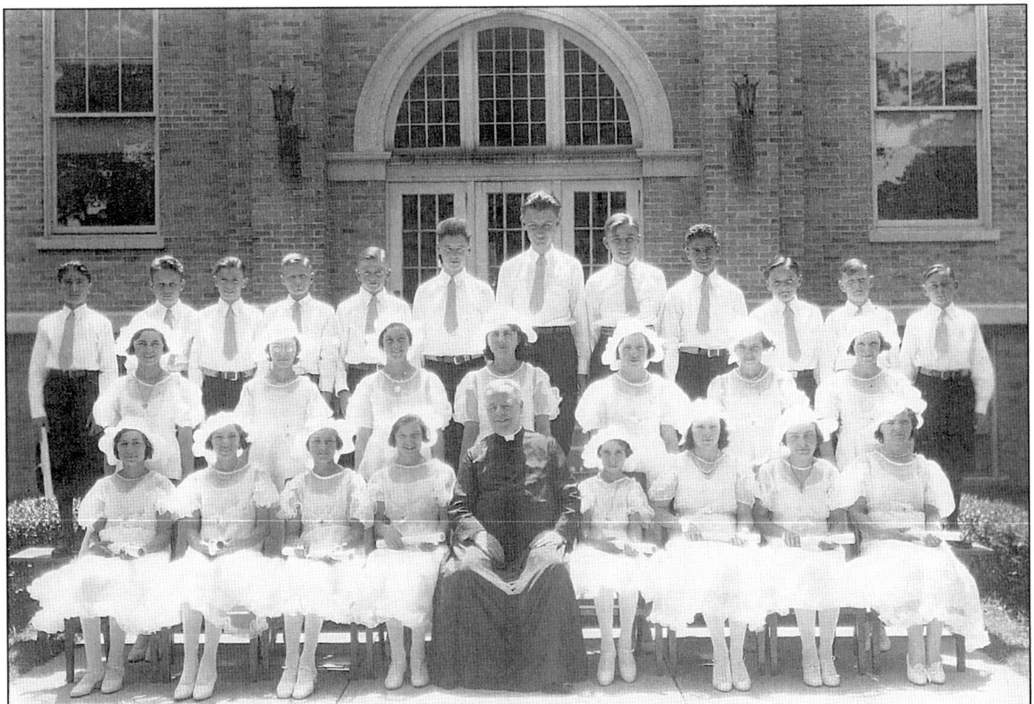

In 1930, St. Joseph's School opened with about 30 children in each of its eight grades. Sr. Mary Angela Walker was the first principal. The first class graduated in 1933 with 24 students. Sr. Virginia McGarry (Sr. Ann Marie) is the only living founder of St. Joseph's School. She currently resides at McAuley Hall at Mount Saint Mary's.

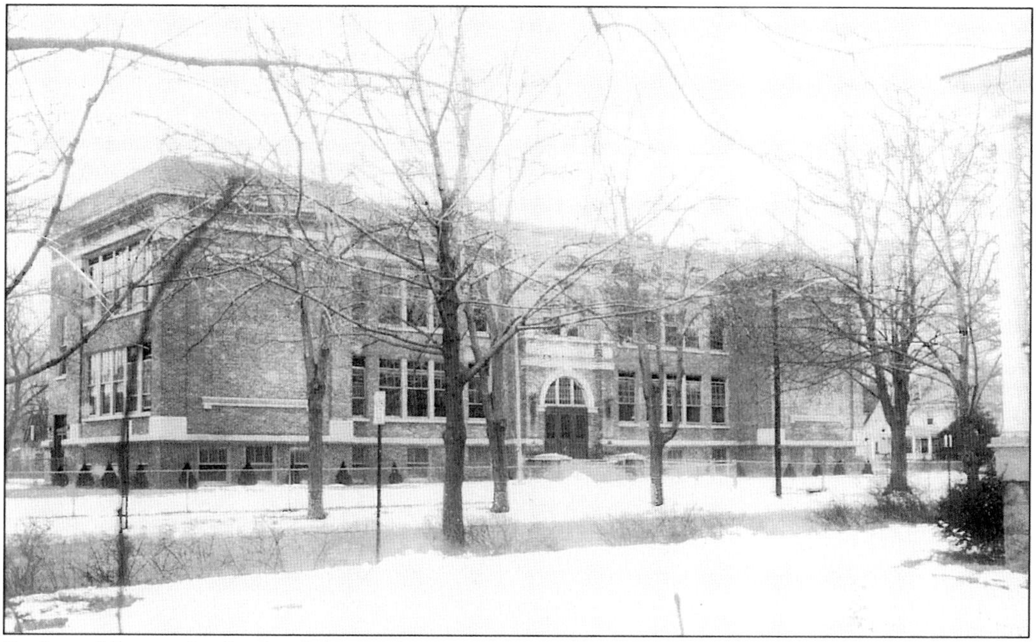

St. Joseph's parochial school, located on Westervelt Avenue, was dedicated June 15, 1930. The elaborate ceremonies were conducted by the Rt. Reverend John J. McMahon, who laid the cornerstone. Sister Angela was appointed principal of the eighth grade school. The parent-teacher association was organized in 1930. Alexander Milne was the contractor for the project.

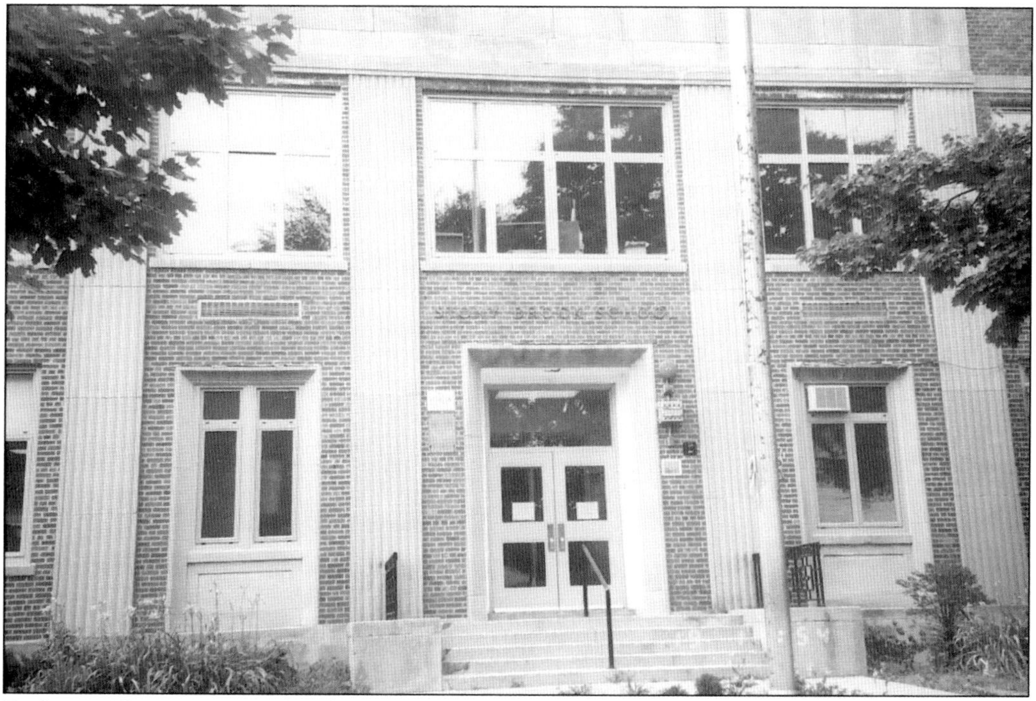

Built in 1951, Stony Brook School occupies property along the brook and adjacent to the high school/middle school complex. It has 12 plus rooms and a gym.

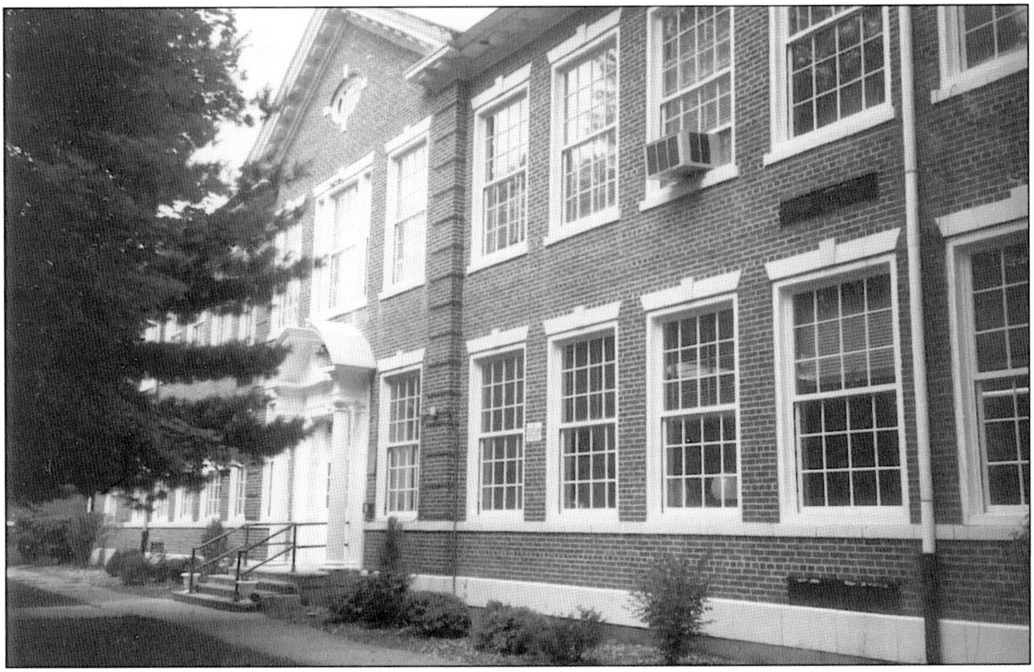

The board of education was authorized to purchase two tracts of land, one at each end of the borough, to be used, when needed, for the construction of elementary schools in 1927. The East End school was built on Oneida Avenue at the foot of Hurley Avenue in 1936. A gymnasium was added in 1966.

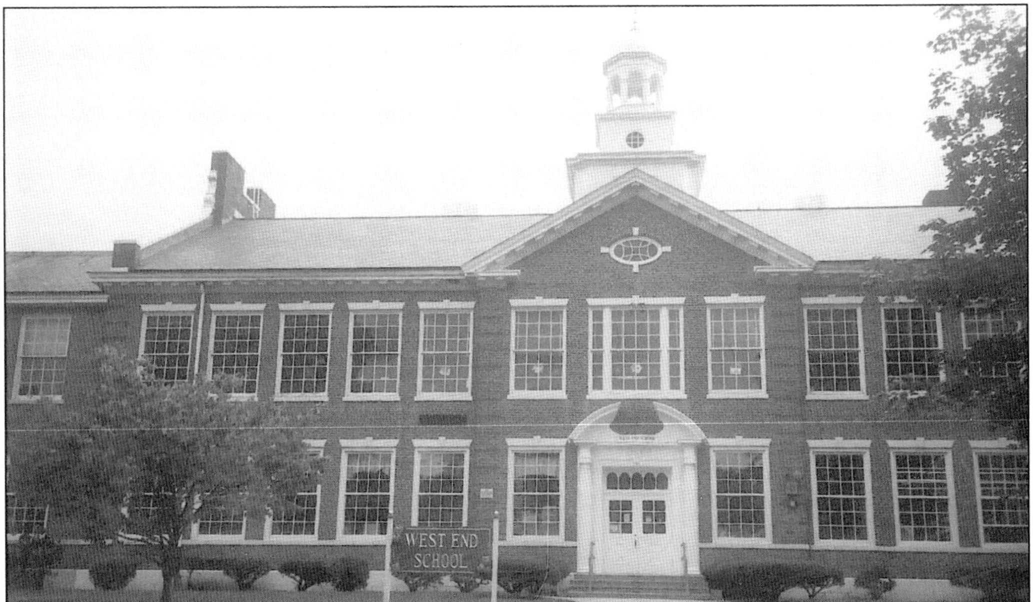

The West End School was built on Greenbrook Road and Harrington Avenue in 1936. Dedication exercises for both schools were held in the Somerset School gymnasium on January 7, 1937. A gymnasium was added in 1966; outdoor tennis courts are a special feature of both the East and West End Schools.

Five

Churches

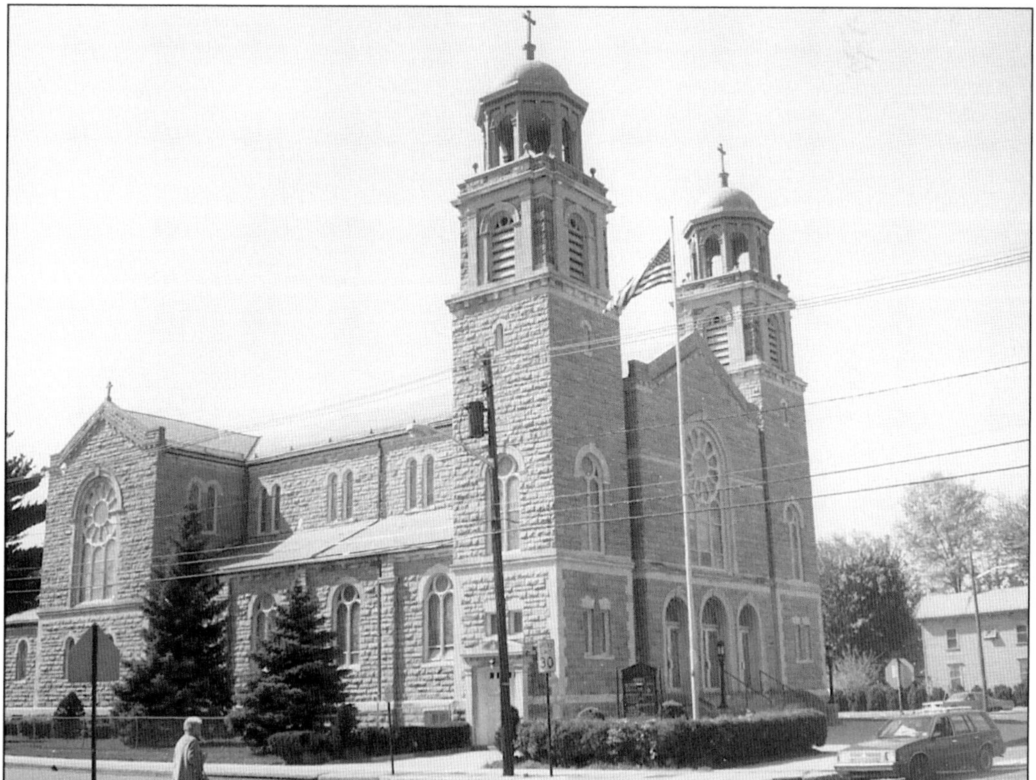

St. Joseph's Roman Catholic Church was established by the late Bishop Farrell in 1881. Mass was first celebrated in North Plainfield in 1851 at the James Verdon residence on the corner of Somerset Street and Summit Avenue. In 1880, the Catholics of North Plainfield found themselves separated from the Plainfield community as members of the newly formed diocese of Trenton. The Borough of North Plainfield became the first parish erected by the new diocese in 1882. The "New" St. Joseph's Church, shown above, was dedicated on April 28, 1912.

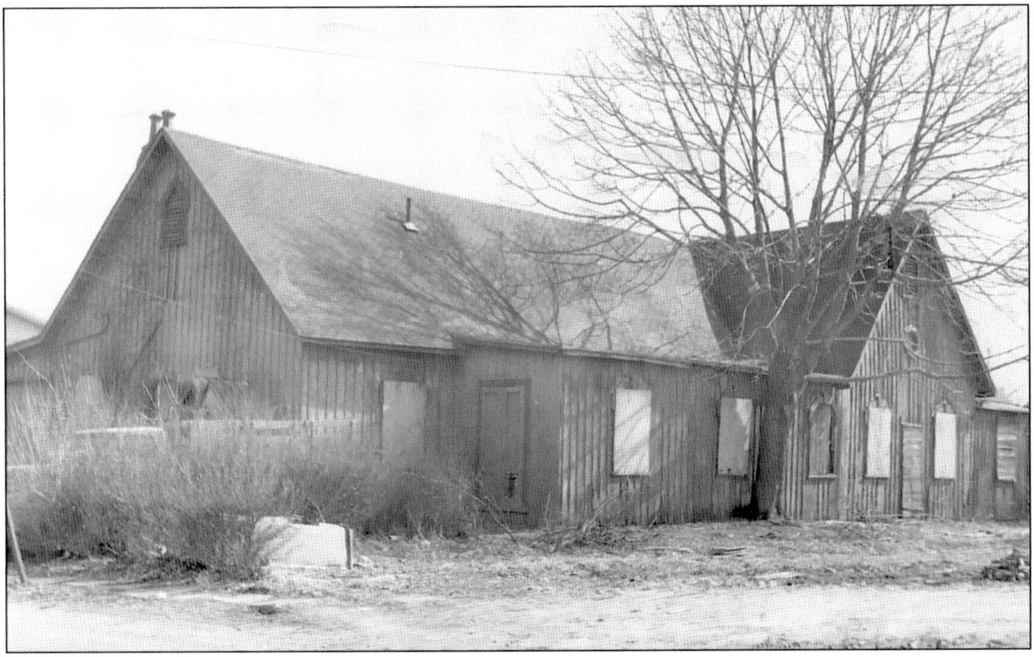

Seen here are the remains of the old Warren Mission Chapel before its destruction in 1974. In later years, the mission was used as a clothing factory, dance hall, and school. The Warren Union Mission Chapel was started by Miss Jeanie Wheeler in June of 1870 on Chatham Street and remained there for many years. The constitution of the chapel stated that the religious services were to be non-sectarian.

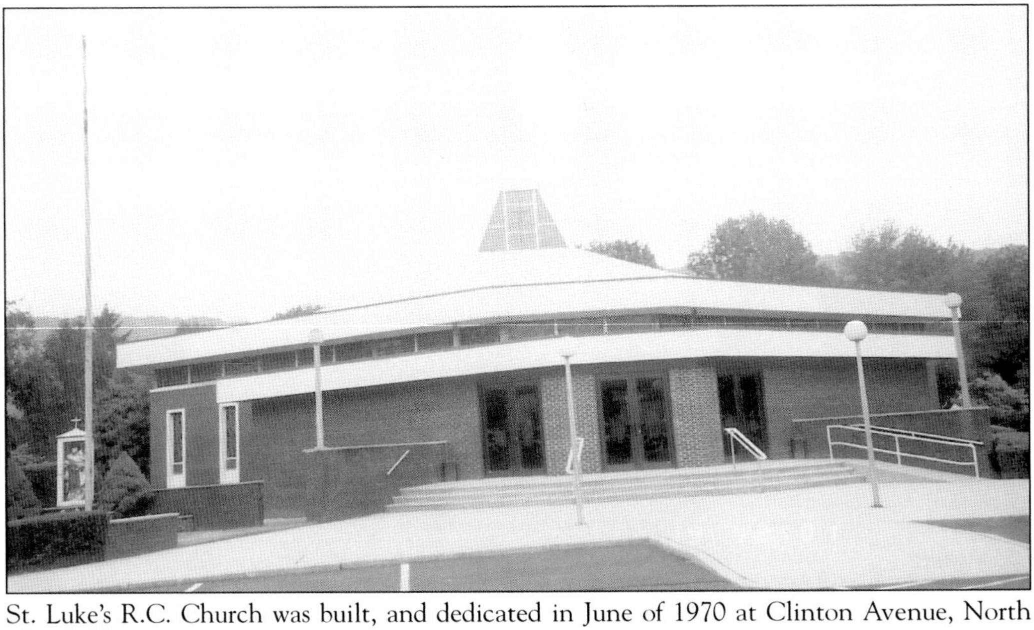

St. Luke's R.C. Church was built, and dedicated in June of 1970 at Clinton Avenue, North Plainfield.

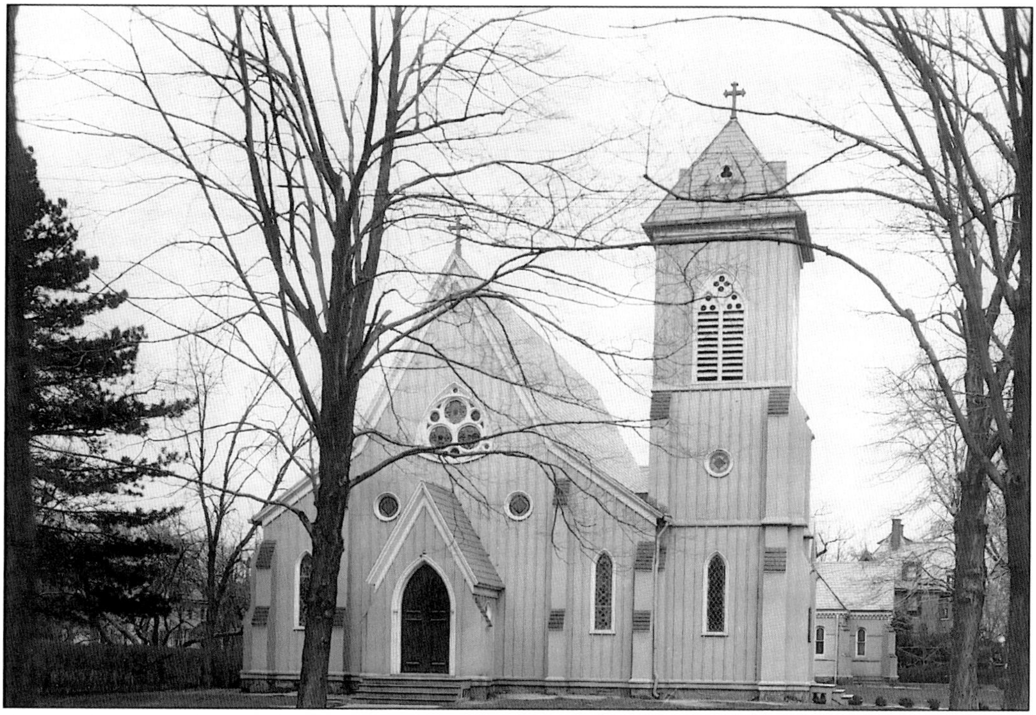

The Holy Cross Episcopal Church was the first established church in the borough. The ground was broken, Tuesday, August 4, 1868, on the corner of Washington and Mercer Avenues. On Sunday, June 13, 1869, the service of dedication was held. Costs for the building of the church were estimated at about $21,000.

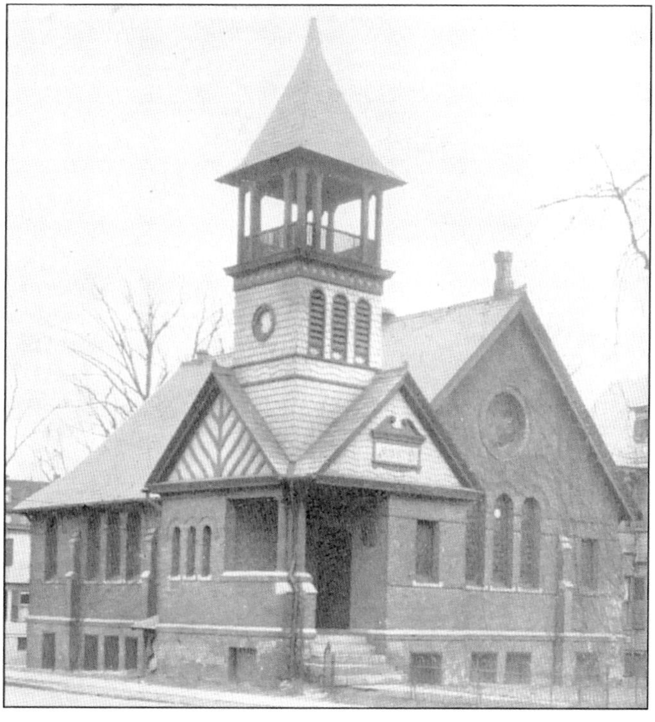

The German Reformed Church on the corner of Duer Street and Craig Place was erected in 1886, and dedicated on February 12, 1888. The church was first organized in 1851, when a group of German families living in Plainfield asked the pastor of the Warren Reformed Church to conduct prayer meetings for them. The first church was organized with 54 members.

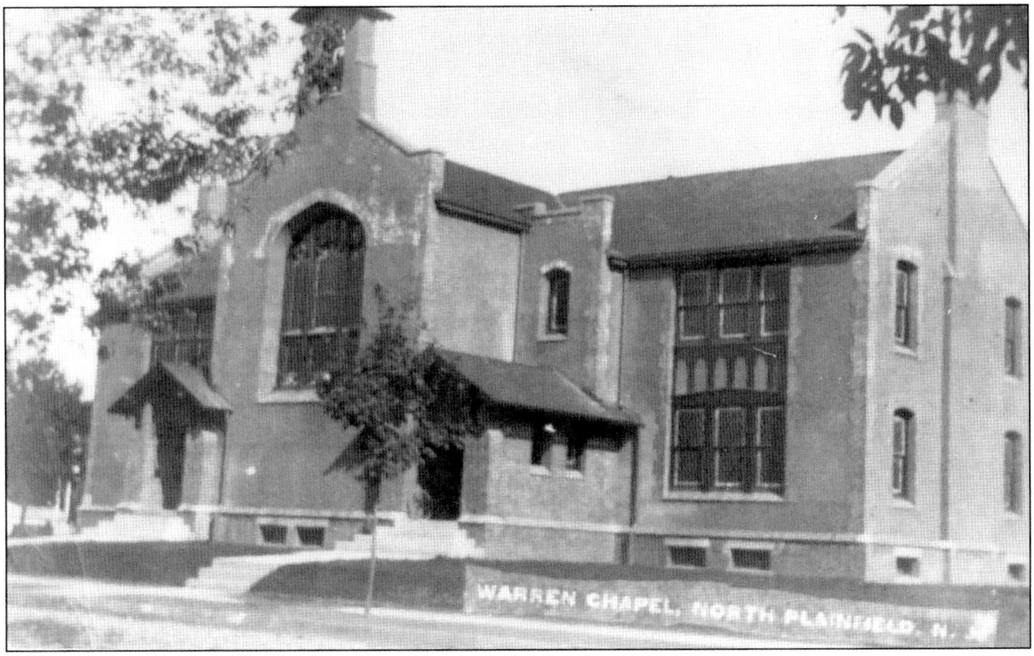

The Watchung Avenue Presbyterian Church was first organized as the Warren Mission Chapel. On April 4, 1893, a meeting was called at which the members present voted that they become identified with the Crescent Avenue Presbyterian Church of Plainfield. In 1907, the Watchung Avenue Presbyterian Church was dedicated, and soon after, a request was granted that made this an independent church.

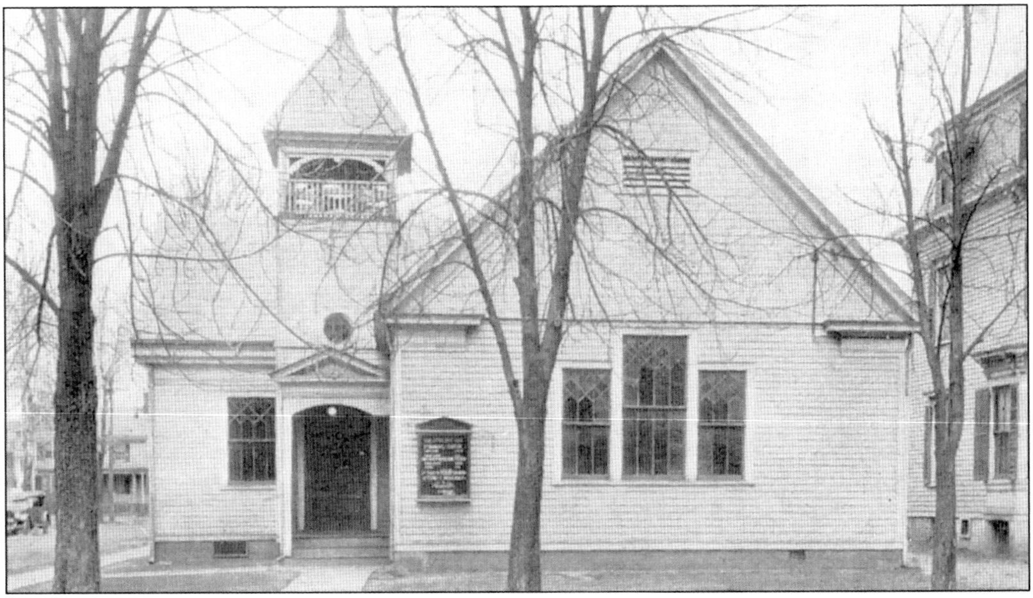

St. Peter's Evangelical Lutheran Church on the corner of Grove Street and Mercer Avenue was incorporated in 1893. Before the church building was dedicated, meetings were held first in the YMCA and later in the Warren Mission Chapel. In the spring of 1893, the property at Grove Street and Mercer Avenue was purchased. By August 27, the cornerstone was laid and by November 1893, the building was completed.

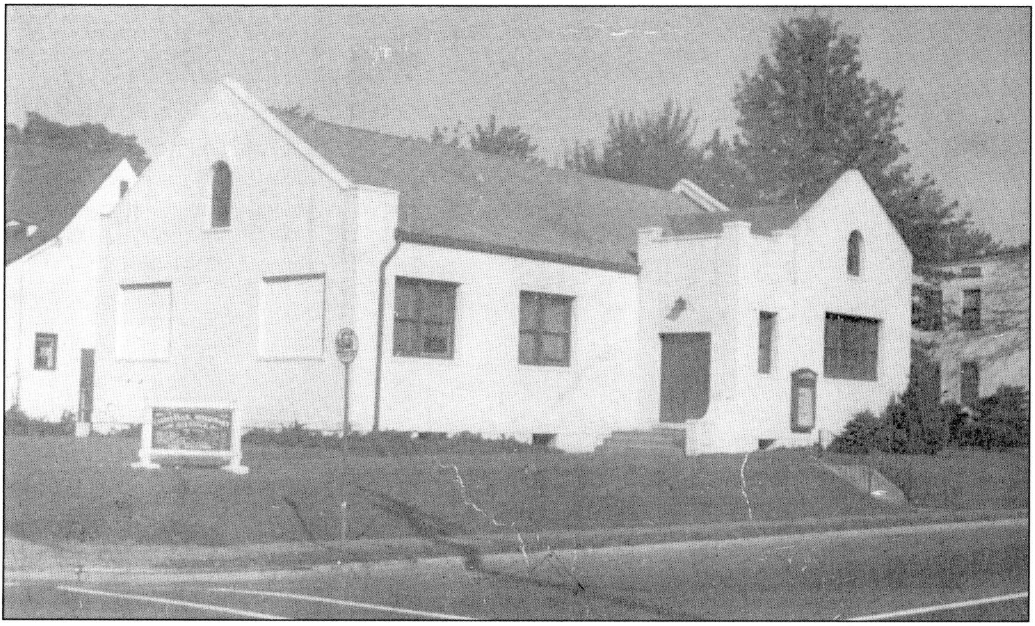

The Christian and Missionary Alliance church stood on the corner of Somerset Street and Mountain Avenue. On Thanksgiving Day 1926, the cornerstone of the church was laid; the building was dedicated on Easter Sunday 1927 and was known as Gospel Tabernacle. This building was later torn down to make way for what is currently Unity Bank.

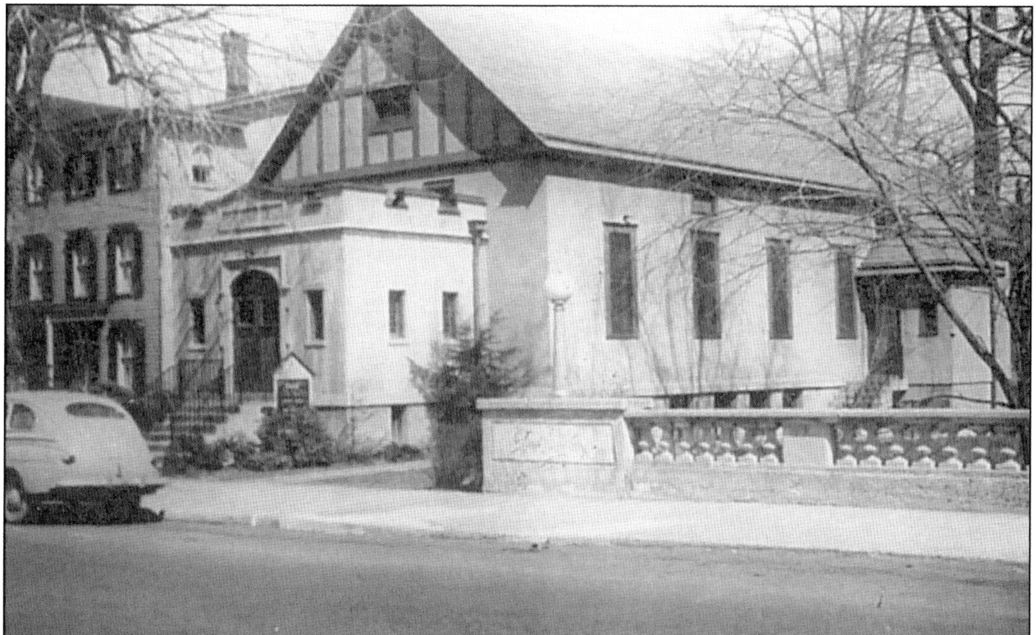

Built in 1892 as the Christian Missionary Society of Ohio, it became the First Church of Christ of Plainfield in 1906. Before 1927, Temple Sholom occupied the building. Once known as the Grove Street Chapel, the Community Baptist church, located at 20 Grove Street, was first organized in 1969 by Rev. William J. Alston and a few dedicated followers.

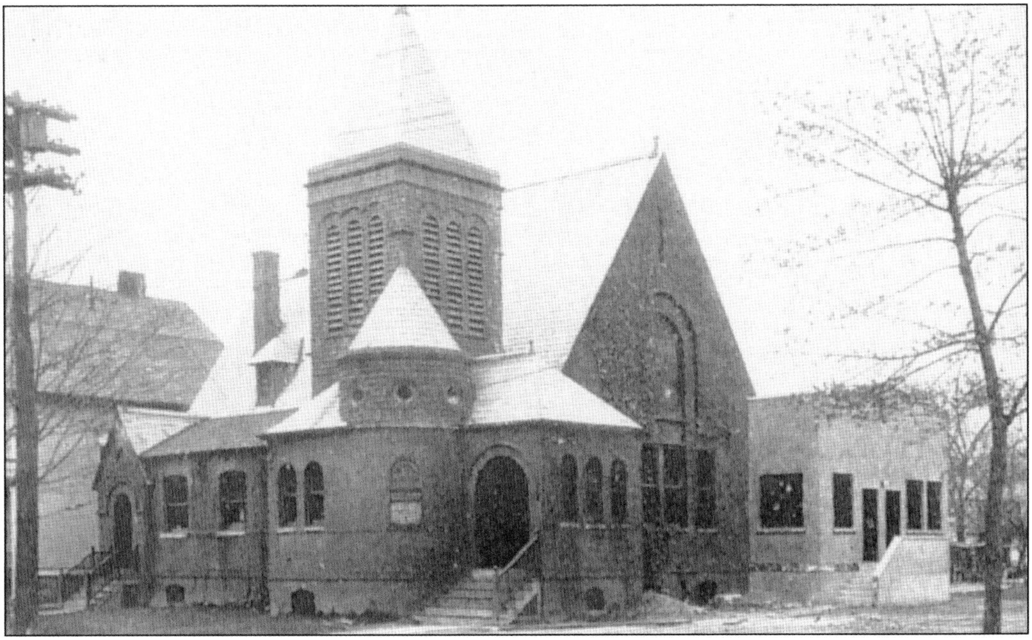

The Grace Methodist Episcopal Church located at the corner of Somerset Street and Park Place was dedicated and opened February 21, 1892, as the Park Place Chapel. This came about from a decision in 1885 from the board of the First Methodist Church in Plainfield to start a chapel in North Plainfield. In 1893, the first minister was appointed to the Grace Methodist Church.

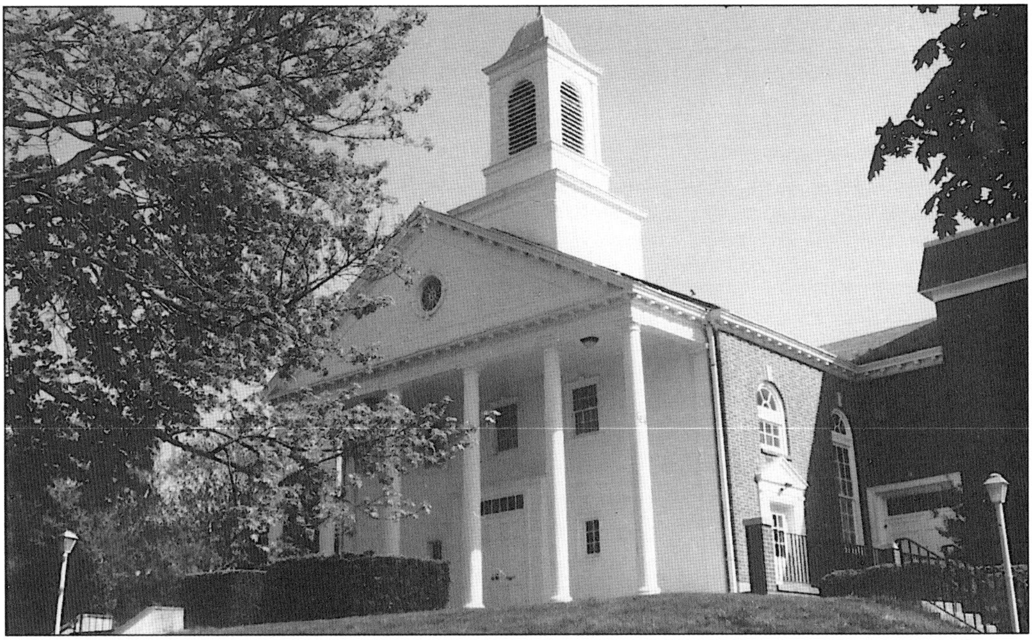

The Hydewood Park Baptist Church was founded in the year 1891 by the Christian Endeavor Society of the First Baptist Church of Plainfield. The present location was purchased from the Hyde family in 1924. On July 22, 1926, the church was incorporated and renamed the Hydewood Park Baptist Church.

Six

MUNICIPAL

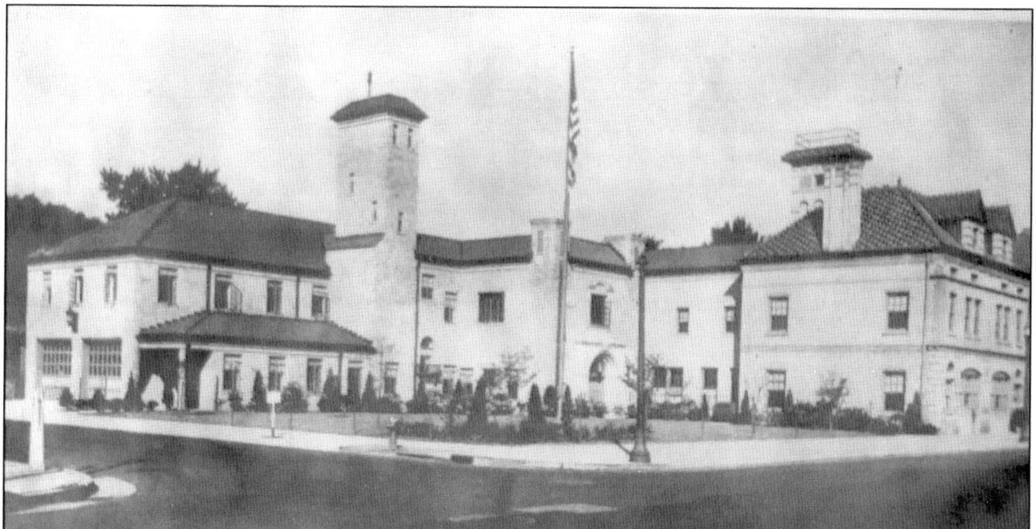

Located at the corner of Somerset Street and Lincoln Place is the North Plainfield Borough Hall. The oldest section, built in 1896, is now the home of the North Plainfield Police Department. In 1937, the main section of the building, displayed in the photograph, was constructed with the aid of the public works administration of the Federal government. In 1958, another addition became the front section.

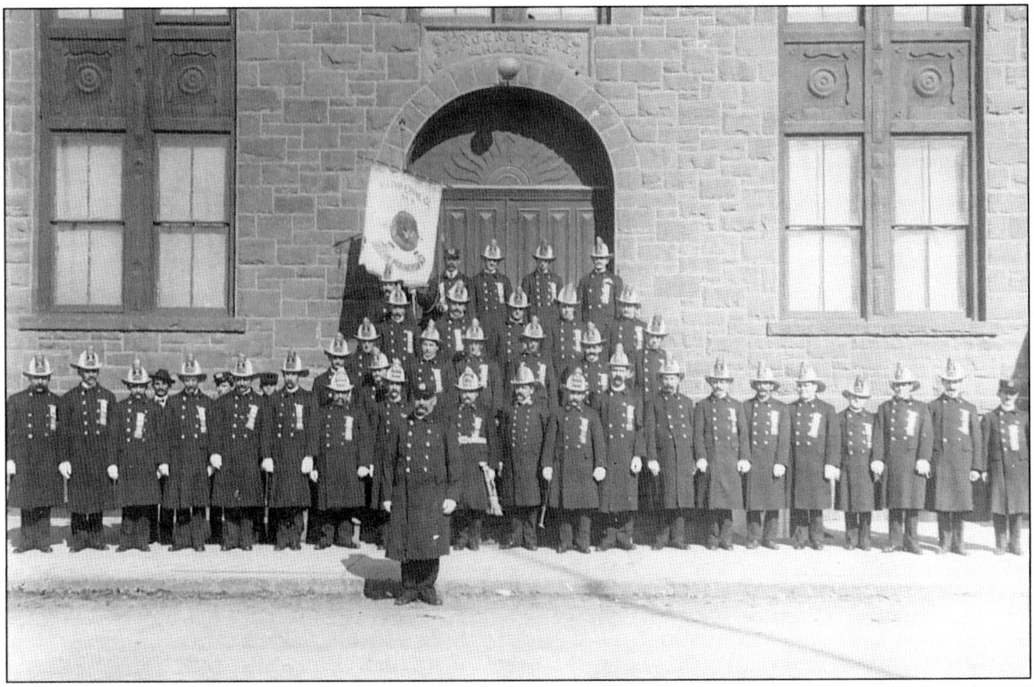

Members of the Warren Engine Company pose for this picture on the steps of Saengerbund Hall in August 1903.

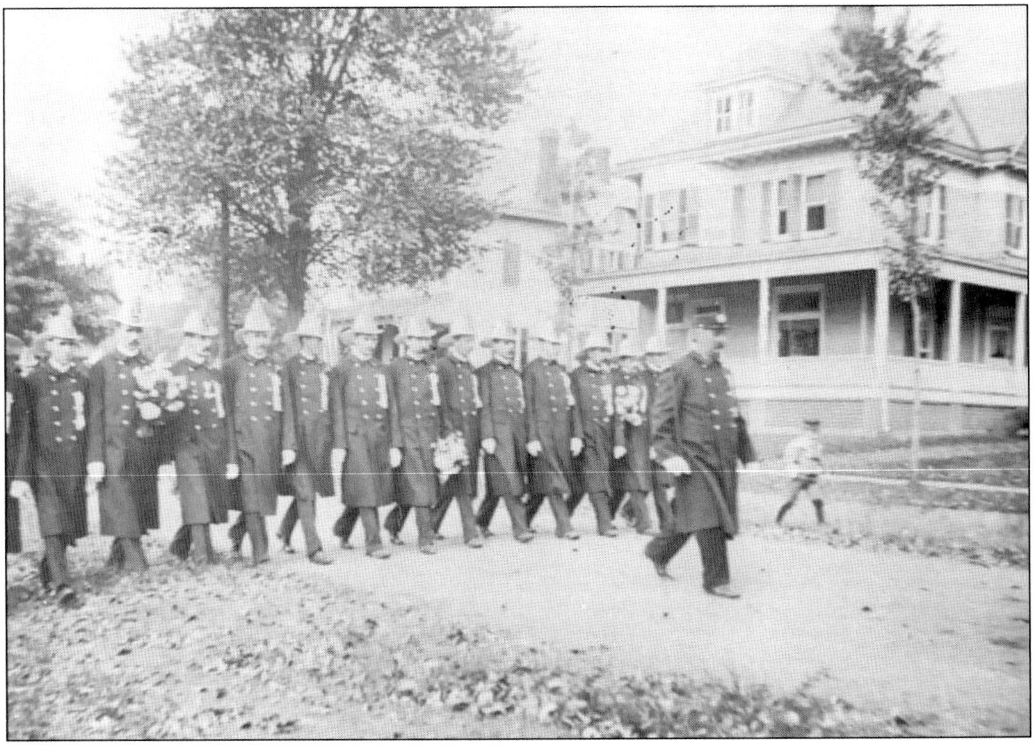

Members of the Warren Engine Company No. 1 proudly strut the unpaved Somerset Street near the intersection of Greenbrook Road during a parade in the early 1900s.

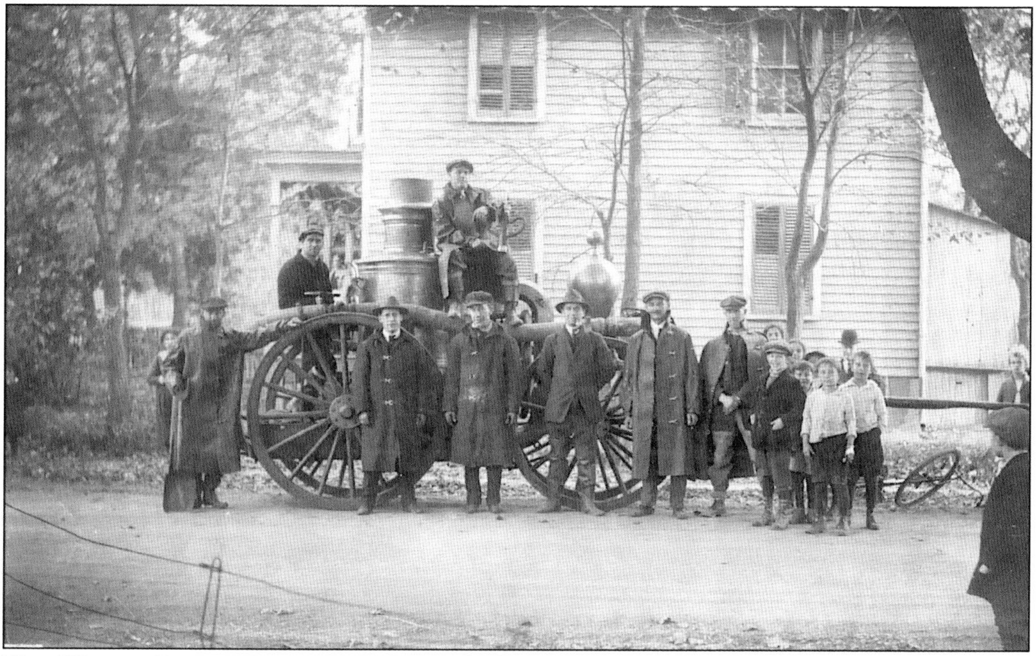

The Warren Engine Company No. 1, which protected residents from fire several decades ago, displayed their firefighting apparatus of the time, which included 3,000 feet of hose, one horse cart, two ladders, tools, two 3-gallon fire extinguishers, and the Amoskeag Steamer shown above.

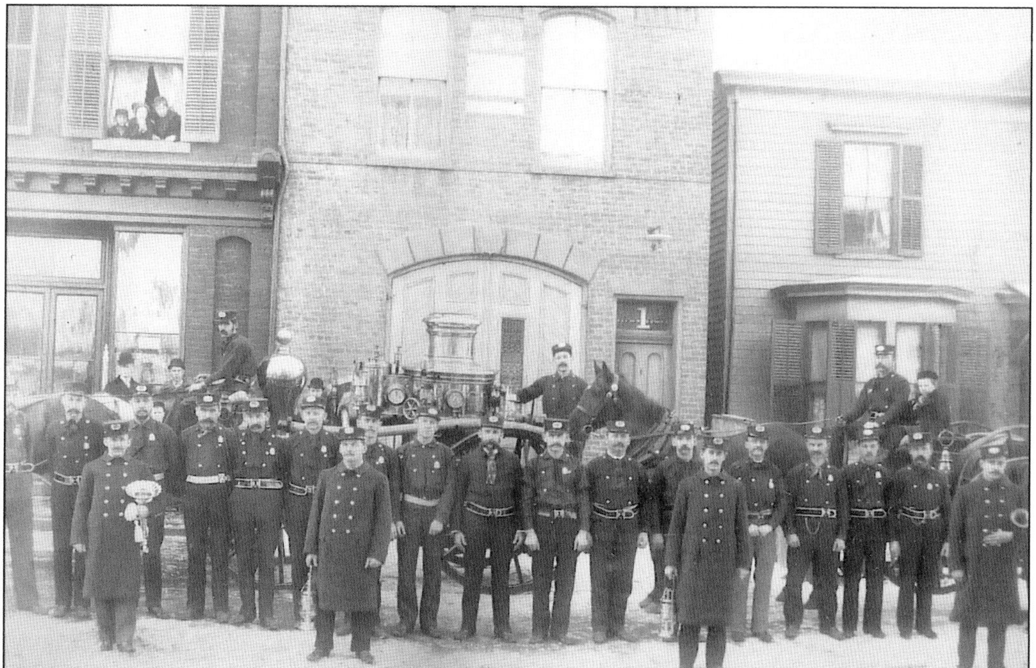

Warren Engine Company No. 1 poses with the famous Amoskeag Steamer in front of their building at 90 Somerset Street.

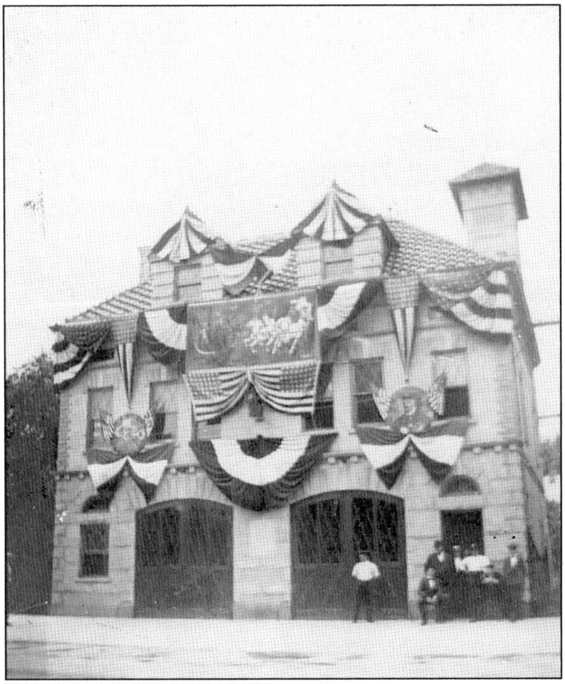

Members of the volunteer fire company are seen in front of the firehouse in the early 1900s at 263 Somerset Street during a Fourth of July celebration. Presently, the police department is located in the building.

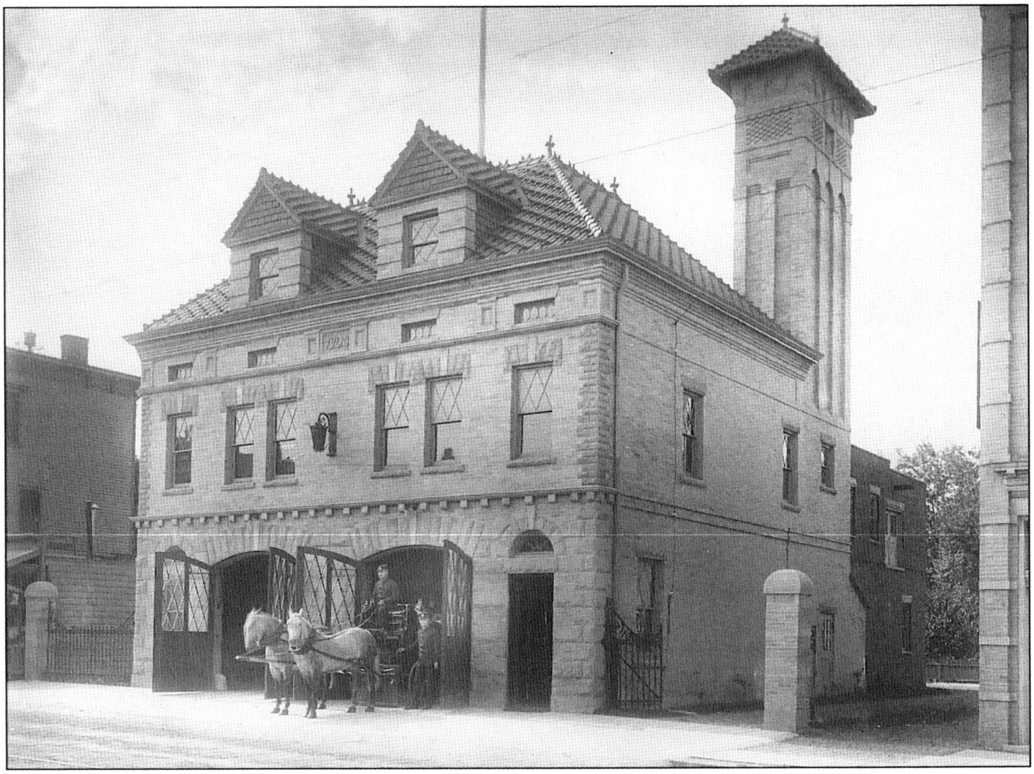

In 1888, the Borough of North Plainfield purchased the building at 90 Somerset Street and the equipment from the Plainfield Fire Department for $3,600. In 1903, a new building was erected at 263 Somerset Street; in 1904, the fire company was relocated.

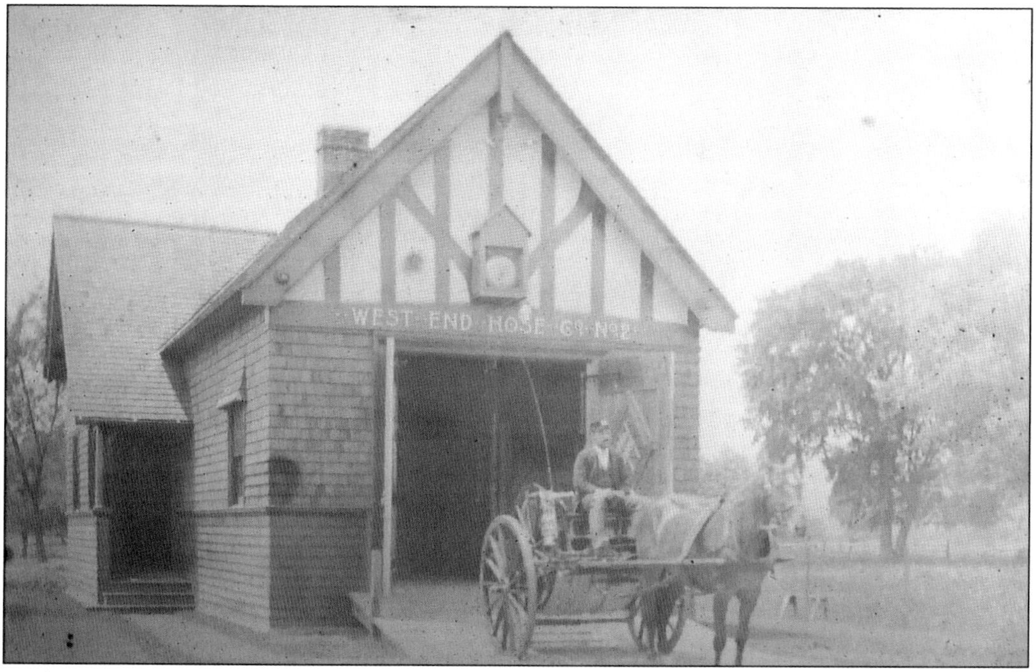

In this picture of the West End Hose Company No. 2, Herman Klinsman Sr. of 62 Harrison Avenue, North Plainfield, drives the two-wheel single hose cart known as the jumper. When the volunteer department was abolished in 1904, Mr. Klinsman purchased the firehouse from the borough and converted it into a dwelling.

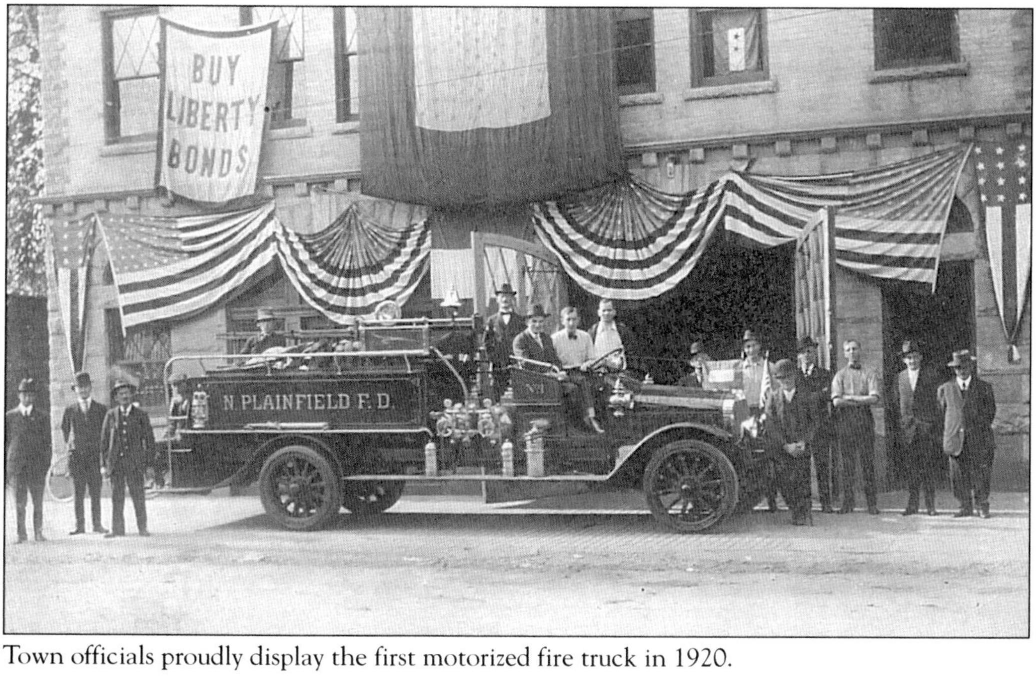

Town officials proudly display the first motorized fire truck in 1920.

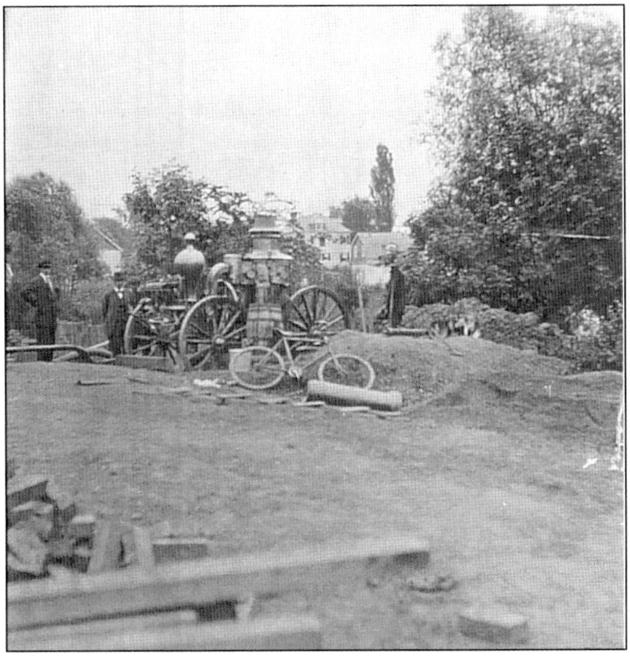

This photograph of the Amoskeag Steamer on West End Avenue was taken on August 1, 1915.

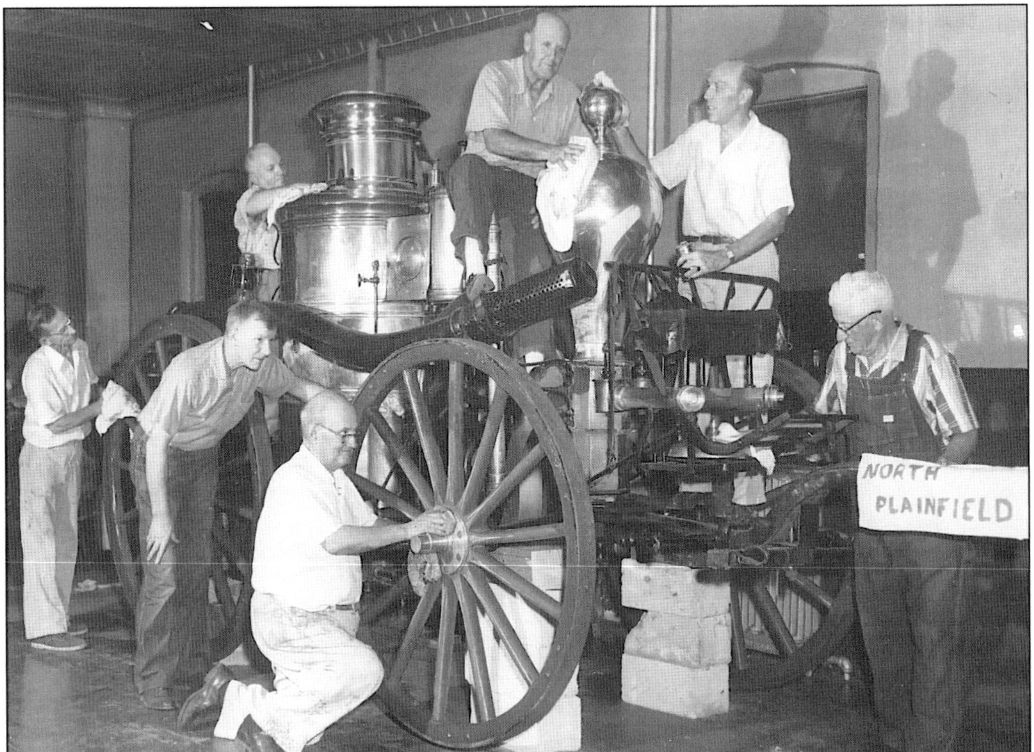

It was a great day when this steamer was purchased from Connecticut for $650 by a committee composed of Charles William Krause and former chief of the Plainfield Fire Department, Thad Doane. It was the unit used when the paid department was organized. The Old Warren Engine Company had its own horses; prior to obtaining horses, the steamer was pulled by hand.

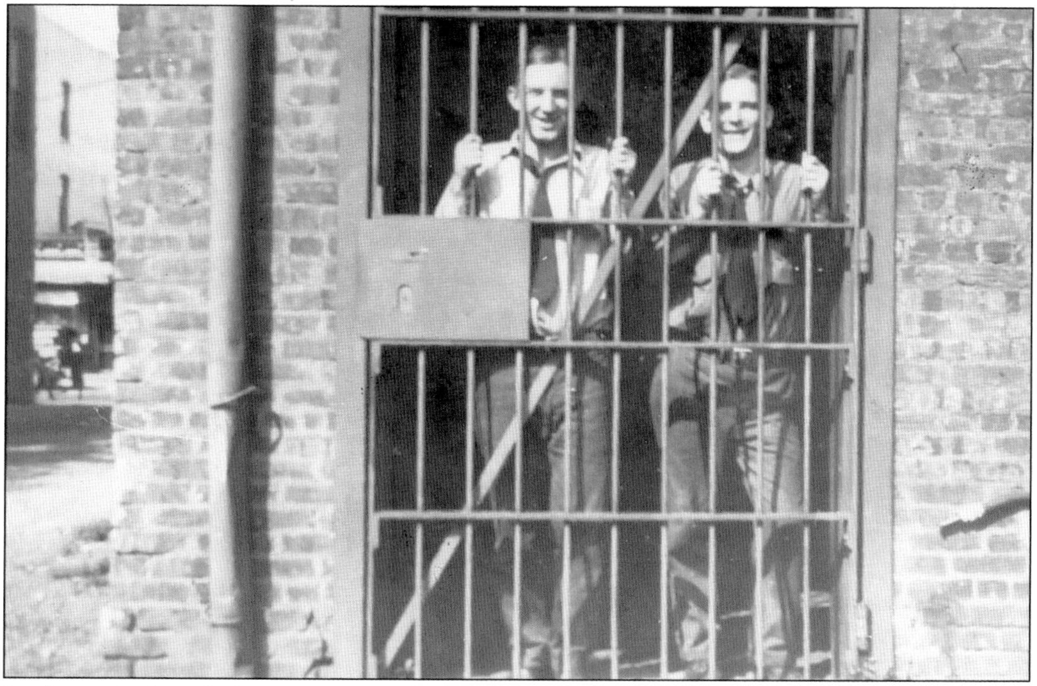

In the early days, before a more modern jail was built, the prisoners were kept in a wooden building on Lincoln Place, in the rear of the present borough hall. Early police headquarters, a courtroom, and a jail were located in the Warren Engine Co. on Somerset Street. In 1916, they moved to the Municipal Rotunda site; they relocated to their present quarters in 1937.

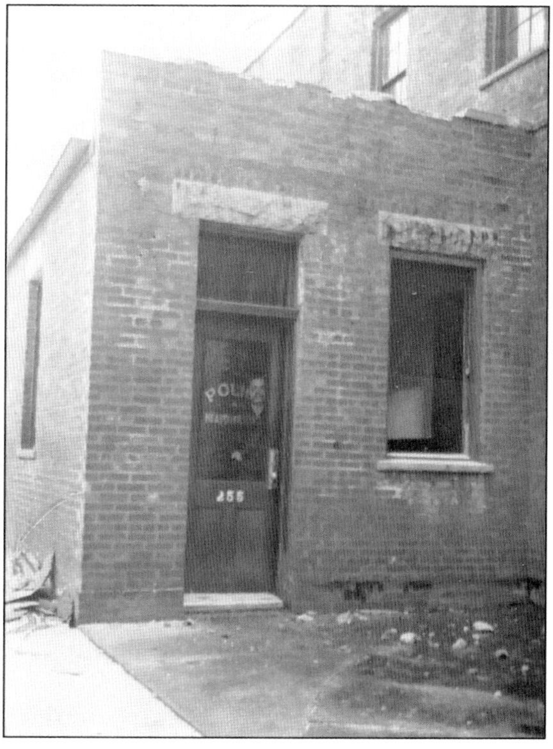

The birth of the police department came shortly after the incorporation of the borough in 1885. In the beginning, the department boasted a force of one. At that time, the peace officer was known as marshal. The first marshal was Peter B. Weaver. In addition to enforcing the law, the marshal lit the gas street lamps every night.

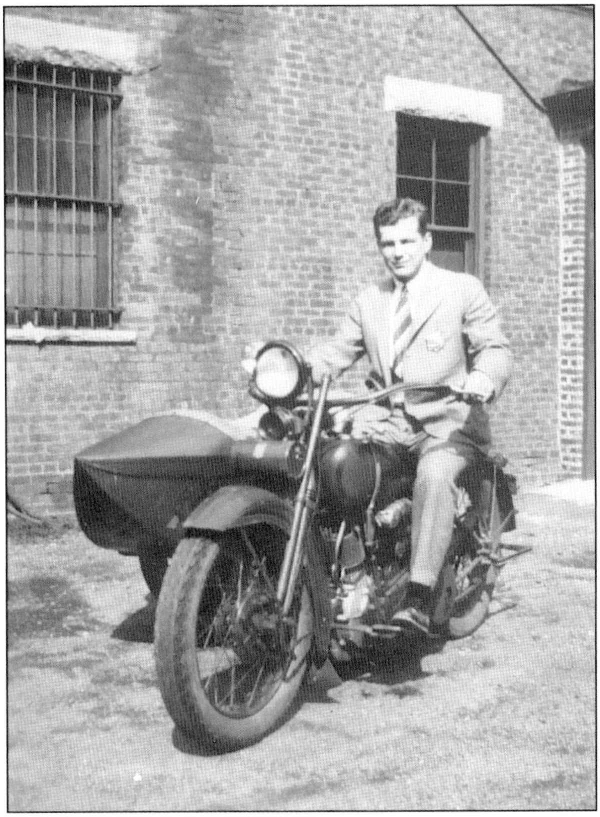

By 1929, the Borough of North Plainfield owned four motorcycles for the patrolmen who could drive. Those who could not drive used two bicycles. Early records reveal bicycle patrolmen were able to catch and ticket speeders driving cars.

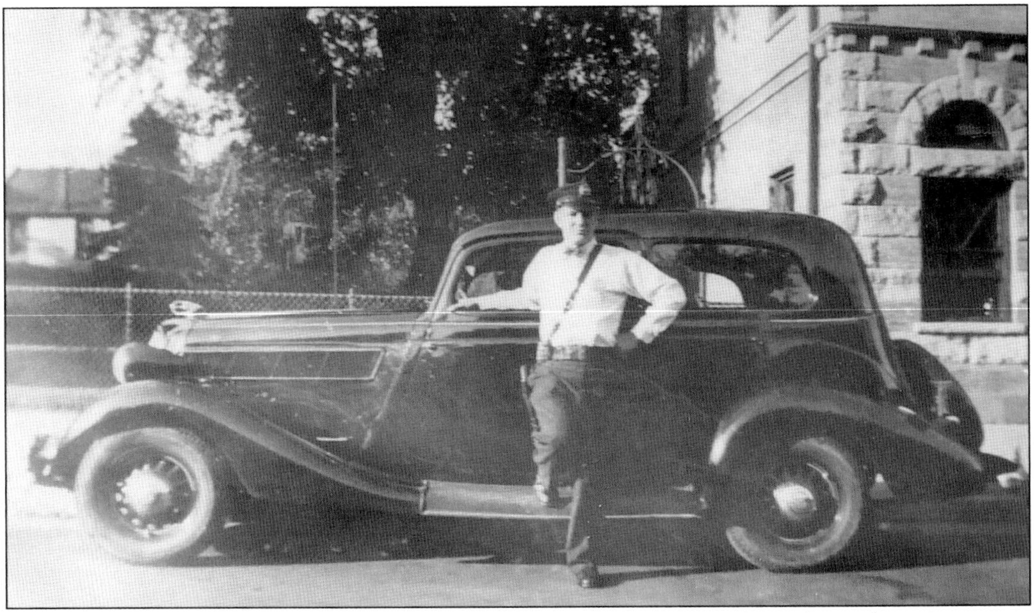

One of North Plainfield's finest is shown next to a police patrol car from the early 1900s.

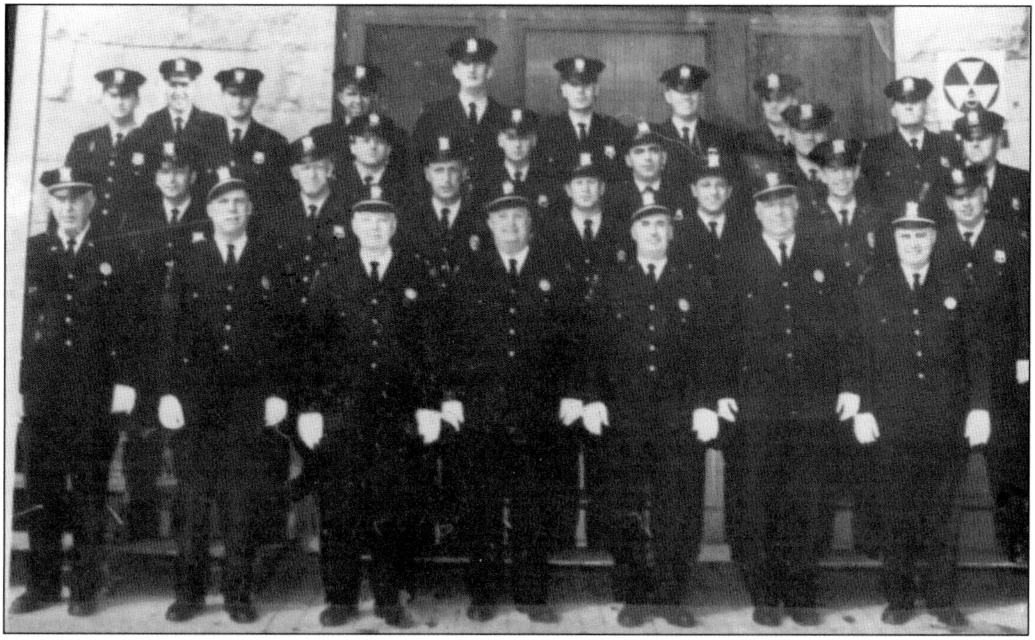

The proud police department of the borough celebrates the Fourth of July by marching in the annual parade. This picture was taken in front of the present-day borough hall after the parade in 1966.

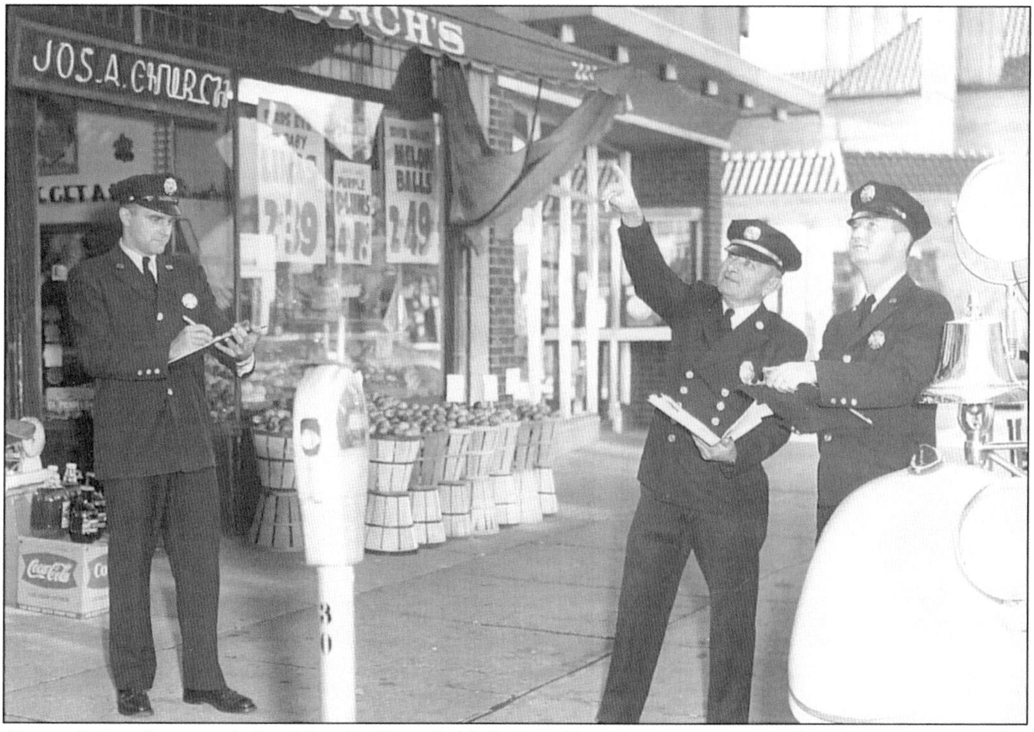

One of the duties of the North Plainfield Police Department was to do inspections in the borough. Included in this photograph, taken November 1961, are, from left to right, J. Wishart, Captain Grosch, and E. Jackson in front of Church's Market on Somerset Street.

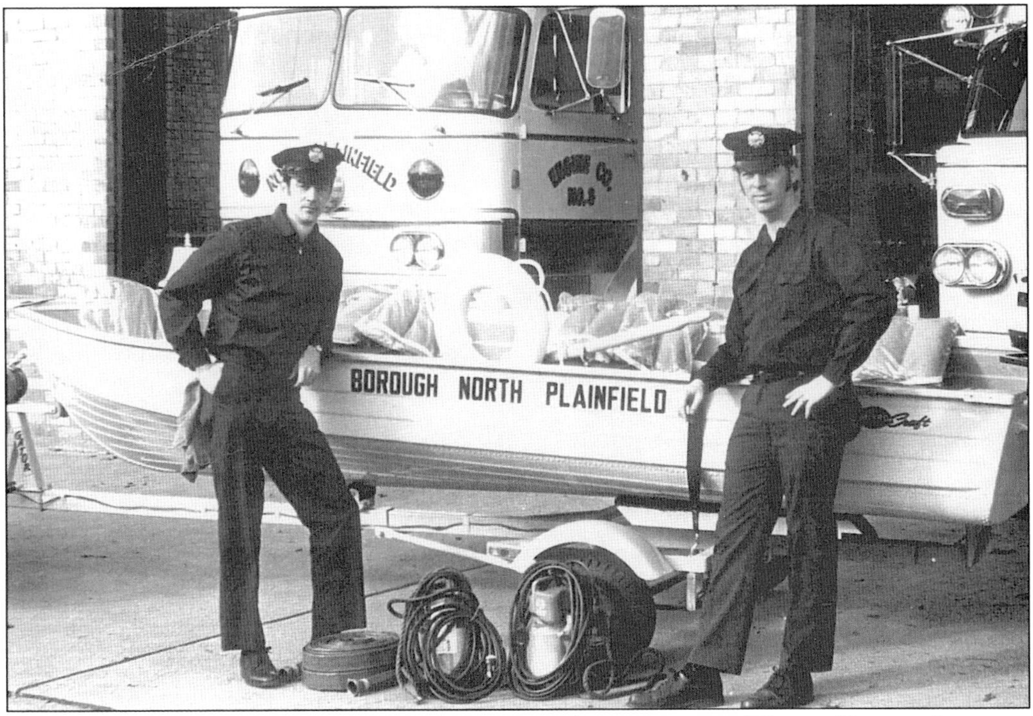

The North Plainfield Fire Department has come a long way since Warren Engine Company No. 1. This photograph shows two North Plainfield firefighters in front of the current fire headquarters.

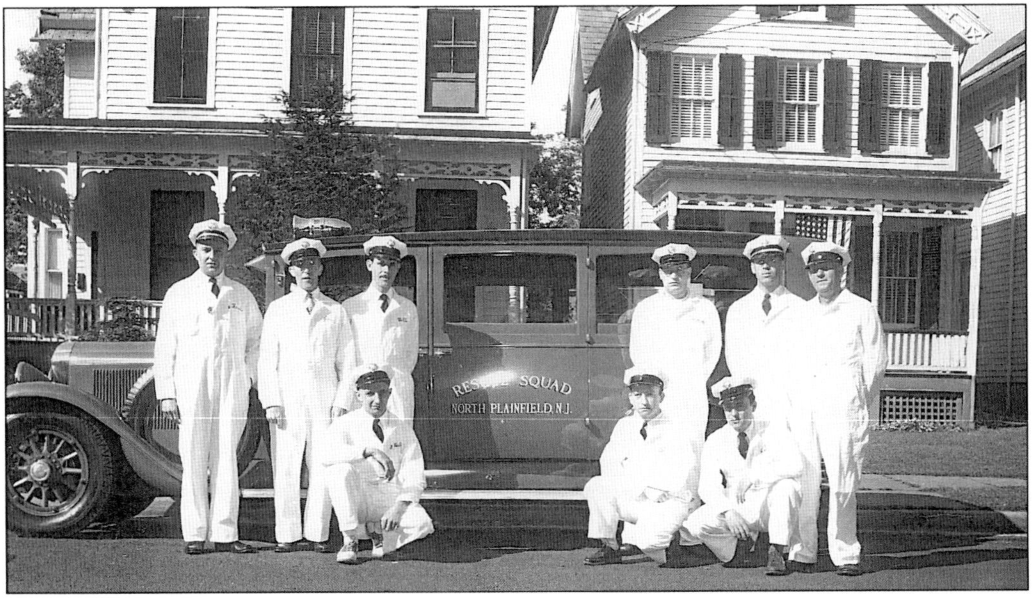

The North Plainfield Rescue Squad was incorporated in 1949 with 23 charter members. The squad was qualified to service the town after completing the first aid training course given by the Dunellen Rescue Squad. Two vehicles were in service at the time. A 1929 Buick ambulance was presented to the squad by Plainfield's governing body; a used 1940 LaSalle ambulance was purchased as a second vehicle on notes signed by several squad members.

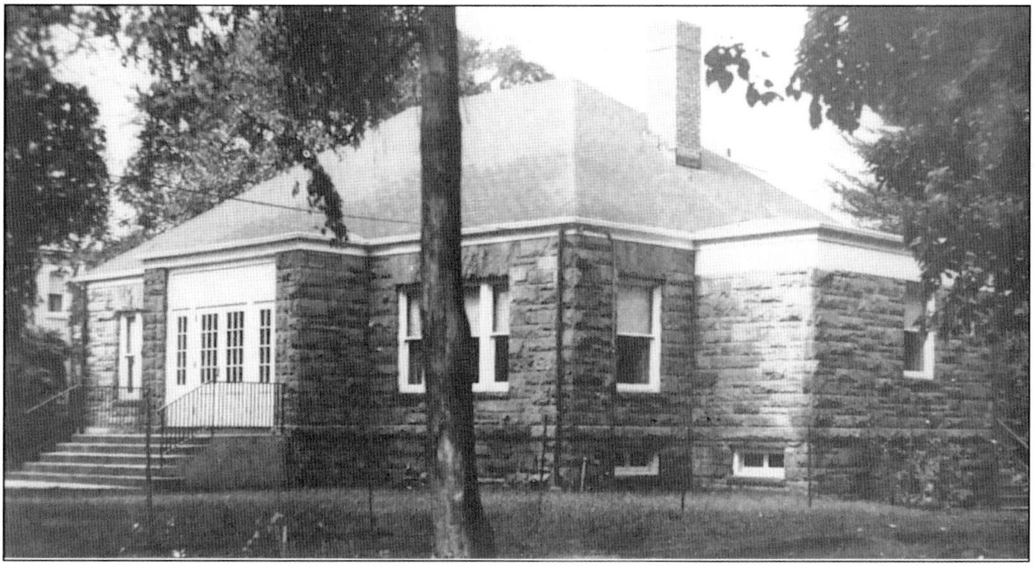

By 1946, the library had totally outgrown the Exempt Fireman's Hall. The North Plainfield Library Association, formed in 1939, organized fund drives to raise $45,000 for a new library. The Borough of North Plainfield bought the house and grounds at 6 Rockview Avenue and gave $5,000 towards its renovations. With an additional $25,000 raised by two fund drives, the $30,000 renovation cost was met and the new North Plainfield War Memorial Library was opened in 1949. In May 1959, the borough council passed an ordinance taking $10,000 from capital funds for the remodeling of the lower level. Today, a new library stands in the place of this building.

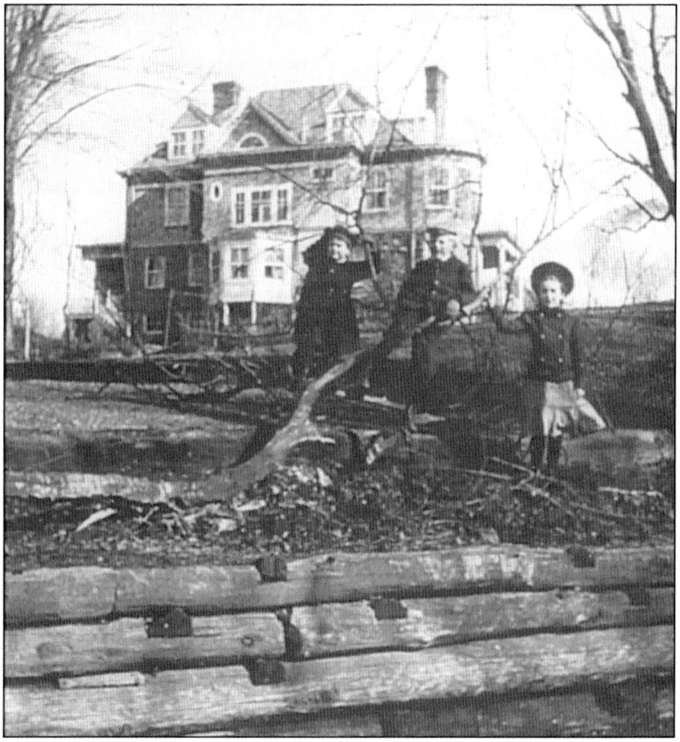

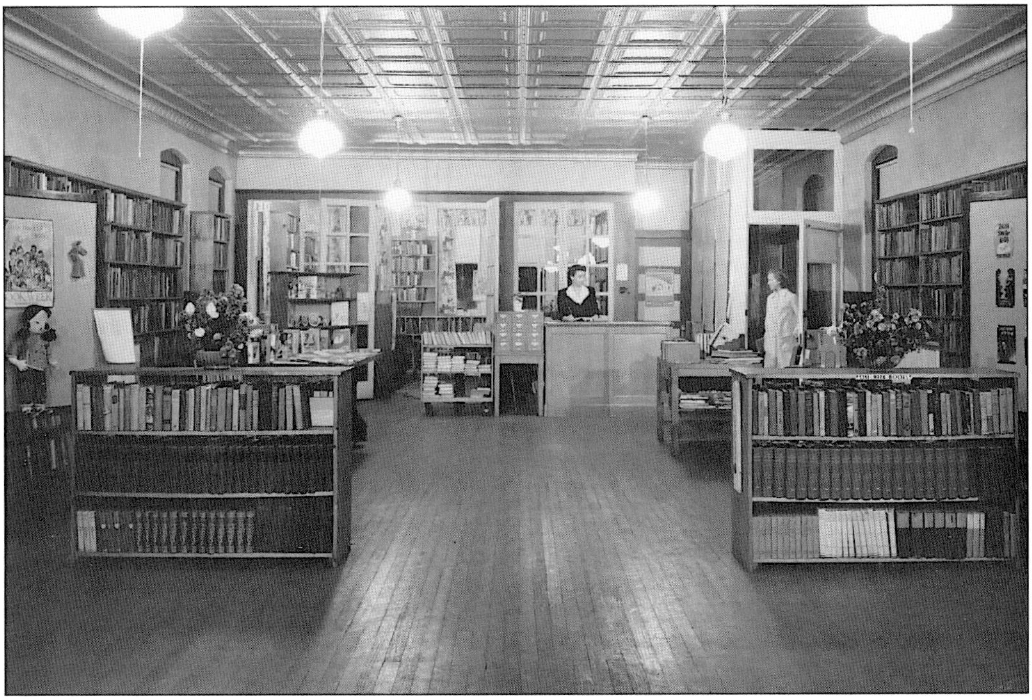

The North Plainfield Library system began with three ladies of the borough's Parent Teacher Associations. The library's first home was the Sunny Shoppe, located on the corner of Somerset Street and Linden Avenue. Six years later, in 1931, the library was moved to Walter's Barber Shop. In 1935, the library was moved to the second floor of the Exempt Fireman's Hall. In five years, the library grew from using a small portion of the second floor to the entire floor.

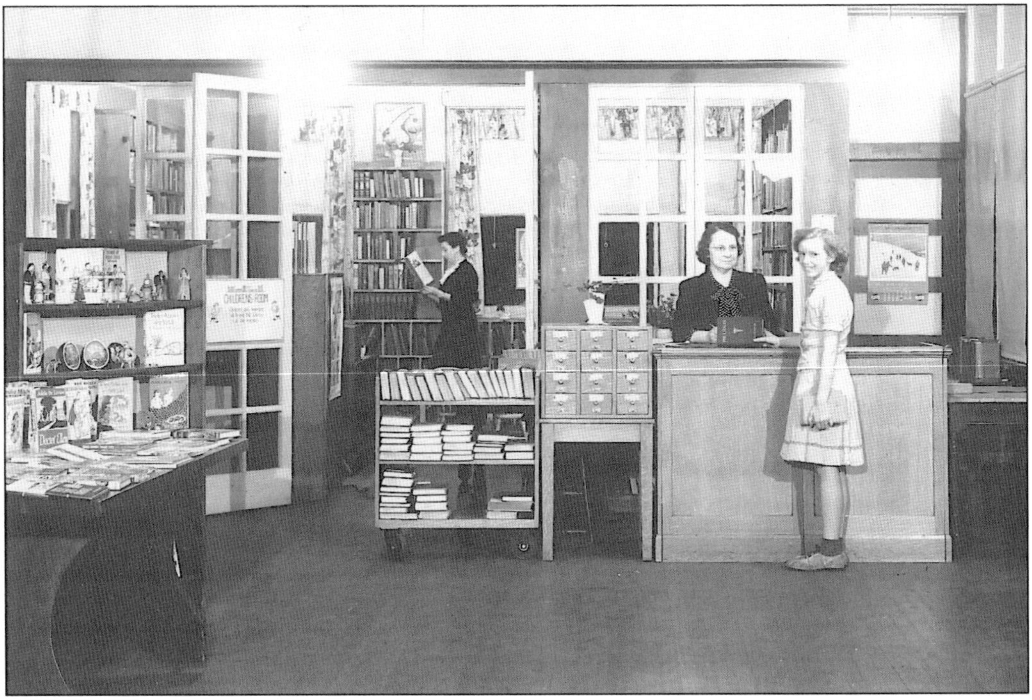

Seven

FIRES AND FLOODS

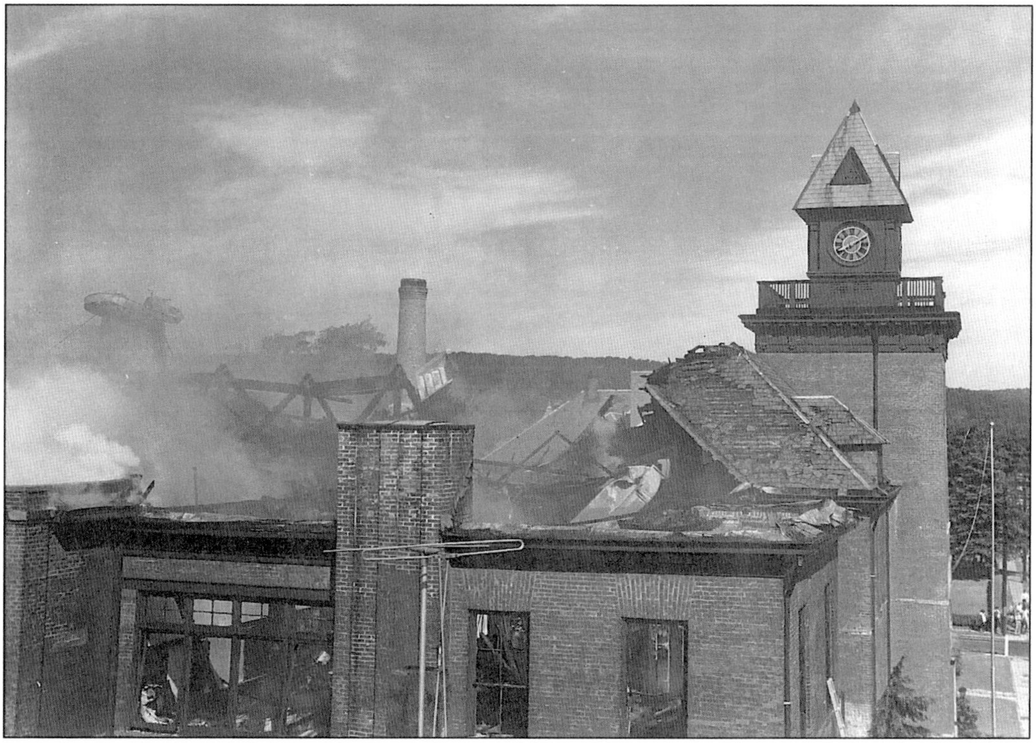

In 1950, flames completely destroyed the southern half of Somerset School. The fire started in the cupola housing the school's clock—a landmark in the structure since it was built in 1883. The school was being repaired, but no workmen were in the building when the fire broke out.

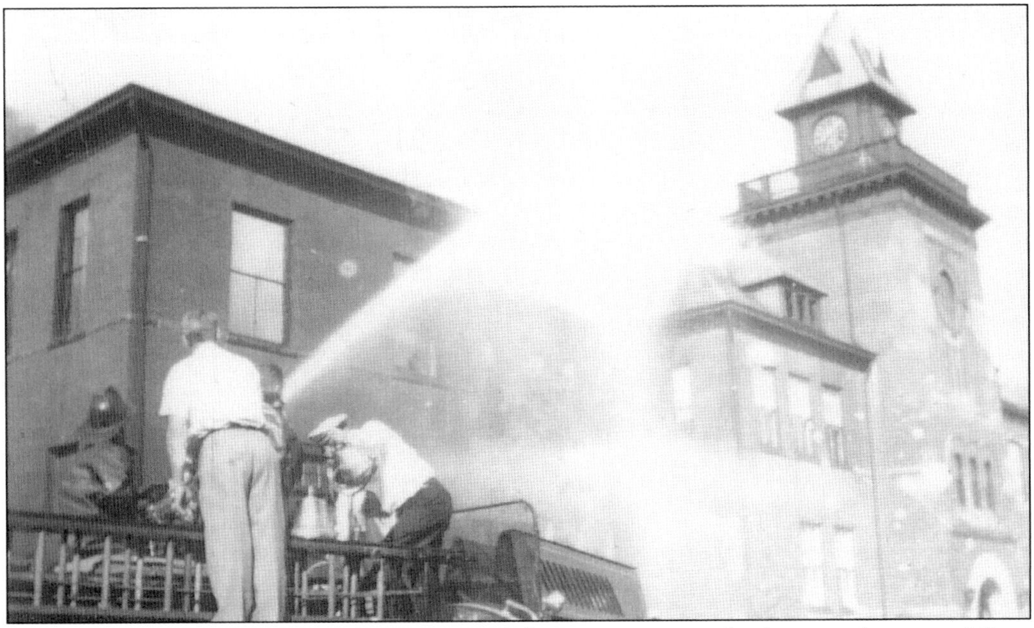

The Somerset School fire gutted seven second-floor rooms; several others on the ground floor were badly damaged by smoke and water. Fire-walls prevented the blaze from spreading into the schools north wing, which had been built in 1900.

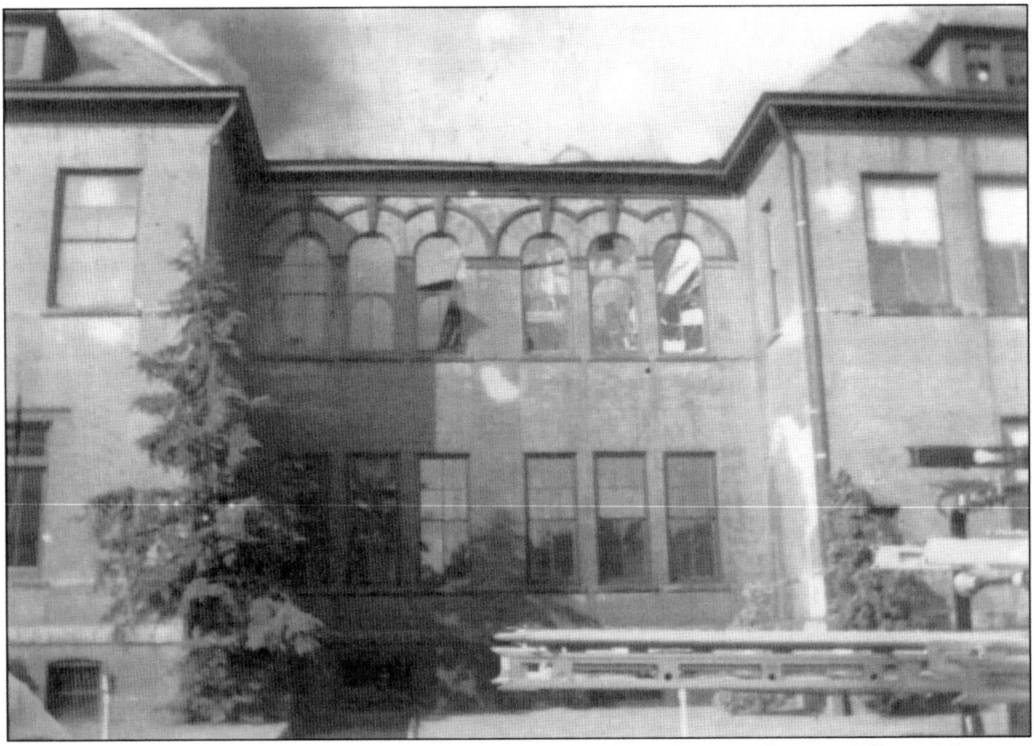

Three North Plainfield fire companies answered the first alarm and were followed by two Plainfield units. Five firemen were overcome by smoke; two others and one volunteer were injured. Hundreds of school children alternately cheered and booed as firemen fought the blaze.

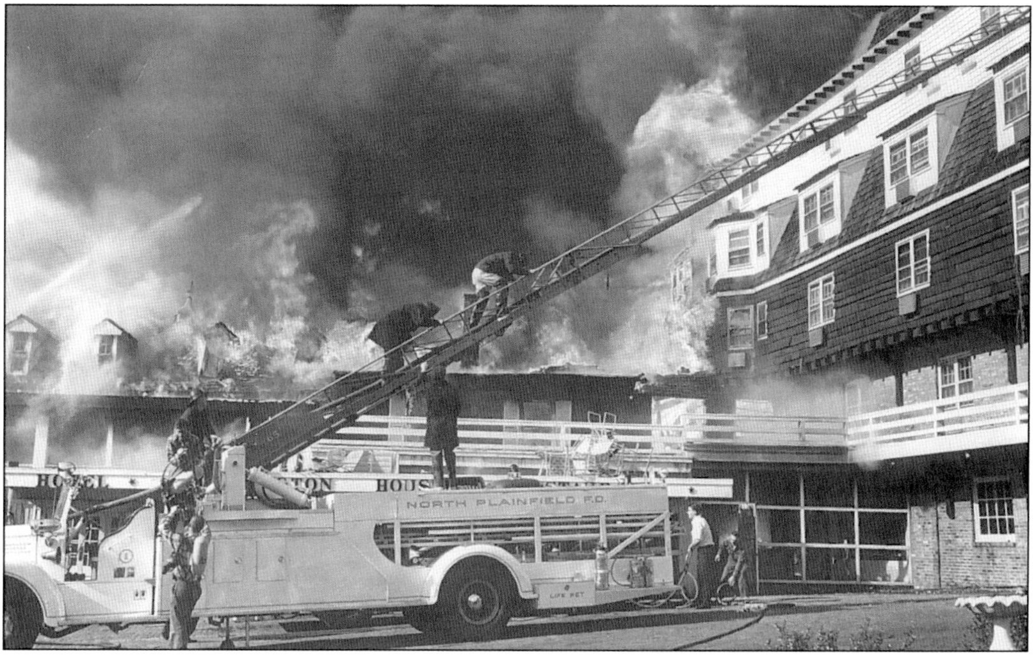

This image of the famous Washington House fire shows firemen wearing oxygen masks and trying to get into the upper floors of the hotel in an effort to confine the blaze to the restaurant area. The heat was so intense they were forced to leave and move their equipment farther away from the building.

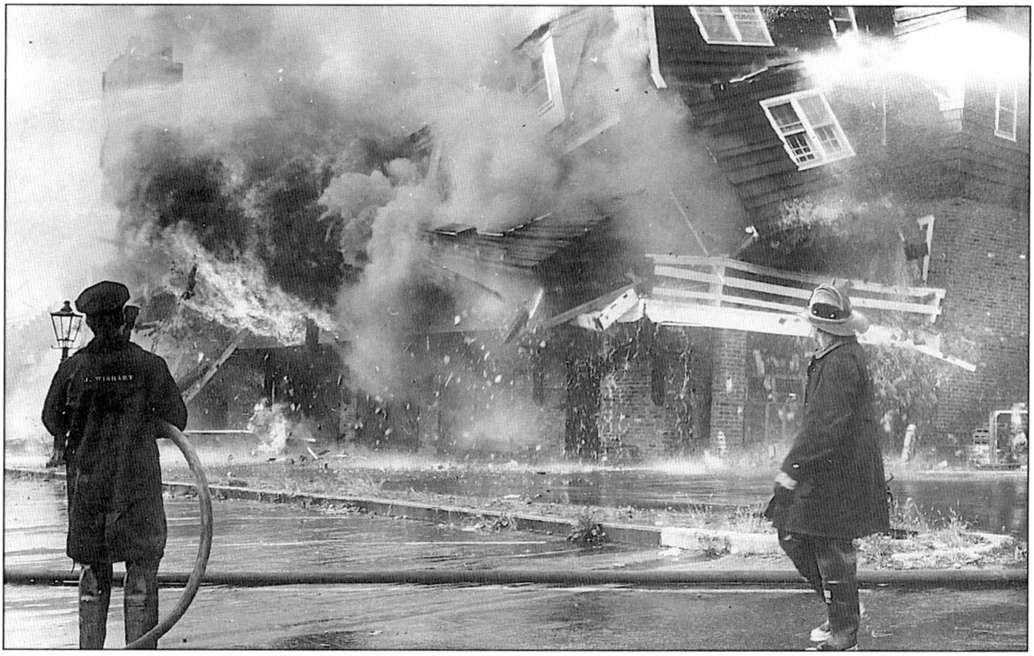

The Washington House blaze was fought by fire companies from Watchung, Martinsville, Plainfield, North Plainfield, Berkeley Heights, Greenbrook, Warren Township, and New Providence. The flames rose 70 feet into the air and the battle soon became just preventing the fire from spreading. The 234-year-old landmark was doomed.

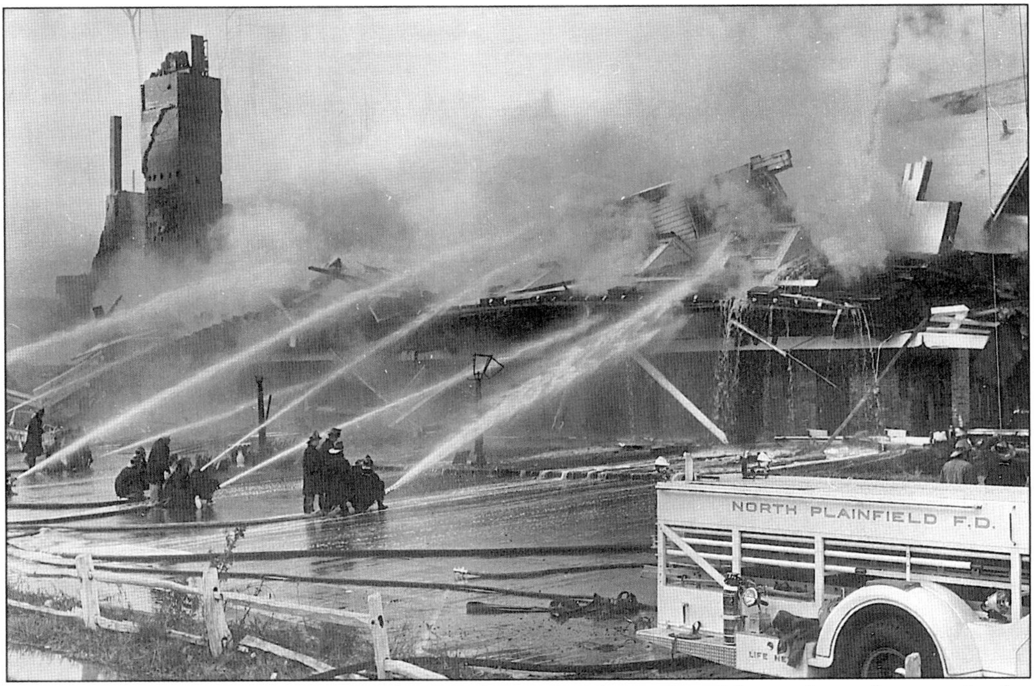

North Plainfield firemen are shown here battling the blaze that destroyed the famous Washington House that was built *c.* 1738 in the notch between Watchung and North Plainfield.

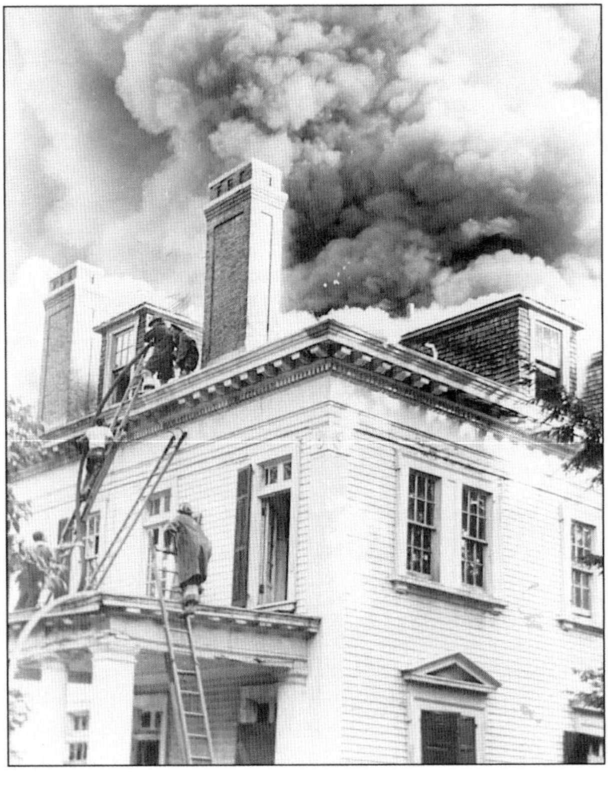

On July 26, 1963, flames gutted the old Hydewood mansion on the north side of Route 22 and North Drive. The mansion, built at the turn of the century, was once part of a huge estate occupied by Mrs. Frances Hyde. The building was slated for demolition when it was destroyed by the fire.

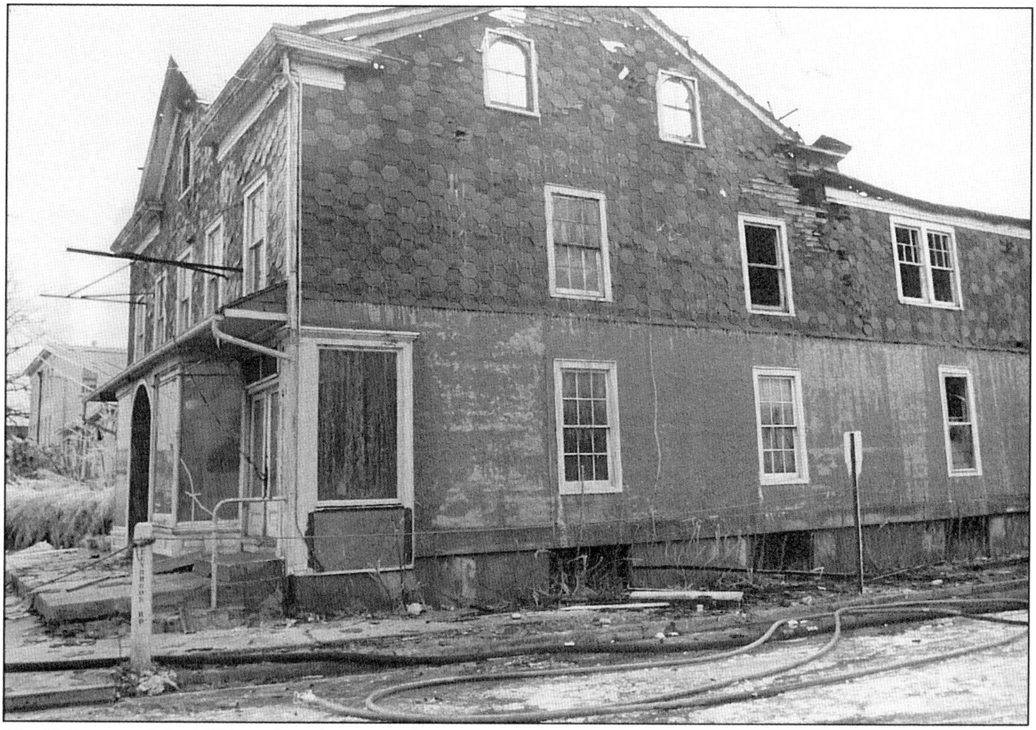

On February 12, 1971, a fire destroyed the building, which was formally the Mountain Inn, at 225–227 Somerset Street at the corner of Greenbrook Road. This location was in the middle of North Plainfield and directly on the trolley line. In its day, the hotel had 22 rooms, 15 of which were bedrooms. Built before the turn of the century, this impressive hotel contained a poolroom and a fine stock of cigars and tobacco. As seen in these pictures, only a burned out shell was left the morning after the fire.

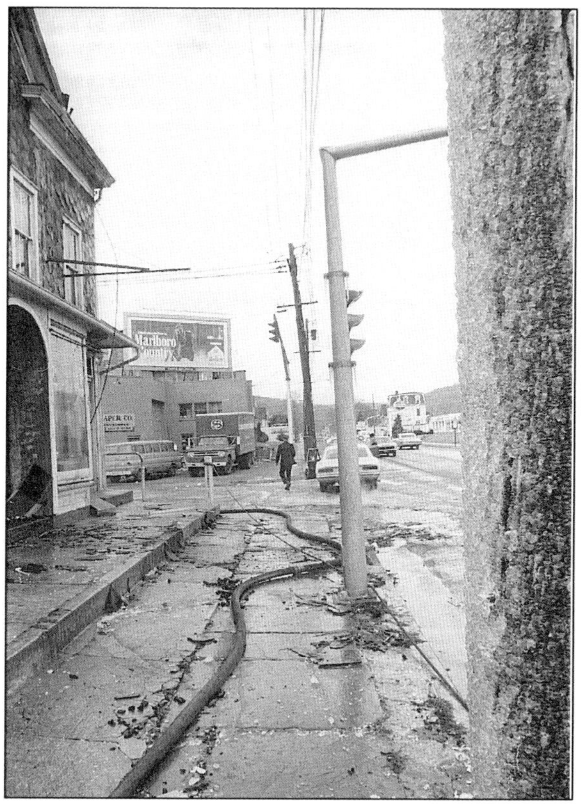

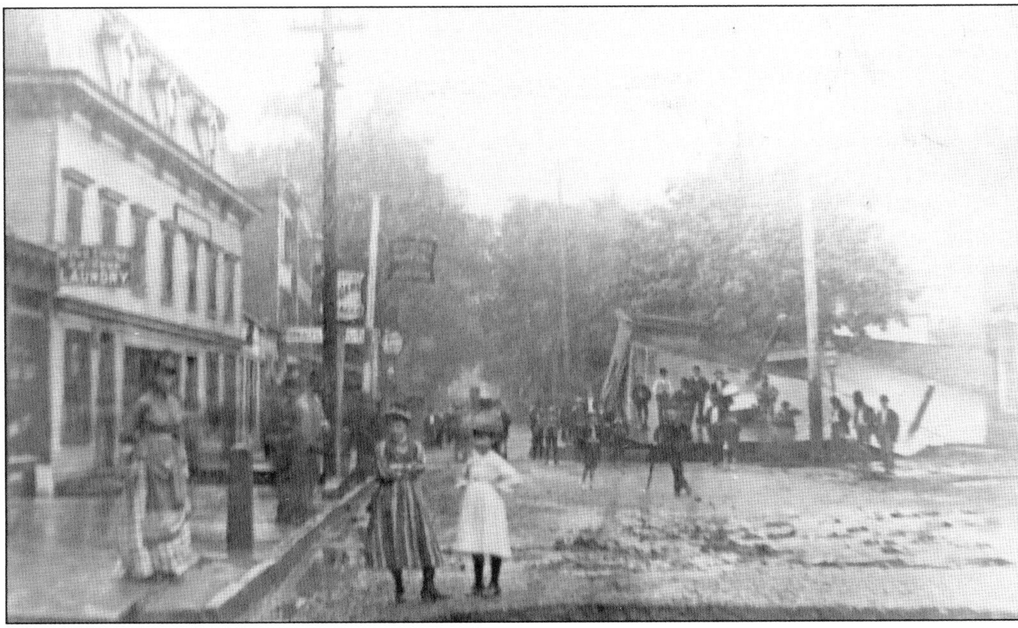

It had rained all day, July 30, 1889; in the mountains, small streams had risen to rivers, and dams crumbled. The Greenbrook and Stony Brook overflowed. Then, a high wall of water rushed down Somerset Street, causing flooding from Pearl Street to Front Street. This photograph taken from Front Street shows Blimm's Hotel on the left. On the right are French's carriage shop, Martin's horse shoeing shop, and Warren and Stewarts wheelwright and blacksmith shop.

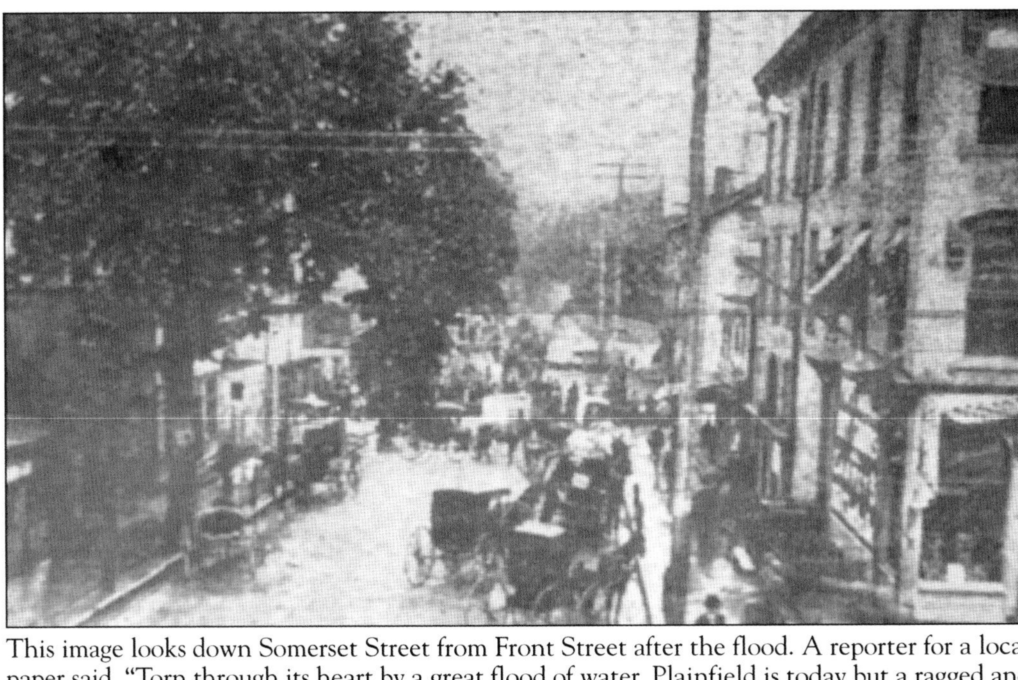

This image looks down Somerset Street from Front Street after the flood. A reporter for a local paper said, "Torn through its heart by a great flood of water, Plainfield is today but a ragged and disheveled likeness of its self [*sic*]. A vast roaring river has surged through our most populous thorough fares."

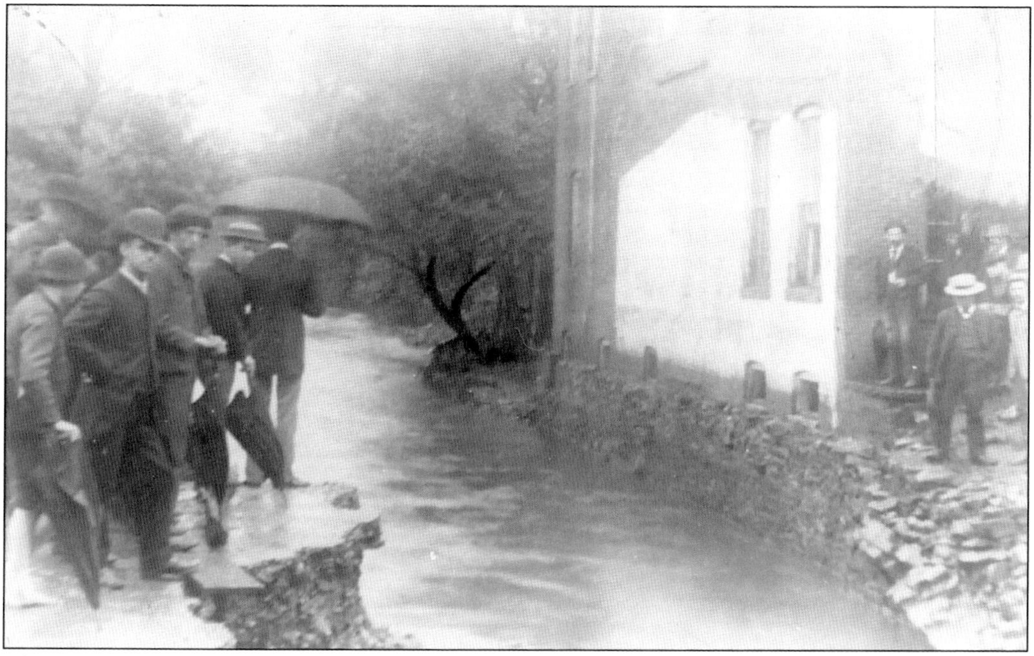

The Grove Street bridge over the Greenbrook was washed away in the flood. Bridges at Duer Street and Washington Avenue were badly damaged. North Plainfield is to the left of this picture.

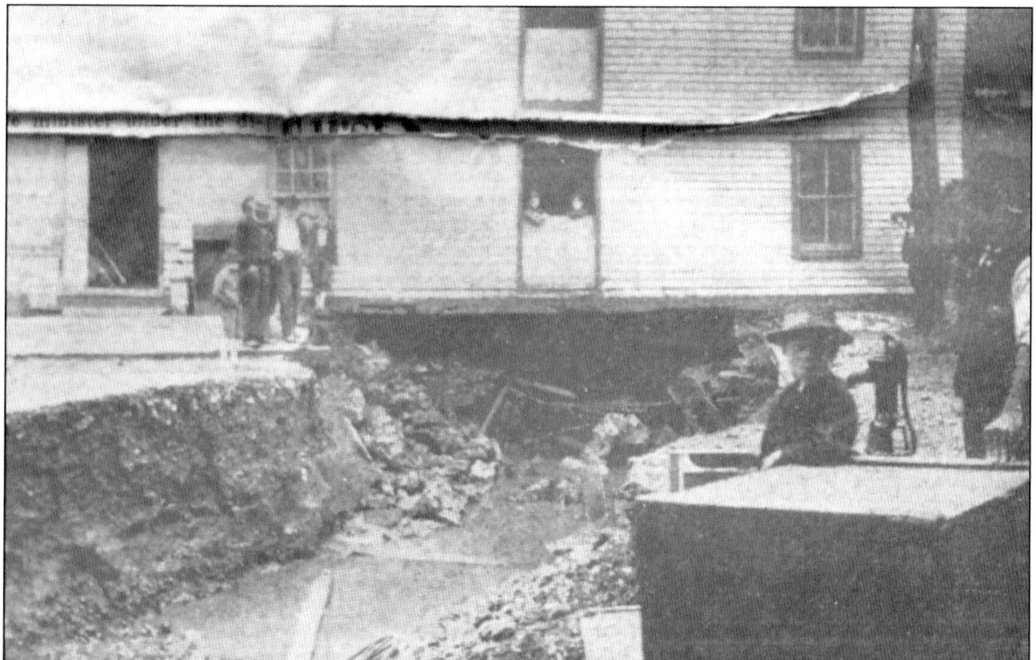

During the flood of 1889, water massed under Somerset Street at the Greenbrook bridge, whose 6-foot-high and 16-foot-wide arches could not accommodate the flood and water. The flood had no respect for historical sites. A great gap 25 feet wide and 8 feet deep was torn through the raceway where French's mill had stood since the late 18th century.

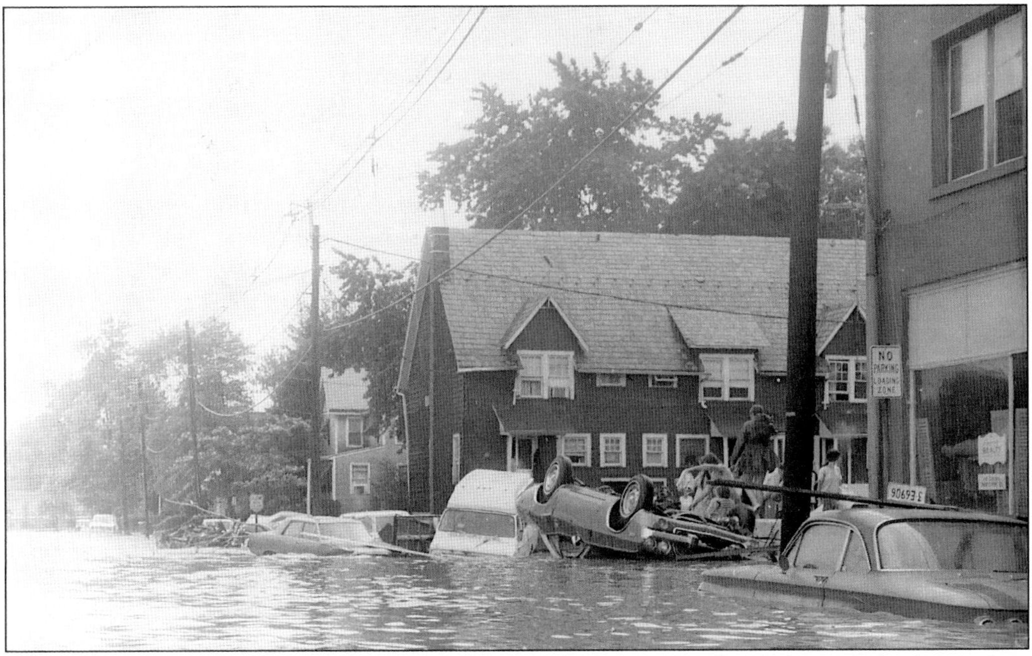

On August 2, 1973, a torrential rainstorm struck the area. The flood claimed the lives of six people and is considered to be one of the worst floods in the borough's history. More than 7 inches of rain fell in less than 5 hours, swelling the waters of the Stony and Green Brooks. Losses were estimated between $4 and $5 million.

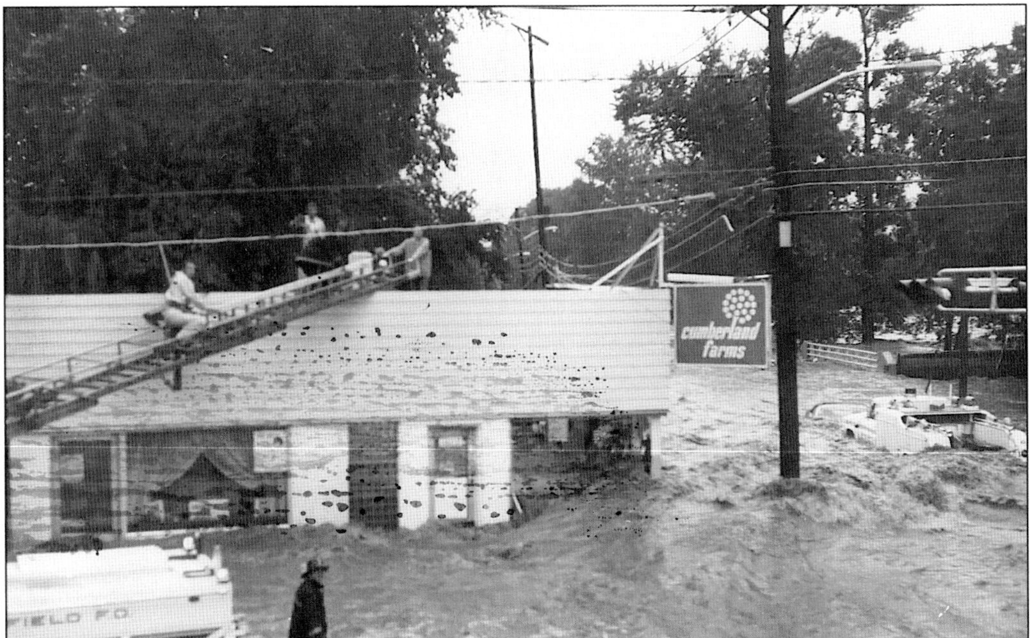

This photograph, taken at the corner of Greenbrook Road and Grove Street, shows the heaviest downpour, which came at 7:30 a.m. By 9 a.m., there were wide spread reports of people needing evacuation. Twenty-four hours later, the water was disappearing and Greenbrook Road was a sea of mud.

Eight

WASHINGTON PARK

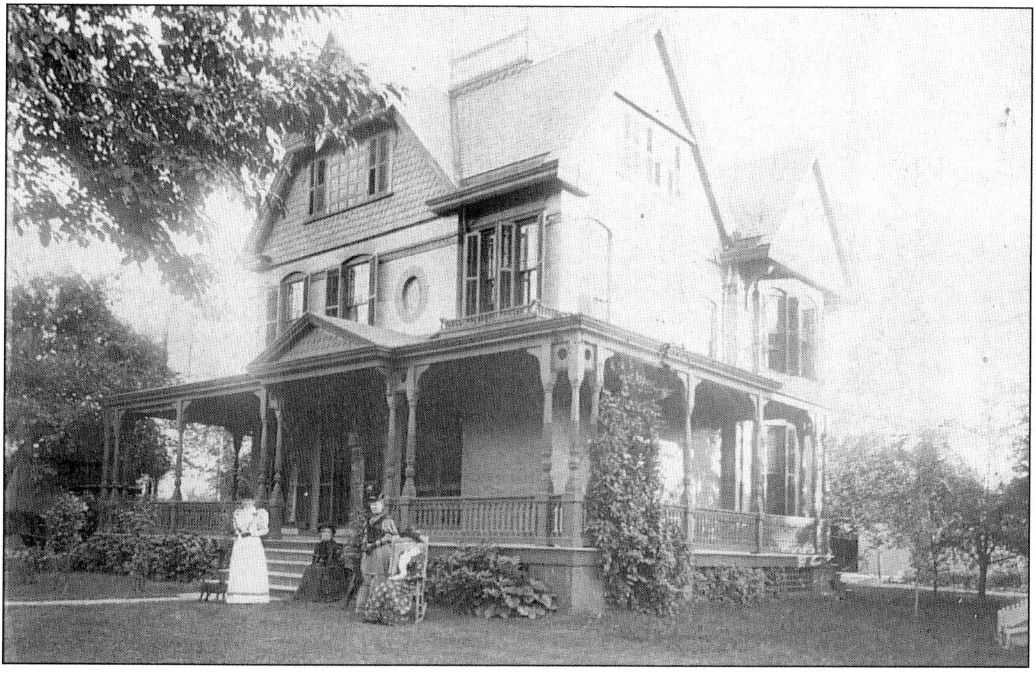

In 1837, Victoria became Queen of England. The ornate style of architecture during her reign (1837–1901) has been designated Victorian. There were many distinct-style trends in Victorian architecture. Some of the main ones were Queen Anne Revival, Romanesque Revival, Italianate, Stick (Eastlake), Second Empire, and Carpenter Gothic. Architects often combined two or more styles in one house creating totally original houses. From c. 1920 up into the 1950s, many fine Victorian mansions were destroyed to be replaced by modern designs. The Washington Park association was formed on May 22, 1980. The purpose of the association is to preserve the heritage of North Plainfield through the preservation of special historic, architectural, and cultural significance. This picture, taken Thanksgiving Day 1894, shows Emma Darby in white with her dog Bubbles. The home of Albert and Emma Marsh Darby stood at 75 Grove Street.

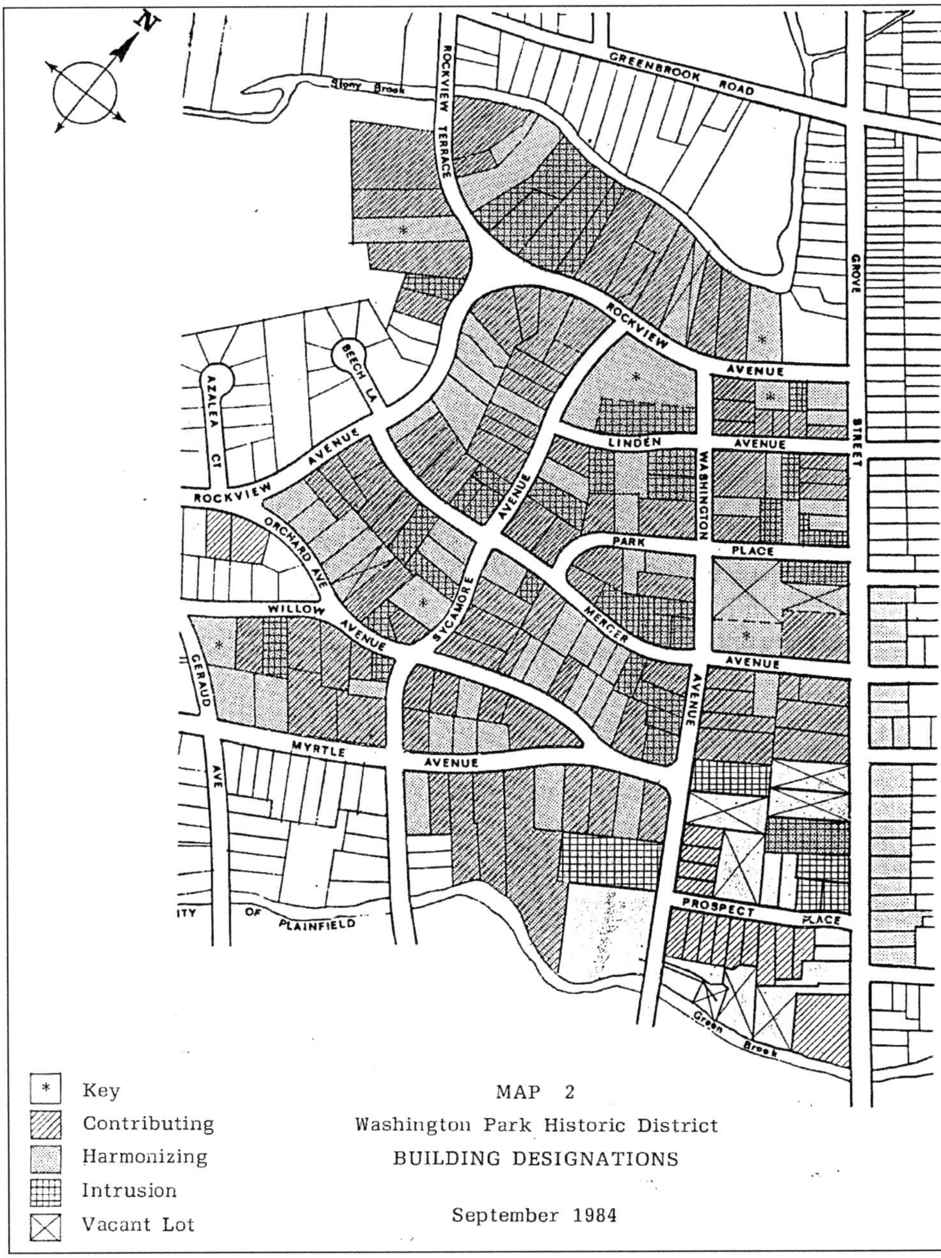

This map comes from the atlas of the city of Plainfield and the borough of North Plainfield, c. 1894. Early 19th-century maps of North Plainfield show the township to be mostly a farming community. The establishment of the Jersey Central Railroad in the 1850s caused many wealthy New York businessmen to build villas in Plainfield and North Plainfield. The population of North Plainfield had grown from 75 in 1832 to 4,000 in 1885. The Washington Park development plan was filed with the clerk of Somerset County on May 12, 1868, as a complete real estate development, which included villa sites for the well-established personages of the New York City business world. In the late 1880s and 1890s, mansions west of Somerset Street were built by such families as the McCutcheons, the McGees, the Warings, Hegemans' Rooms, the Cooleys, and the Mungers.

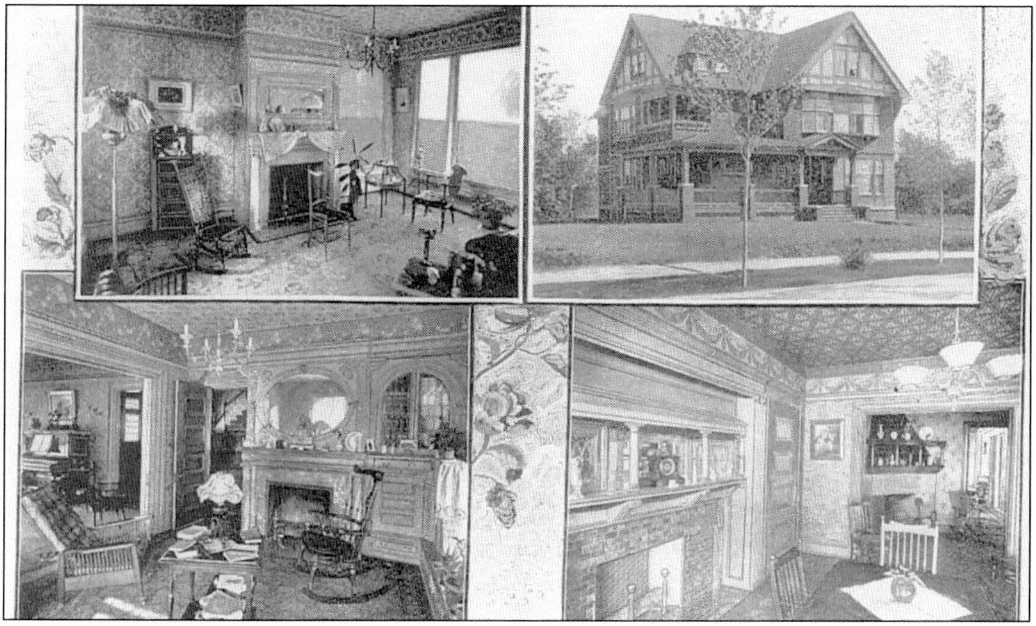

Attorney C.A. Reed built the house at 27 Myrtle Avenue in 1857. The late-19th-century residence included some Stick-style, ornamental-cut woodwork, stained and leaded glass, and diamond-shaped shingles. Mr. Reed was corporation council member for the borough of North Plainfield from 1888 to 1901; he was president of the Park Club of North Plainfield; in 1895, he was elected to New Jersey House of Assembly, becoming a state senator in 1896, and president of the senate in 1899.

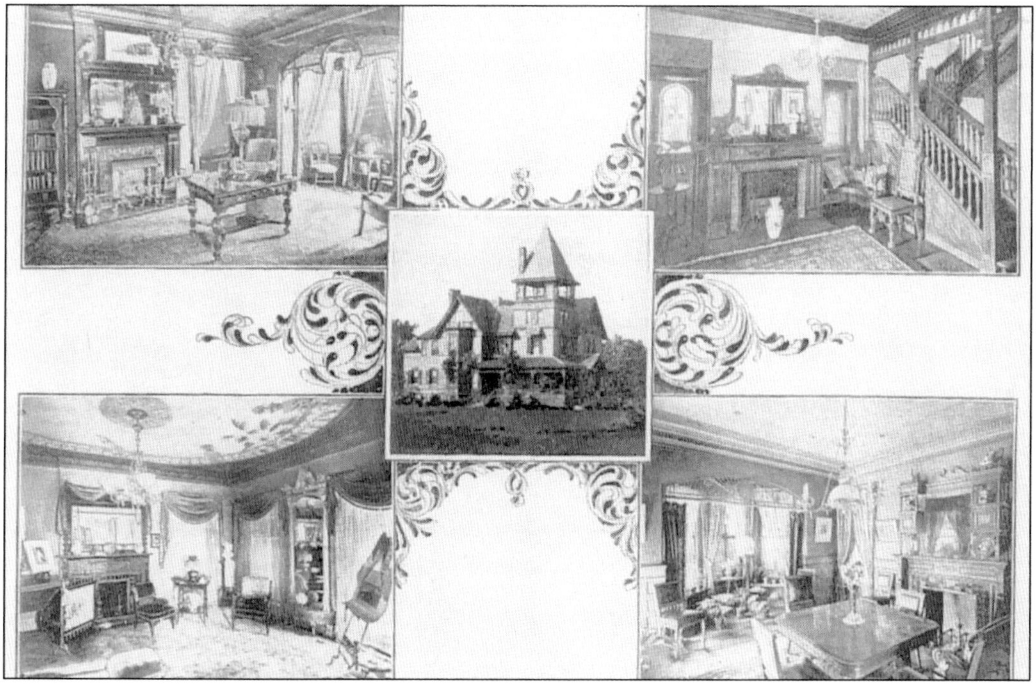

This home of W.W. Howland is located at 82 Rockview Avenue. At the turn of the century, this residence was known as "Notre Retraite."

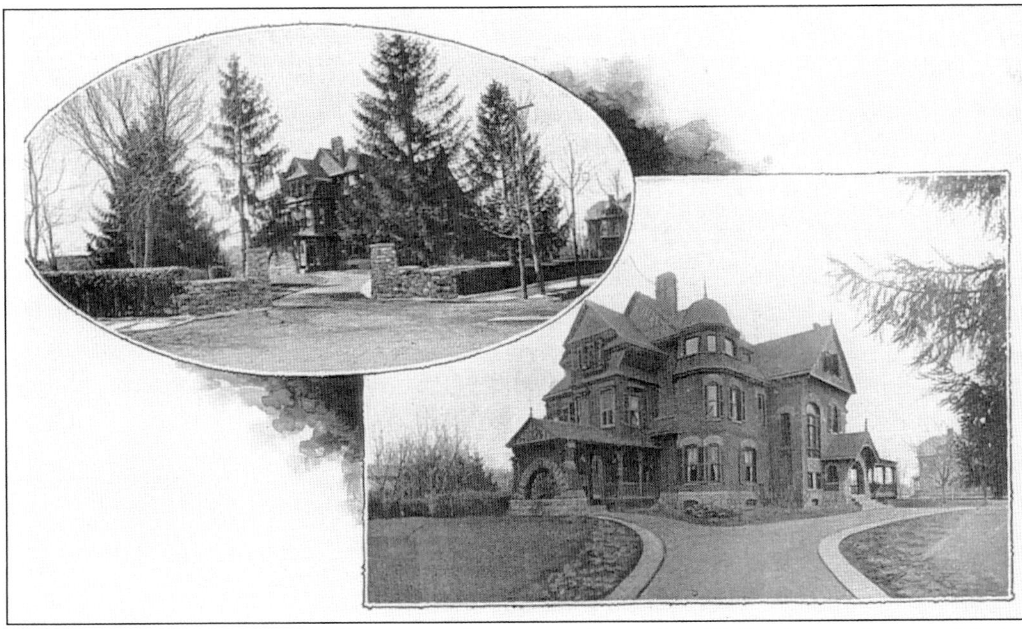

One of the finest Queen Ann houses in the state is located at 21 Rockview Avenue. Notice the irregular shape usage of the bricks and the stones at ground floor; the rusticated cut stone foundation shows an English influence. A combination of an English Country house, American material, and Japanese influence is quite evident in this nationally unique building. Charles H. Smith was the architect. The 1894 atlas shows that the house was owned by C.W. McCutchen. Mr. McCutchen was in the export business with Holt and Co. in New York City. In 1948, after the death of Mrs. McCutchen, Miss Margaret McCutchen gave the residence to the Religious Society of Friends to be used as a home for elderly people.

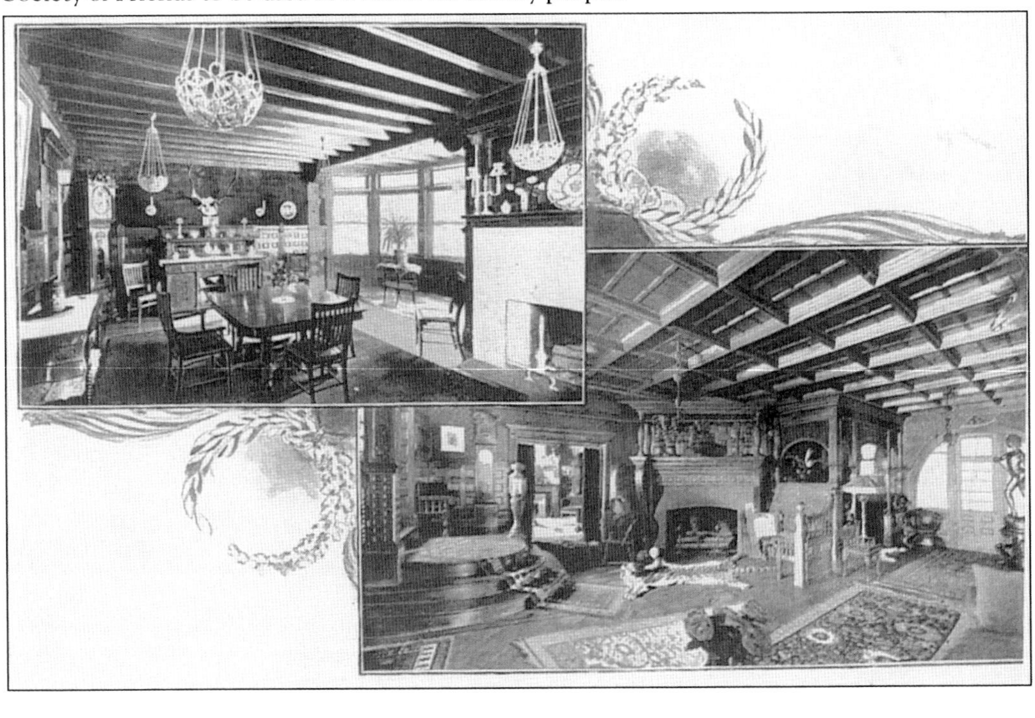

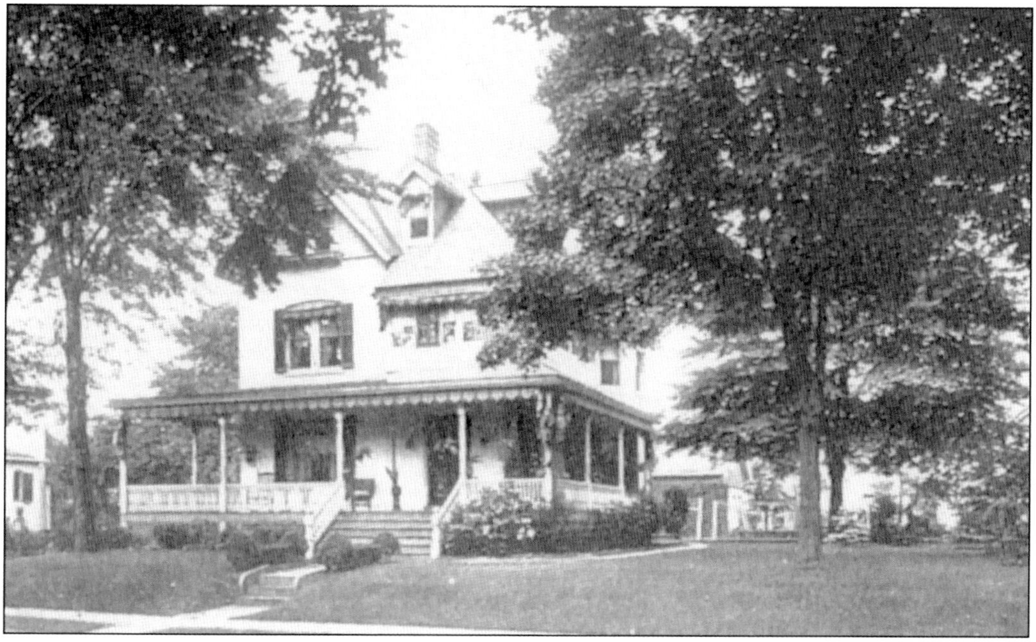

The 1894 atlas shows that the house at 112 Sycamore Avenue was owned by Hegemann. This two-and-one-half-story Queen Ann has stucco on the first floor, with shingles on the second and third. This original home had a wrap-around porch with turned posts, a slate roof, and double-beveled glass doors in front.

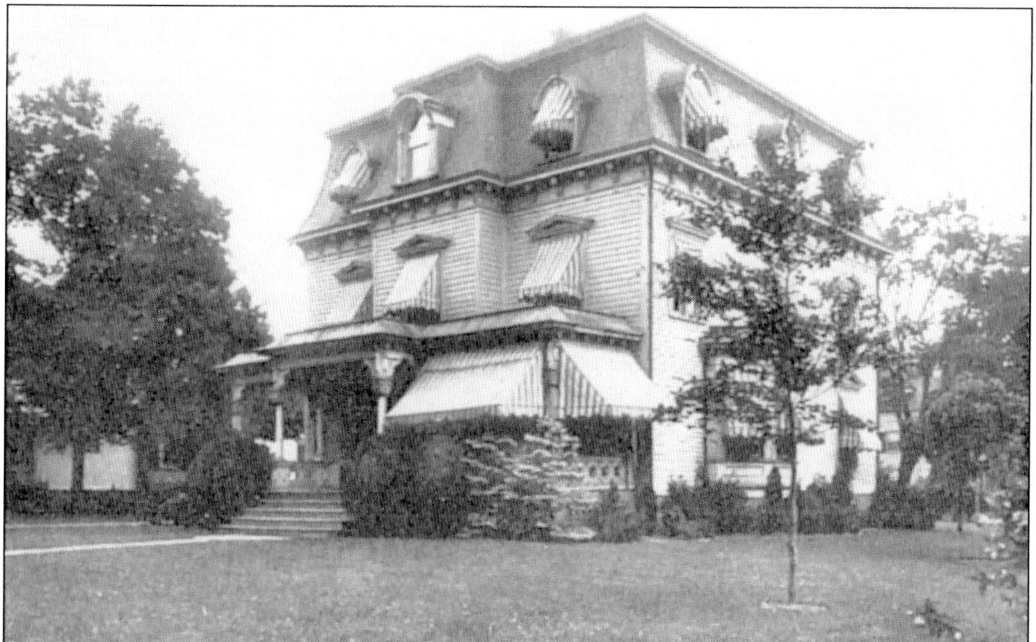

The residence at 57 Willow Avenue is a two-and-one-half-story Second Empire design. It has good railing detail, cut scroll brackets, roping around the mansard roof, and arched dormers over the windows. The house is shown in the 1894 atlas as owned by E.J. Waring. It was once owned by Alexander Milne, who was mayor of North Plainfield from 1914 to 1926.

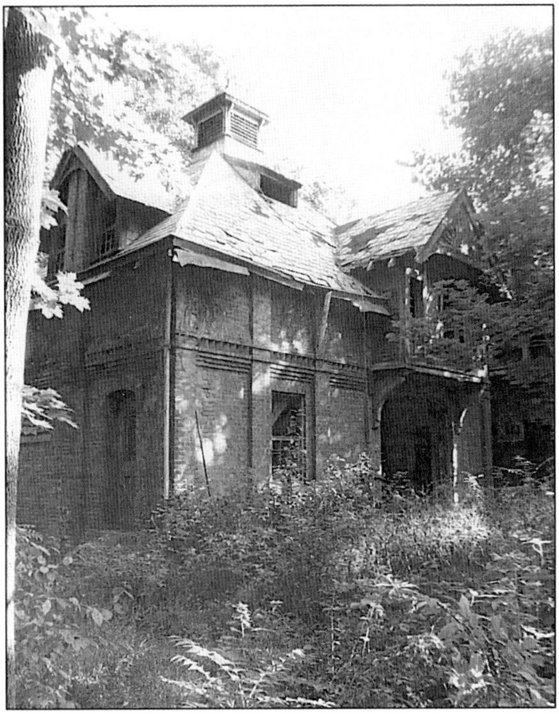

Restoration commenced in November 1982 on this carriage house located at 30 1/2 Rockview Avenue. The build has Queen Ann–style detailed brickwork; brick arches and bandcoursing; a high Queen Ann roof with very interesting dormer windows and cupola; dormered loft doors, which project out over entry; and an intricately carved large board over doors. The building appears to date back to the mid-1860s. The 1894 atlas shows that George P. Dupee owned the land.

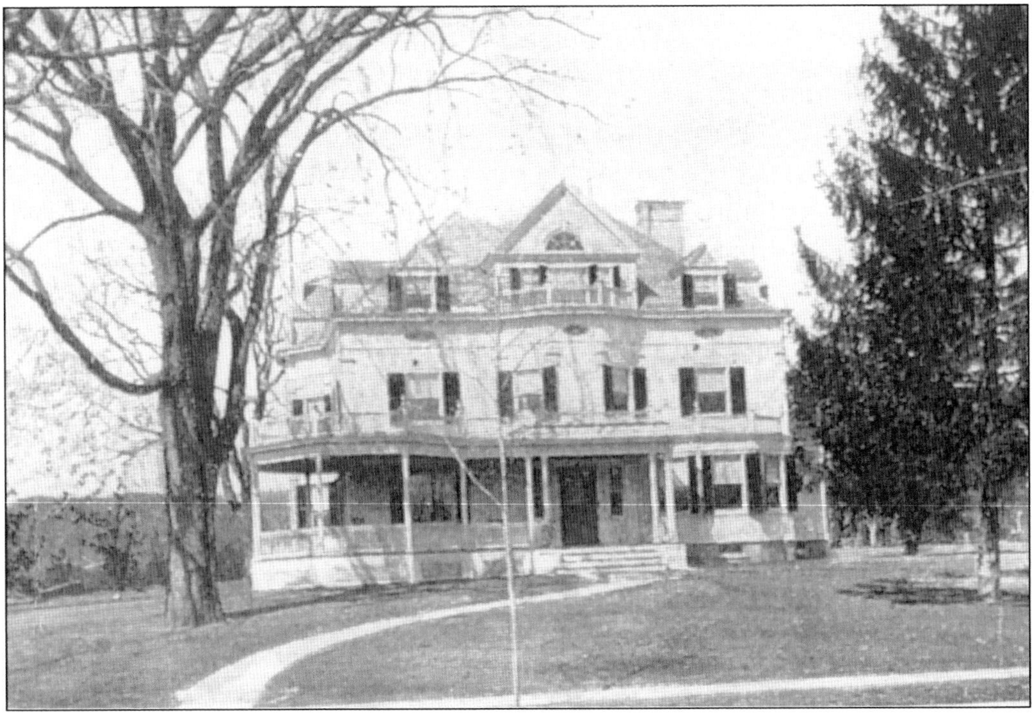

Fifty-four Myrtle Avenue is the site of a much-altered Colonial Revival–style building. A modified palladian window is on the third floor. According to the 1894 atlas, Samuel Townsend owned the house shown in this photograph. A number of homes had been converted into multiple dwellings during the World War II period.

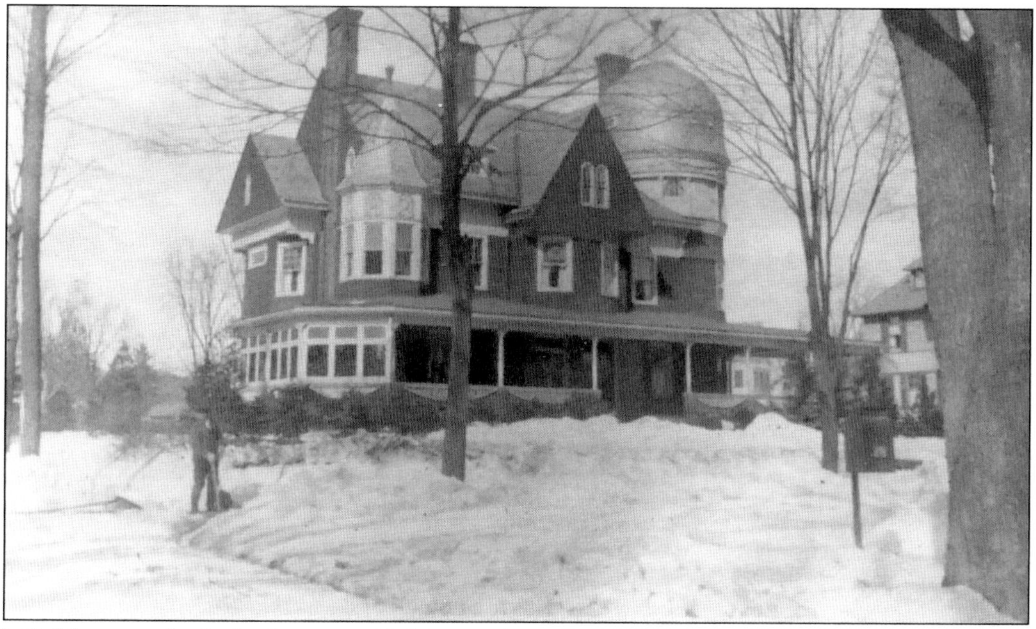

J.G. Musgrove built the house at 80 Mercer Avenue, *c.* 1894. Upon its completion, this high Queen Ann had a port cochere, and natural wood shakes on the second and third floors, gesso work above the window on the corner tower, beautiful leaded and stained glass windows throughout and on the stairway, and a large "onion dome" tower.

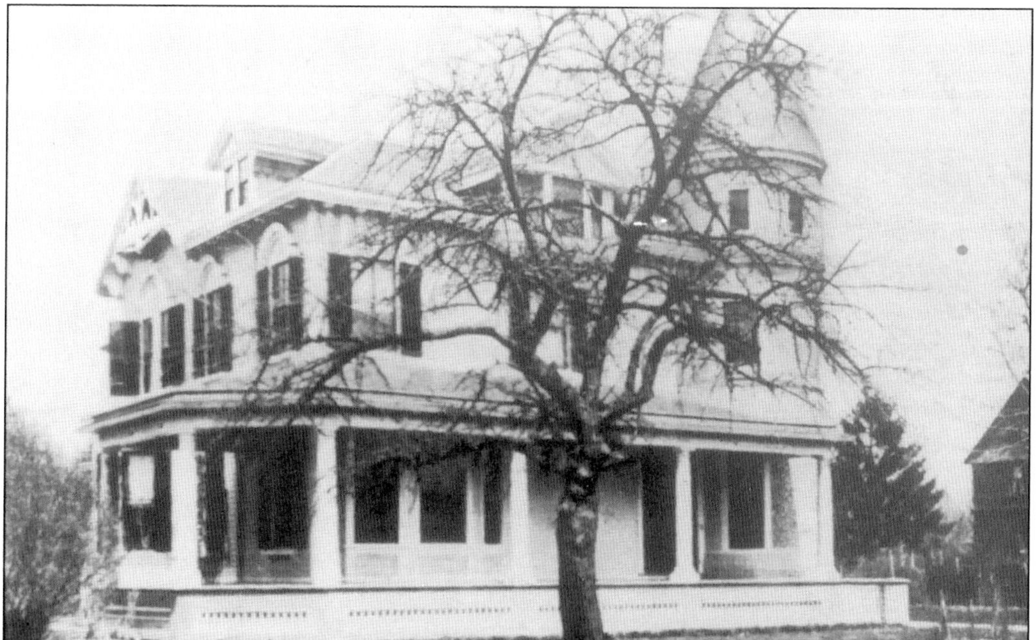

English-born mason and master builder William White constructed the house at 40 Willow Avenue, *c.* 1868. The house is rectangular, three bay, side hall plan with a hipped roof, slate shingles, and a three-story round tower. Greek masks of comedy and tragedy are integrated into the tower.

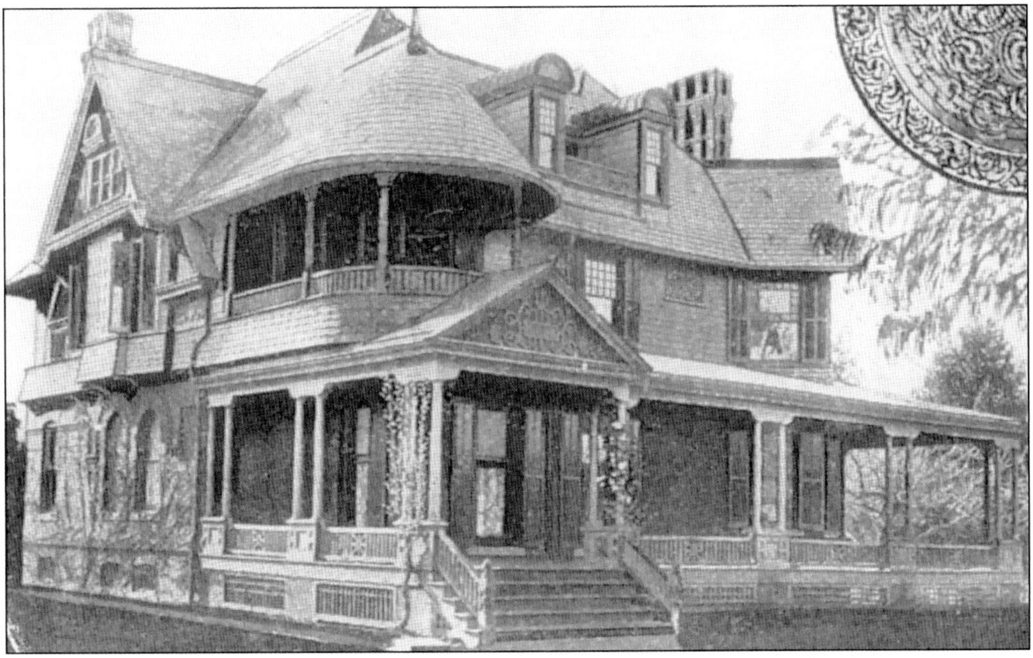

Located on the corner of Rockview Avenue and Orchard, the owner of this lost treasure was listed on the 1894 atlas as H.A. McGee.

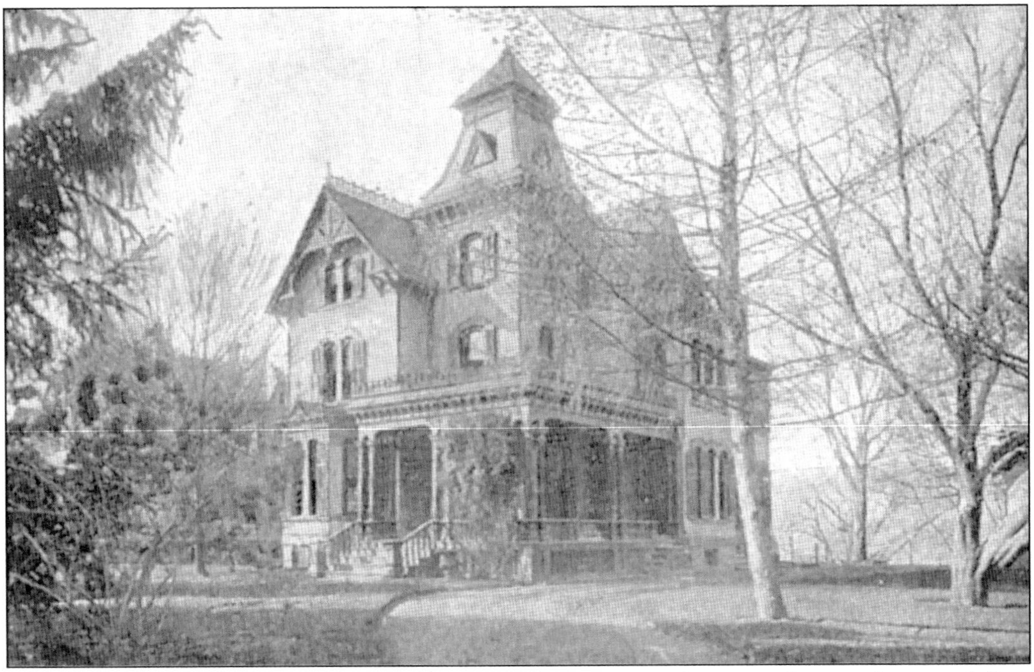

Located at 12 Rockview Avenue is this smooth stucco with triangular windows and East Lake detailing complete with port cochere and carriage house. The 1894 map lists the owner as Mary Loomis.

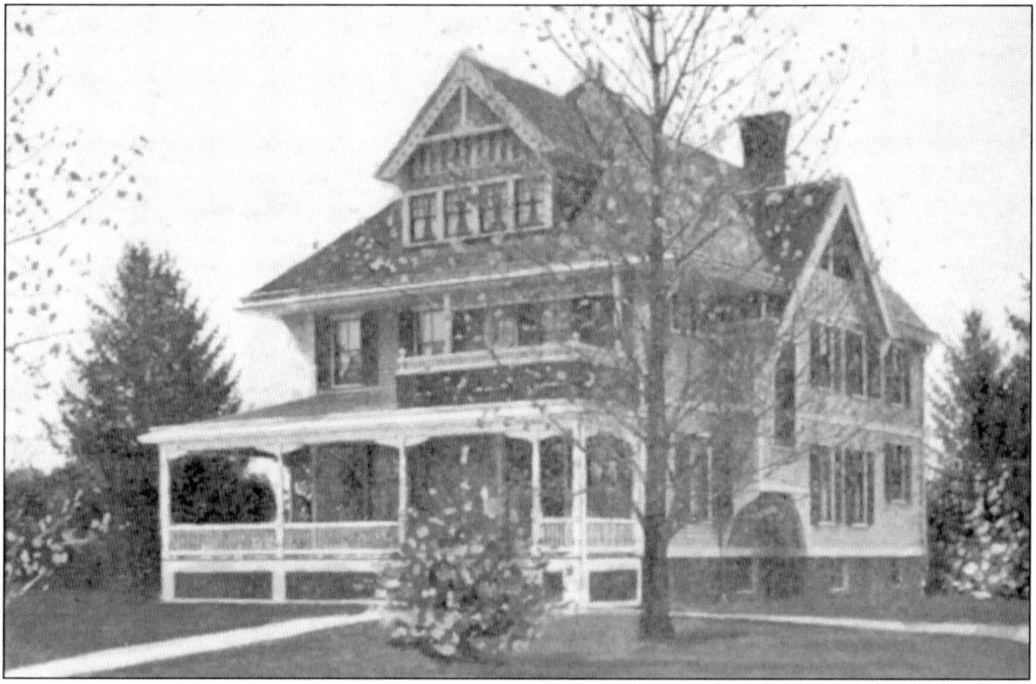

Mr. Hallock built the house at 39 Willow Avenue, *c.* 1886. It has an outstanding Queen Ann style and Japanese influences on the second and third floors, beautiful parquet floors, natural wood trim throughout the house, many fireplaces, and exquisite stained-grass windows.

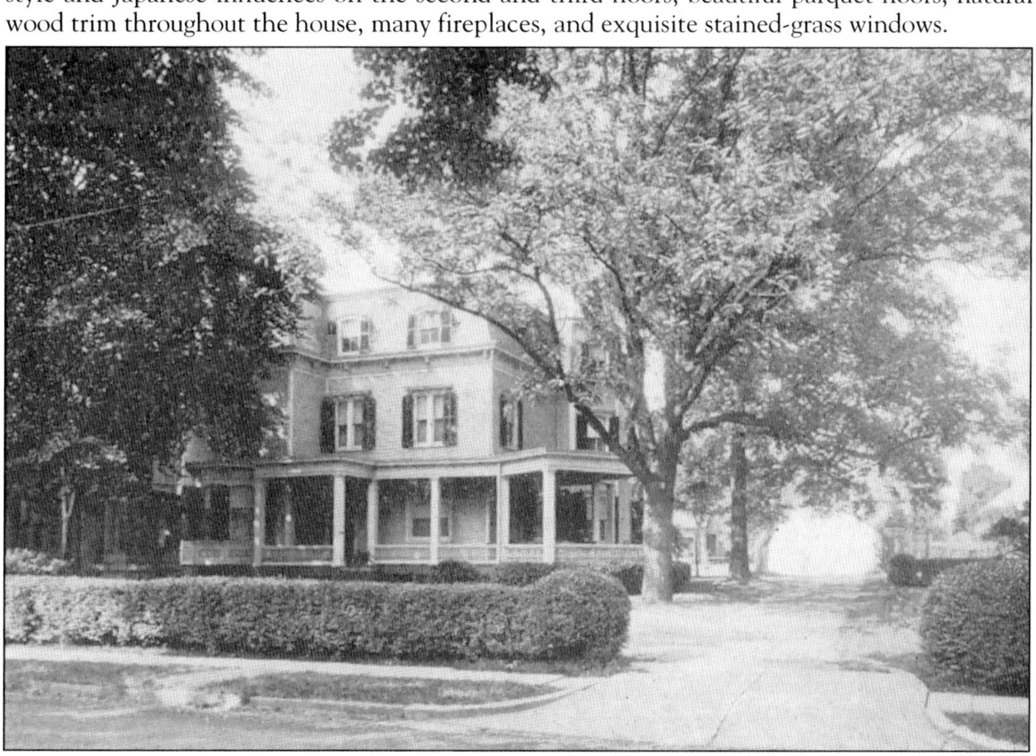

H.R. Munger built this Second Empire style with a painted slate concave mansard roof and wrap-around porch, *c.* 1871 or 1872. The house has beautiful stained-glass windows.

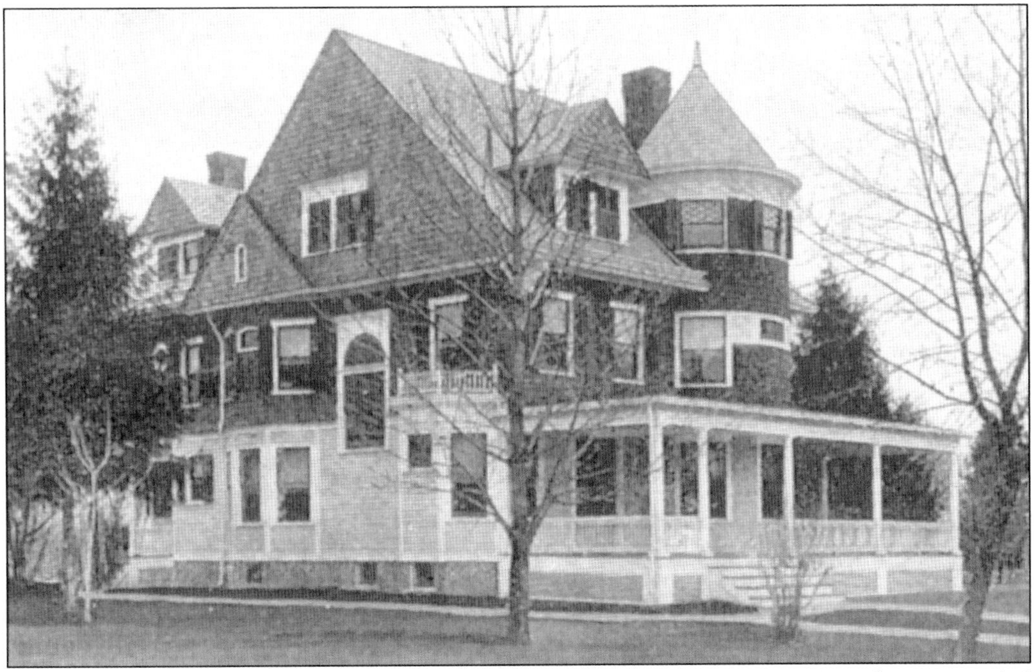

George O. White owned this home at 41 Willow Avenue. This Queen Ann has a rounded tower, cut diamond sawtooth and fish-scaled shingles, stained-glass windows, and wrap-around front porch.

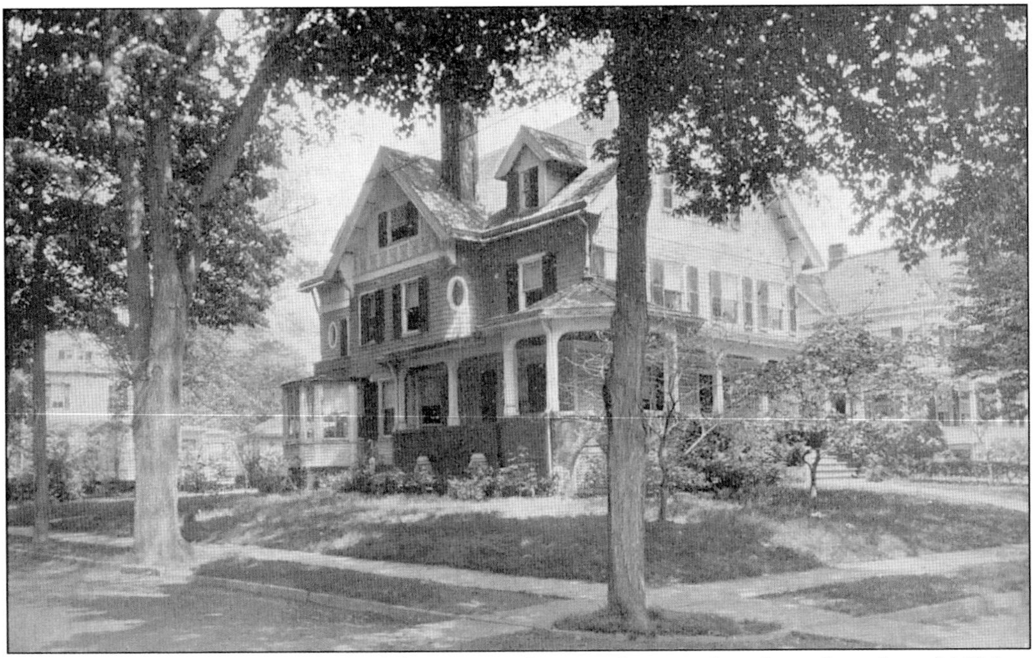

Thirty-six Myrtle Avenue was built by Wm. J. Roome, but was listed on the atlas of 1894 as property only. This Queen Ann frame house with Jacobean elements was constructed with half timber and a Japanese influence.

Nine

Street Scenes

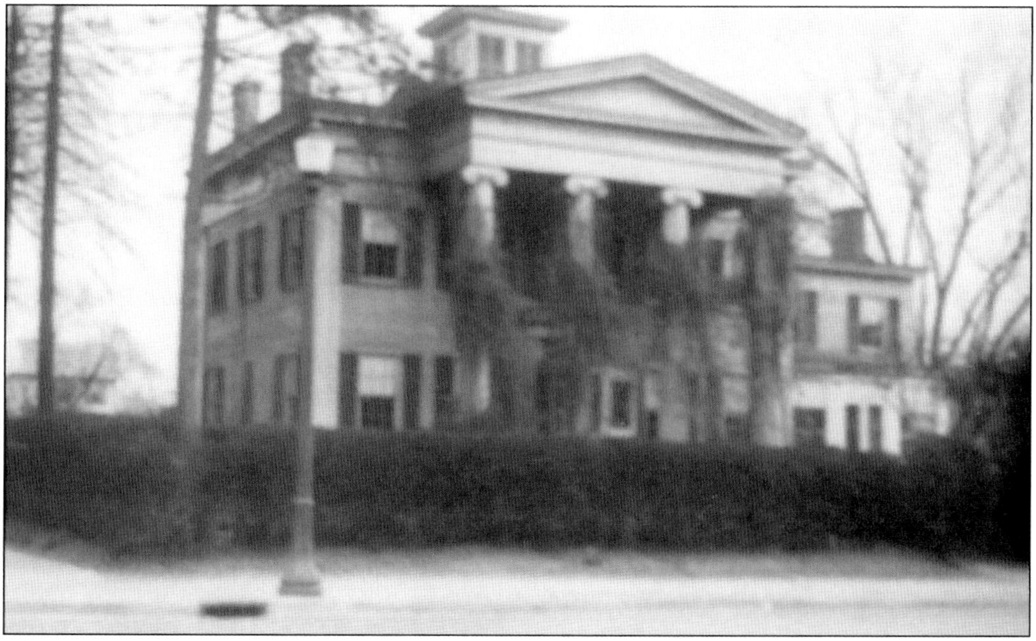

This beautiful old home of Phineas M. French stood at the corner of Somerset and Pearl Streets in North Plainfield. The dignified Colonial home was the largest house anywhere in the area. People came from far distances to see its four great Ionic pillars and large cupola. Phineas French owned all the property from Front Street to Pearl Street and was known as the "borough patriarch."

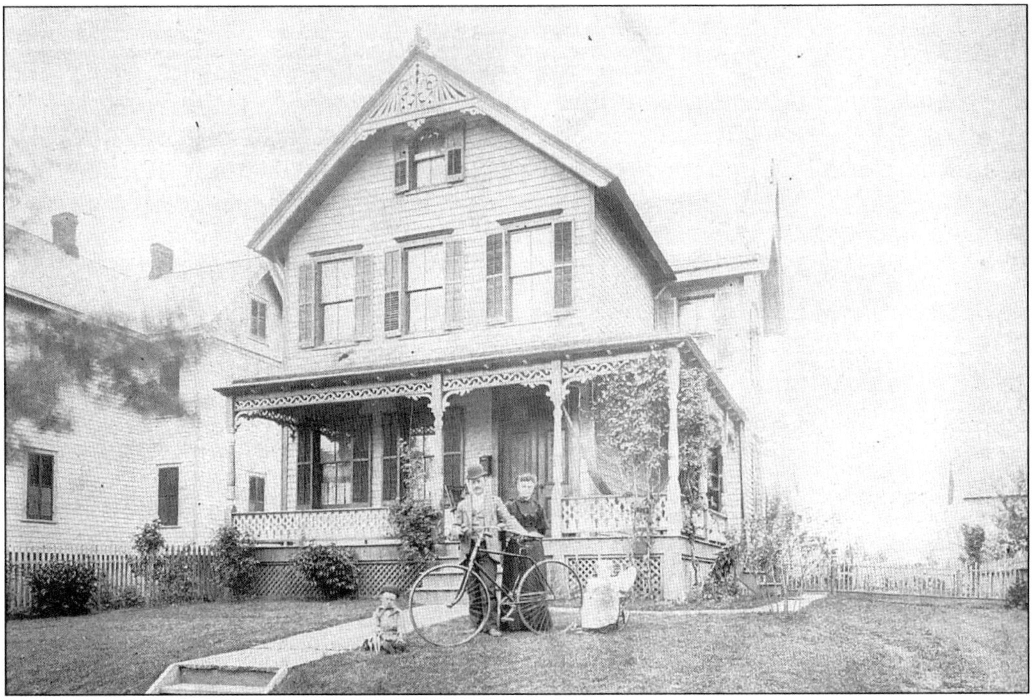

The Hub Stine House, located at 10 Mountain Avenue, is a good example of a smaller Victorian home, complete with gingerbread moldings.

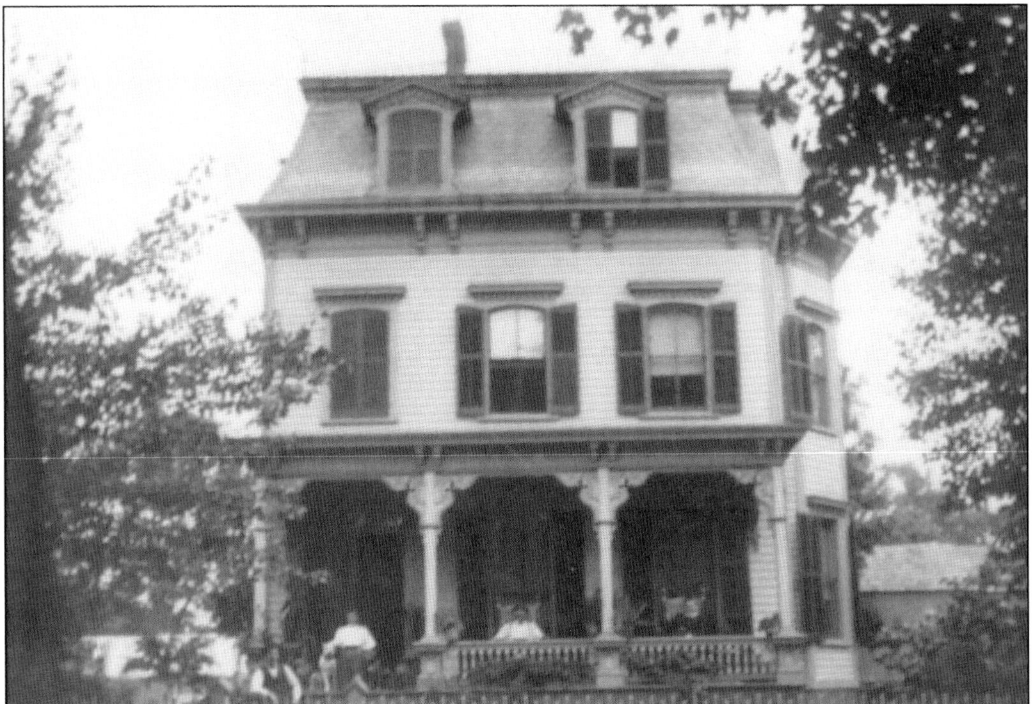

This Victorian home with mansard roof was located on Pearl Street near the corner of Somerset Street. The Feller family lived in the home for many years.

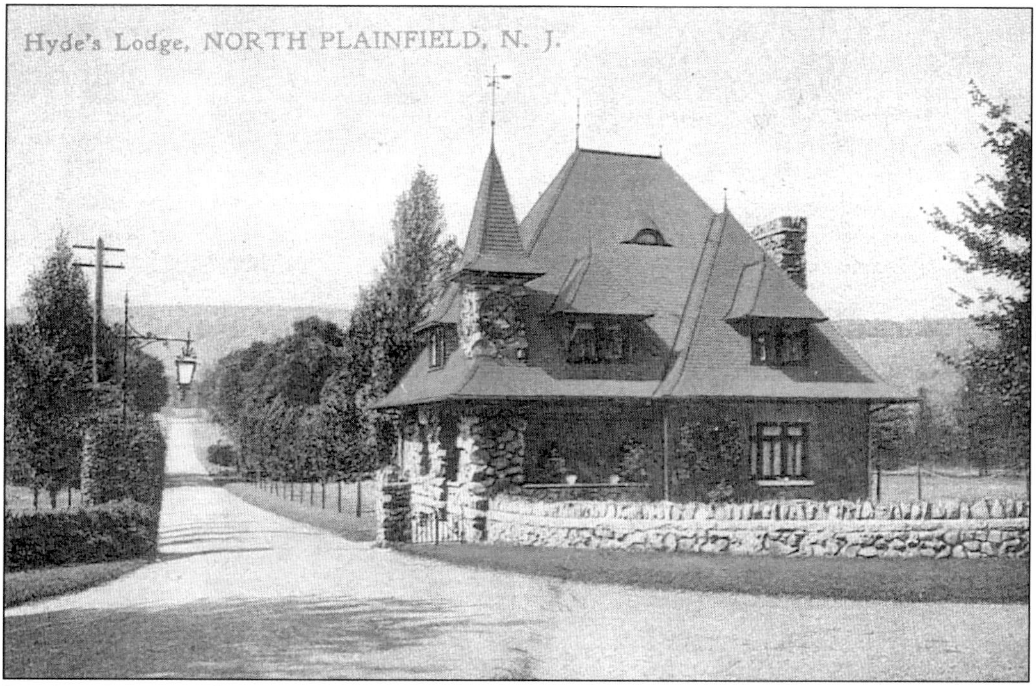

In 1911, Louis Hyde, son of Francis Hyde, built a mansion on the top of the mountain. Mr. Hyde decided to have an approach to this mansion from Norwood Avenue and had a "Gate House" built of stone, complete with a clock tower. The long drive up the mountain was called Hyde's Drive.

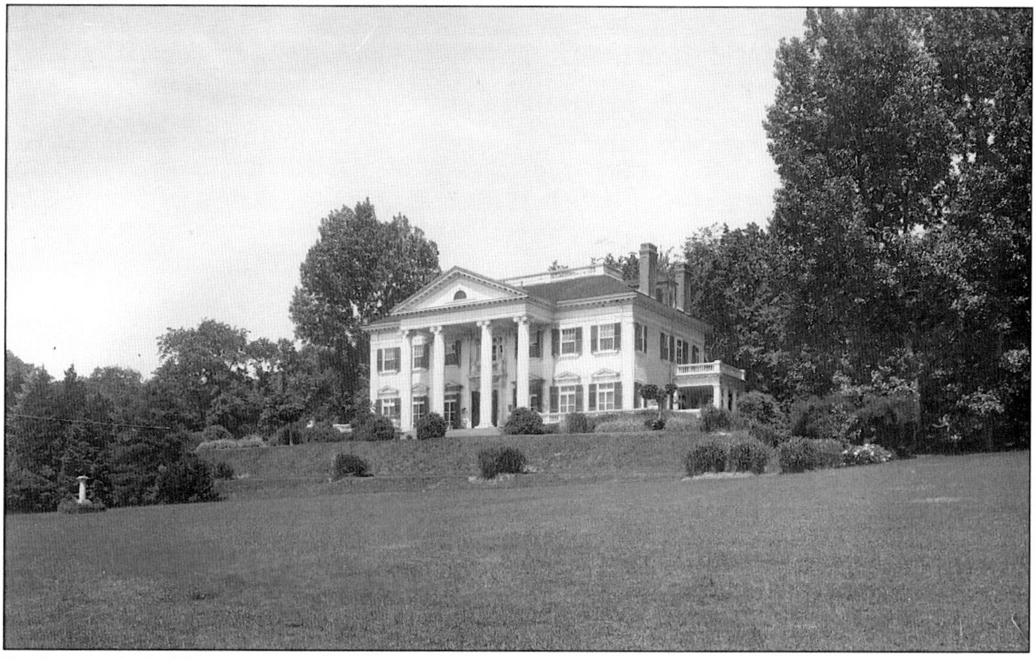

Early in 1900, Francis DeLacey Hyde built "Hydewood Hall," at the foot of the Watchung Mountains. This approach was from Westervelt Avenue. Mrs. Hyde entertained Teddy Roosevelt at this home. Regency Village now occupies this property.

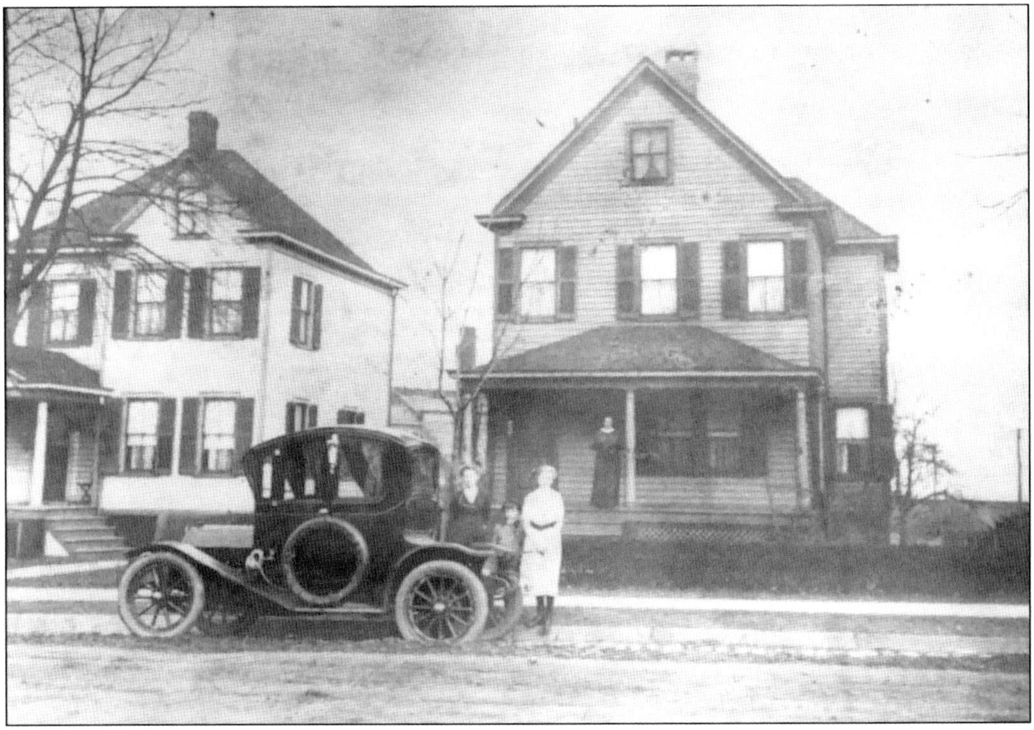

At the turn of the century, automobiles were starting to be seen on the streets in North Plainfield. People had gone from buggies, trolleys, and bicycles to the horseless carriage.

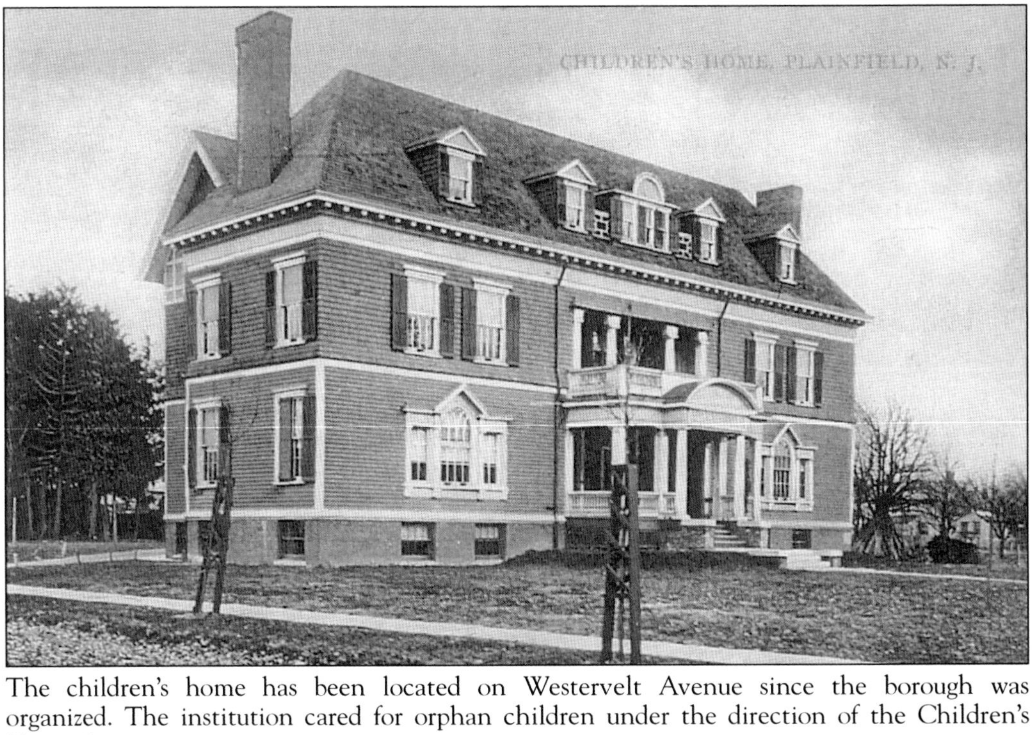

The children's home has been located on Westervelt Avenue since the borough was organized. The institution cared for orphan children under the direction of the Children's Home Association.

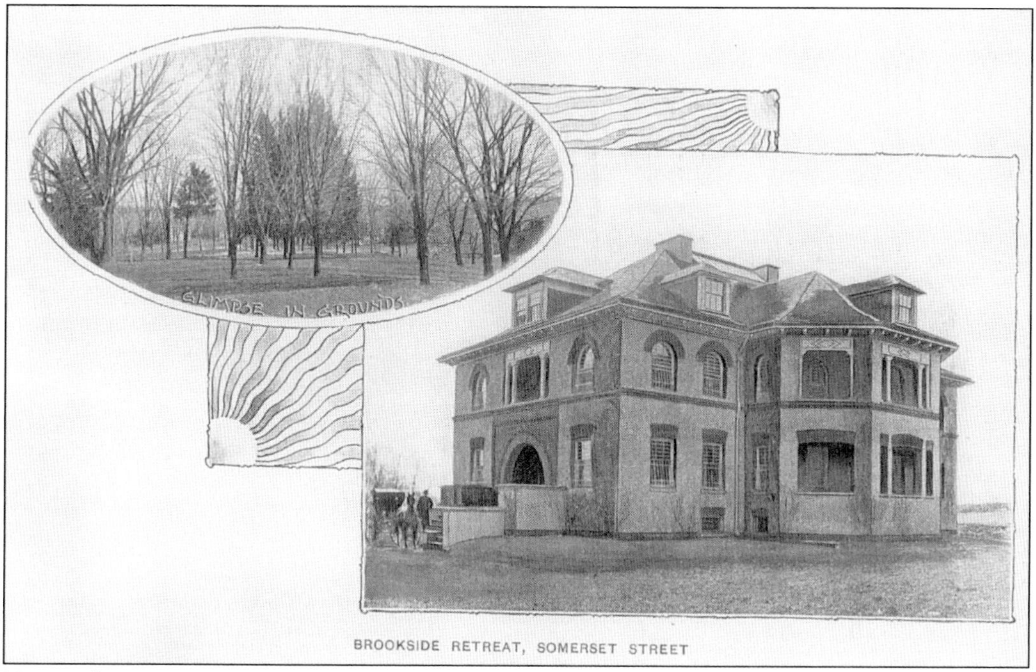

Now Villa Maria, Justice H. Cooley built his Brookside Sanitarium at the corner of Somerset Street and Interhaven Avenue in 1876. For several years, it served as the Arthur Pitney Home for aged and invalid. In 1939, seven nuns from Germany purchased the property.

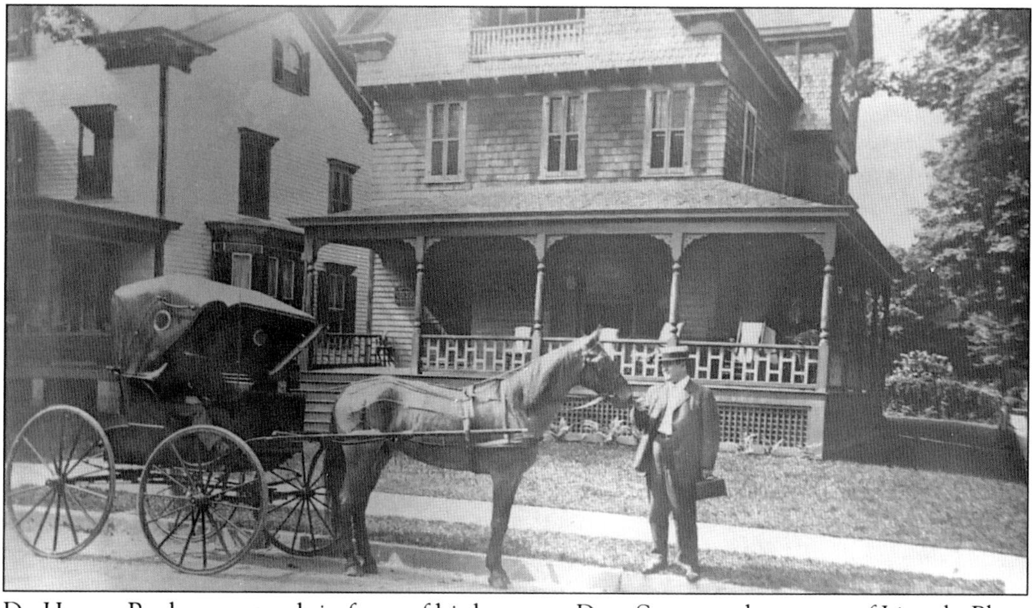

Dr. Harvey Buchanan stands in front of his home on Duer Street at the corner of Lincoln Place in this c. 1898 photograph. Dr. Buchanan practiced general medicine for about 20 years in North Plainfield.

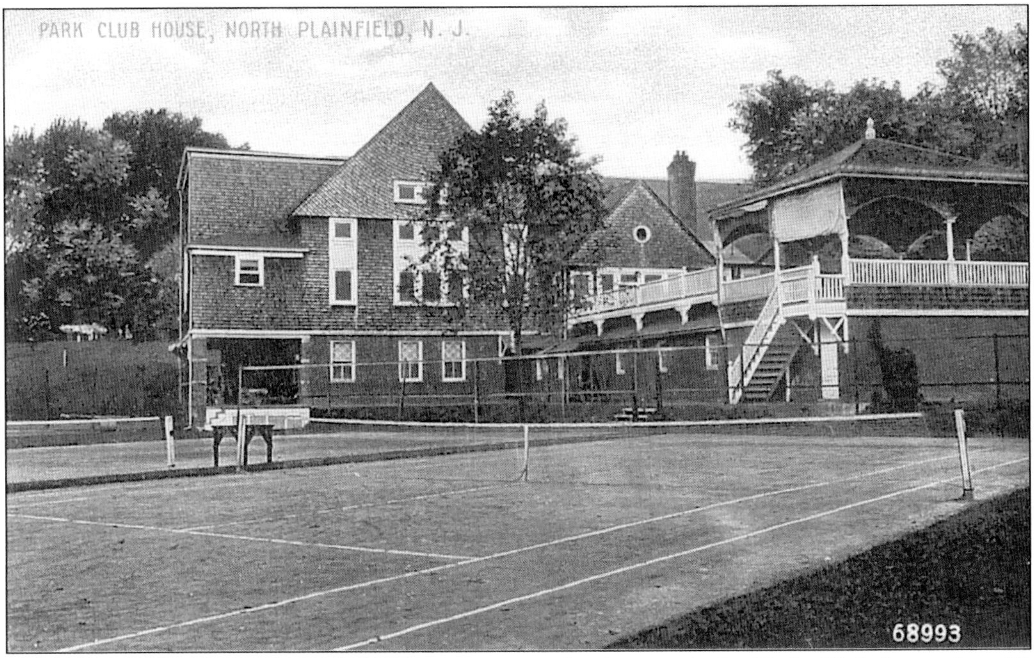

For many years, the center of social activity revolved around the Park Club located at 20 Washington Avenue. Built in 1889, the club promoted tennis, bowling, and other sports. It was later known as Pythian Hall and the North Plainfield VFW.

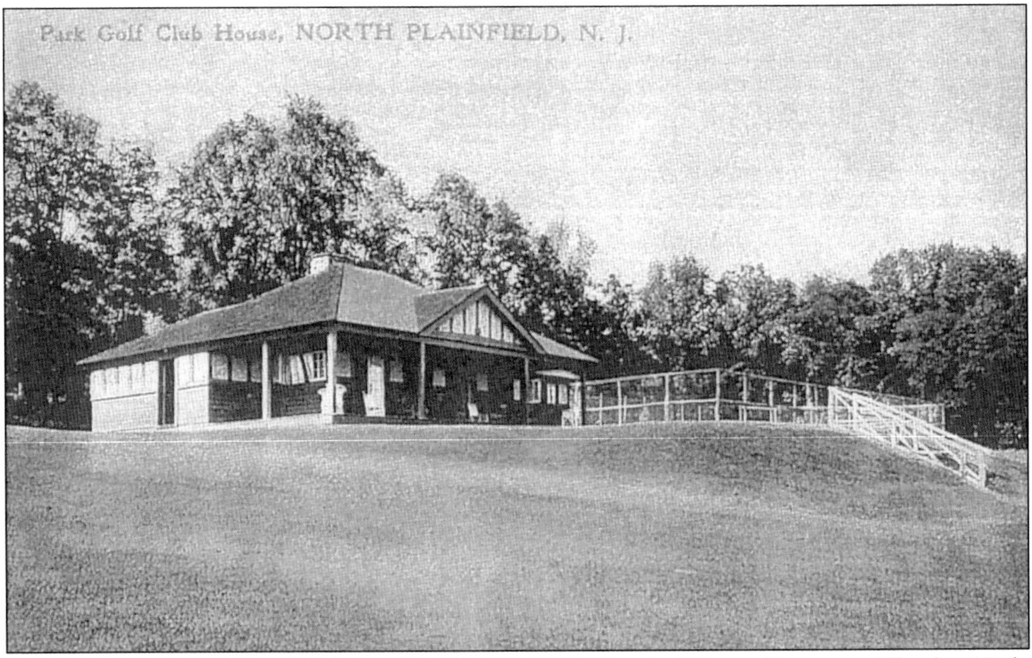

In 1892, a group of men from the Park Club decided to build a golf course. Charles Hyde donated a section of his property at the base of the mountain and a nine-hole course was laid out. The course later moved and became Watchung Valley Country Club, which is now known as Twin Brooks.

This view shows Greenbrook Road in North Plainfield Township after it had been retreaded with small crushed stone. The stone was furnished by Bound Brook Crushed Stone Co., Wilson Quarry Co., Smalley Stone Co., and Morris County Crushed Stone Co.

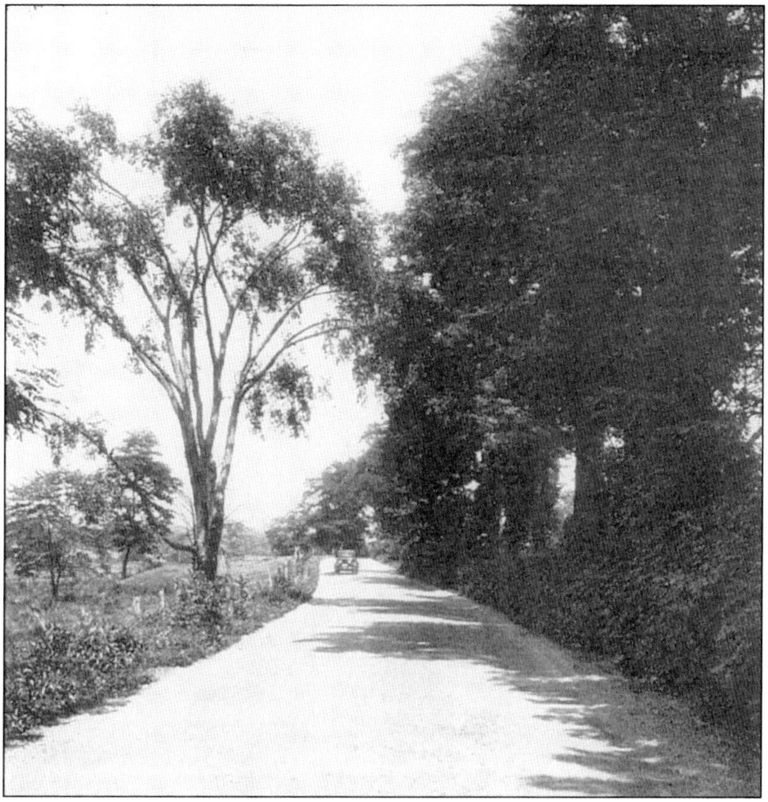

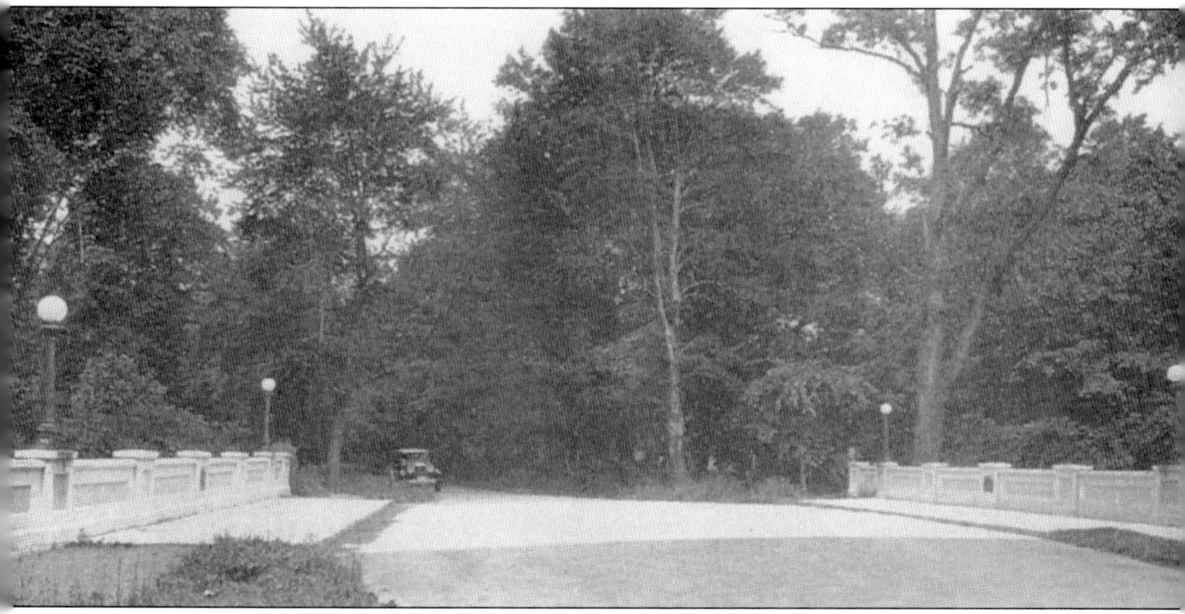

This picture of the Netherwood Bridge was taken in 1928. The bridge connected the Borough of North Plainfield with the city of Plainfield. The builder of the bridge was Arthur E. Smith.

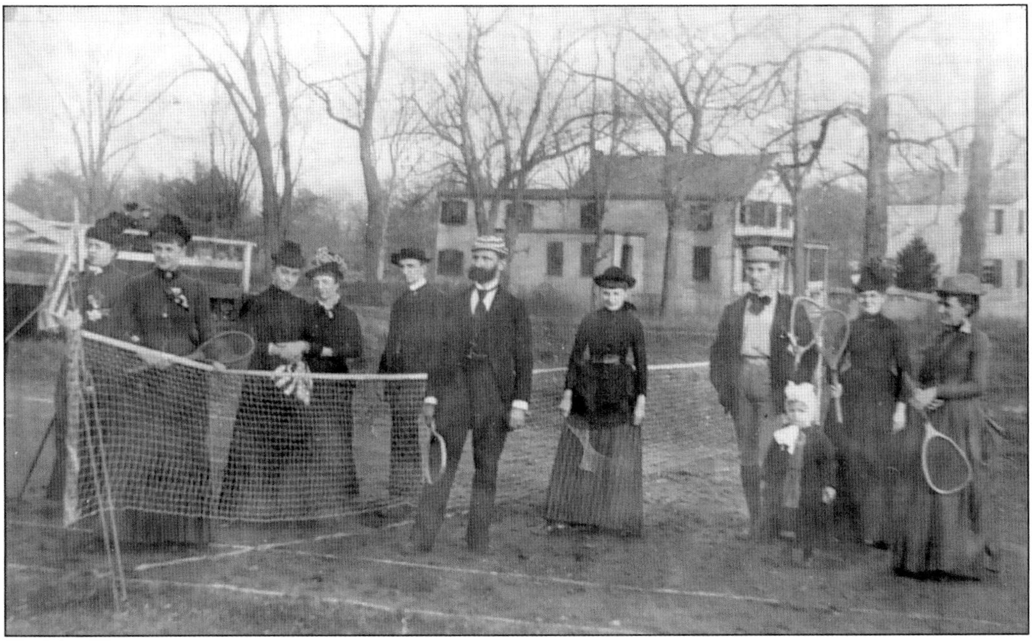

In the 1880s and 1890s, tennis was becoming a popular sport in the Plainfield area. This photograph was taken at the Elm Street tennis court on the border of North Plainfield and Plainfield. Elm Street is now Roosevelt Avenue.

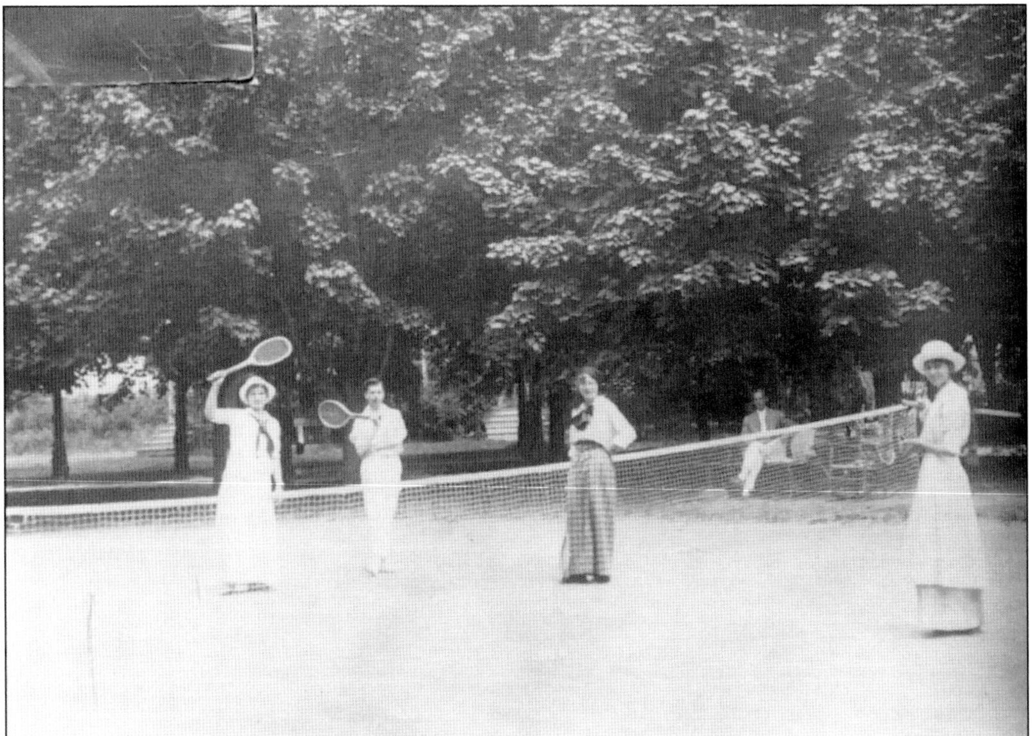

Tennis attire has certainly changed since this photograph was taken at the turn of the century. No respectful citizen would be seen on the courts without a hat, a coat and tie, or a long skirt.

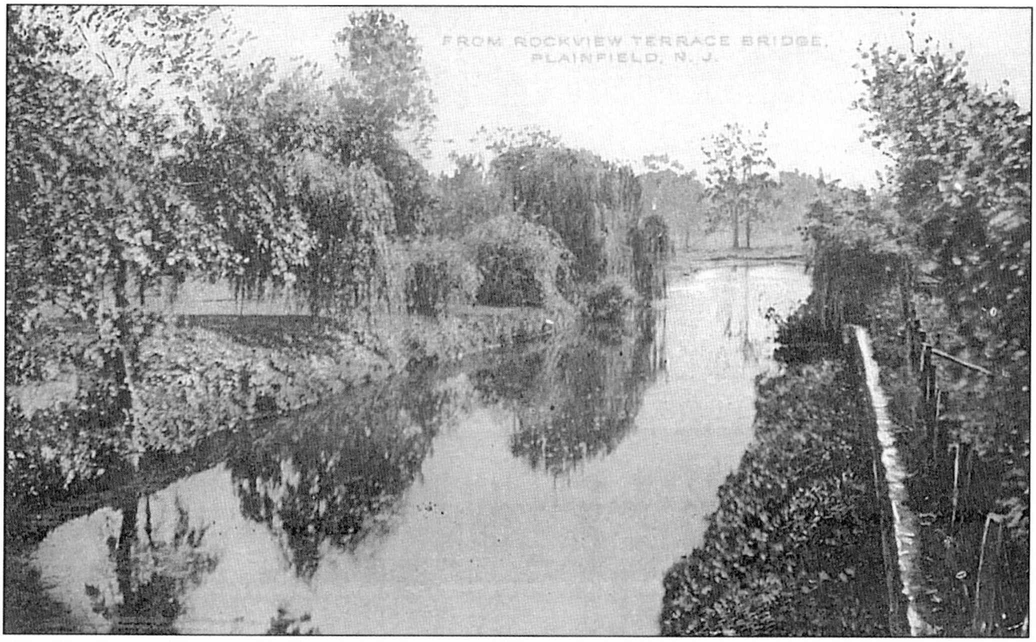

The Rockview Terrace Bridge can be seen in this early 1900s photograph.

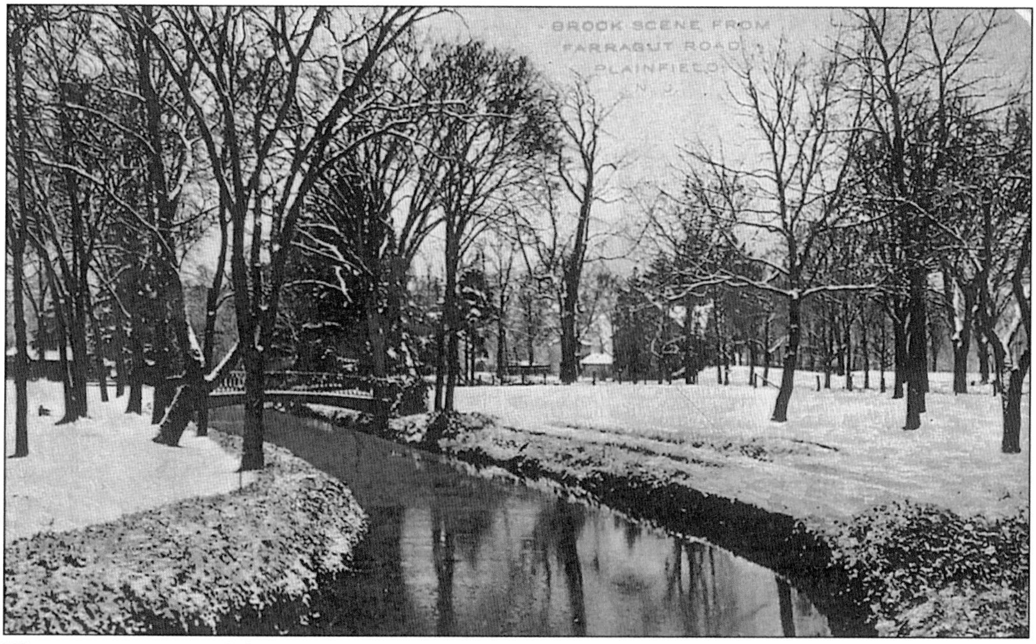

This winter scene of the Green Brook was photographed from Farragut Road, *c.* 1906. A few homes were built in the area at this time.

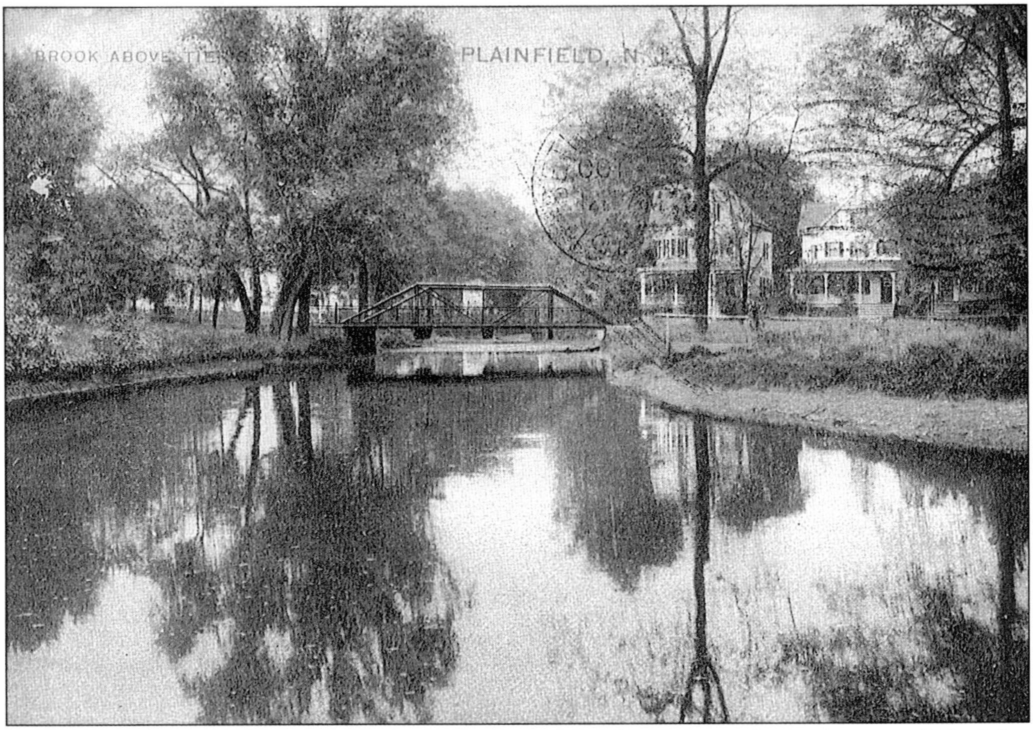

This photograph shows the brook just above Tier's Pond. Tier's Pond was the site of Mr. John Vail's former mill pond. Today, there is no trace of what was once Tier's Pond.

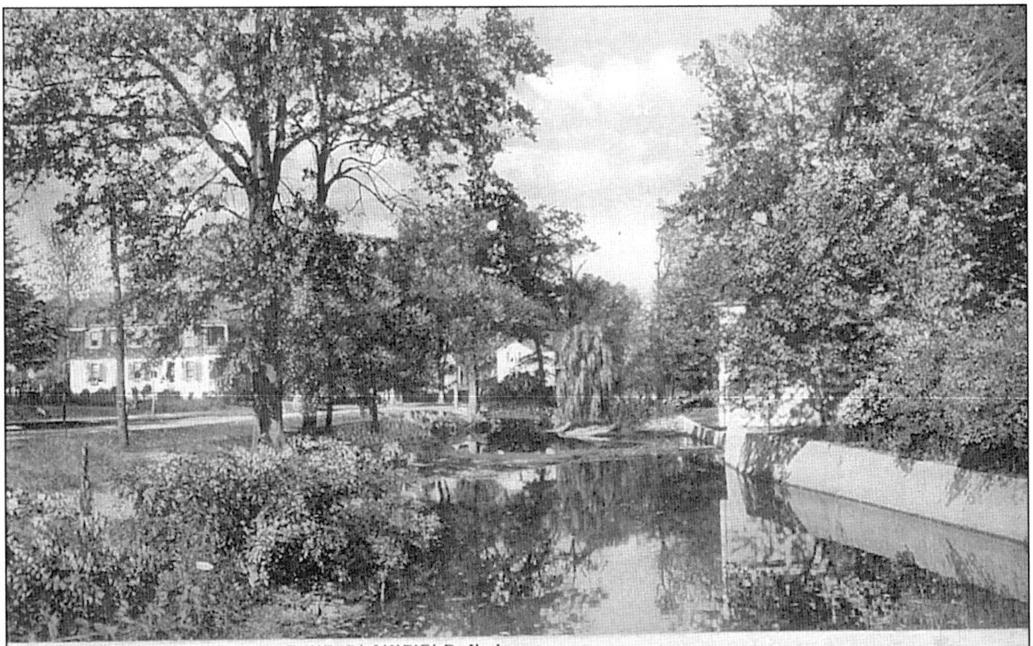

Green Brook, shown above, divides North Plainfield from Plainfield and Somerset County from Union. This view from Westervelt Avenue shows rural North Plainfield, *c.* 1900.

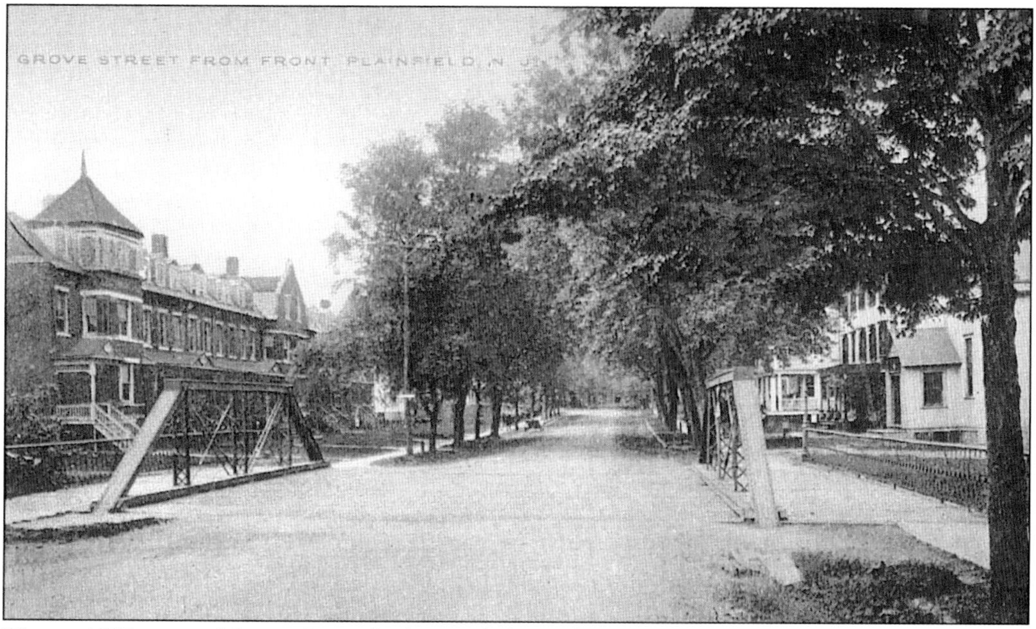

This *c.* 1900 view of Grove Street looks north from Plainfield. This once narrow tree-lined road has become a wide thoroughfare and heavily congested area. The Grove Street apartments can be seen in the photograph.

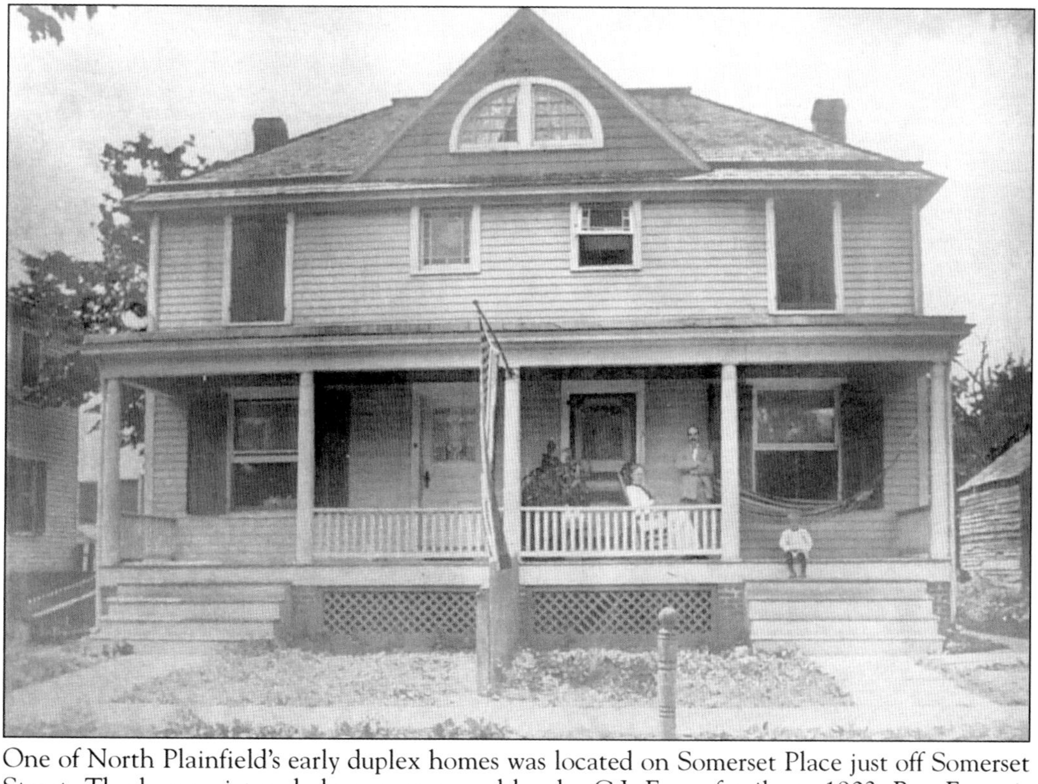

One of North Plainfield's early duplex homes was located on Somerset Place just off Somerset Street. The home pictured above was owned by the C.J. Force family, *c.* 1903. Roy Force is sitting on the porch. Sarah Jane Force, mother of C.J. Force, is in the rocker.

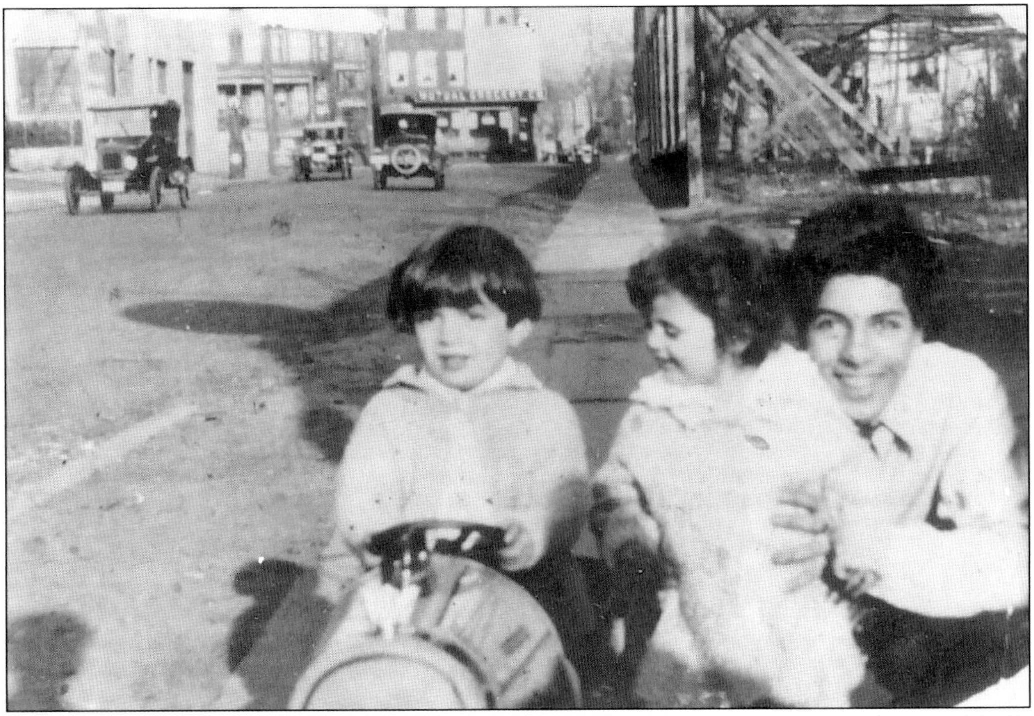

This view shows Greenbrook Road in 1928. The Vitelli family can be seen in front of Vitelli Bottling; Fran is in the car with two-year-old Evelyn, and Dennis nearby.

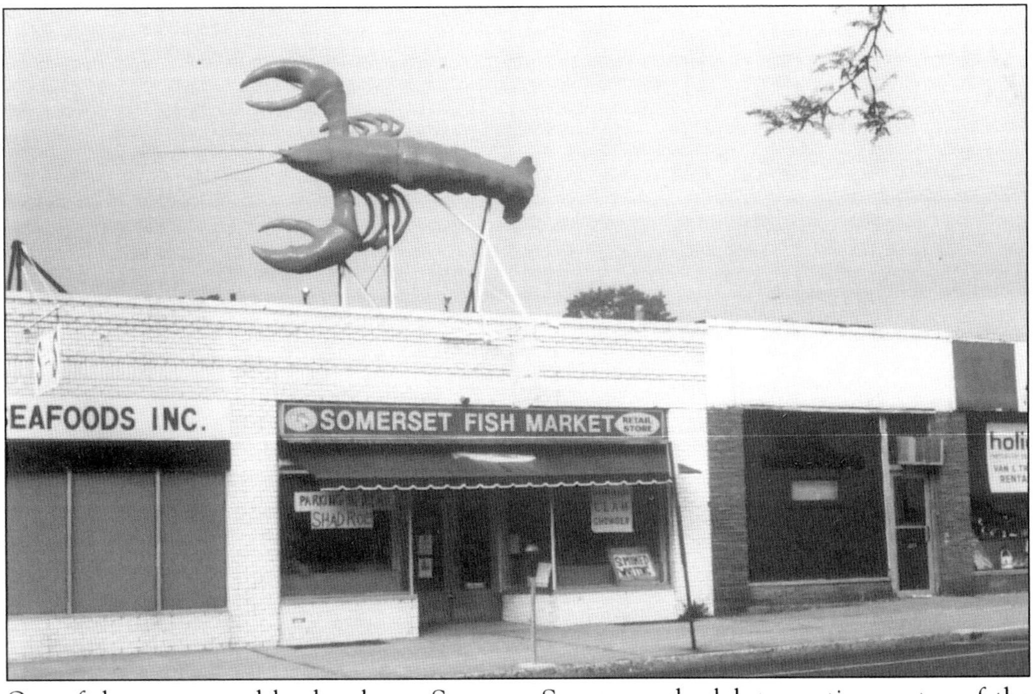

One of the most noted landmarks on Somerset Street was the lobster resting on top of the Somerset Fish Market, located on the corner of Somerset Street and Craig Place. The lobster has recently been removed (c. 1990s) to make way for a new establishment.

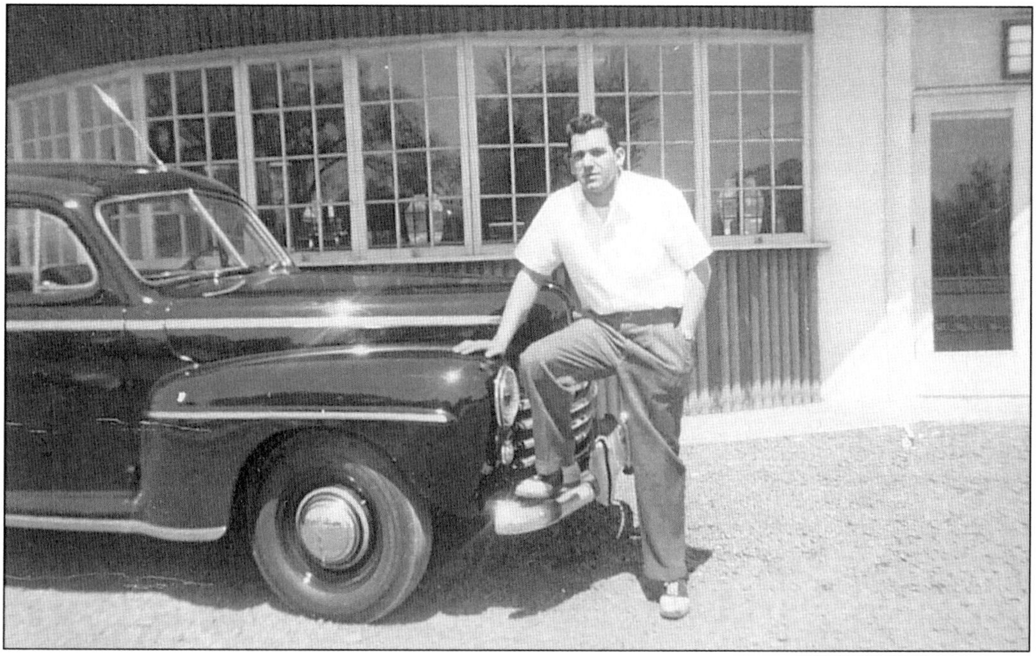

With the development of Route 22 came many new businesses. In the early 1950s, the Blue Star Drive-In was located on the corner of Wilson Avenue and Route 29. Owned by the DeMatteo family, one could drive in and order a hamburger, fries, and a milkshake.

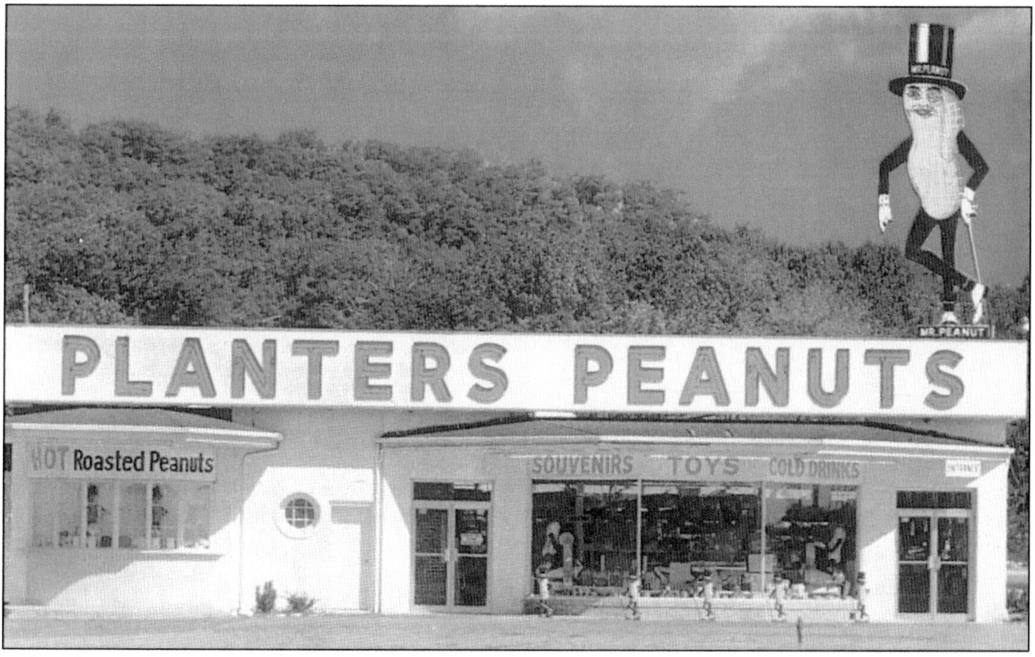

After the Blue Star Drive-In closed, Planters Peanuts operated on this site. On any given day, a large walking peanut would wave and beckon you into the store as you drove by. Today, this is the location of Fabric Land.

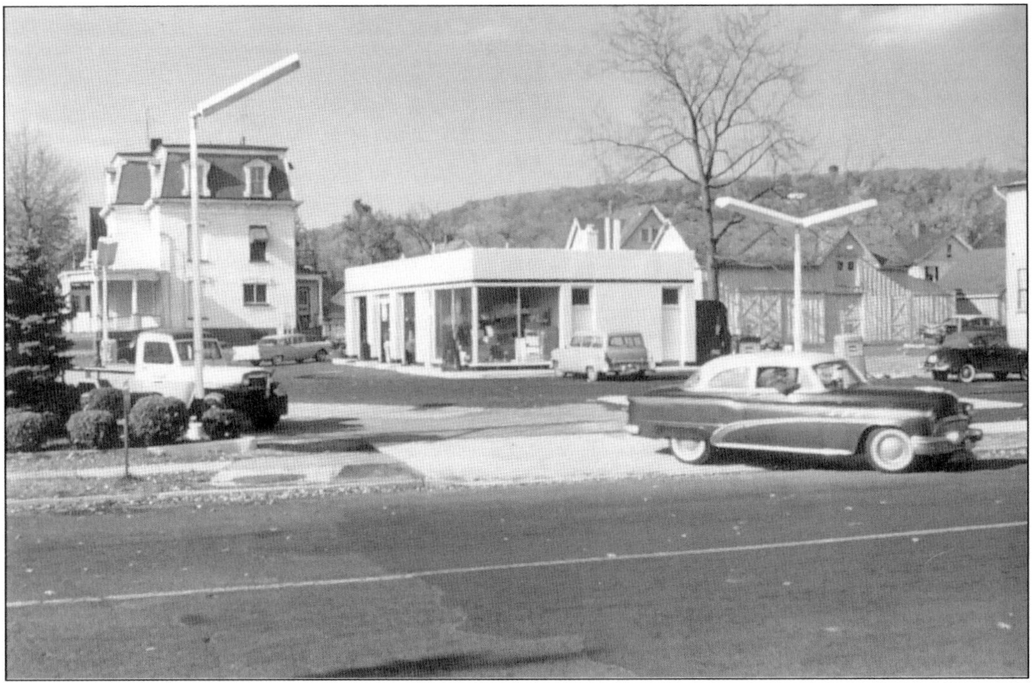

Early in the 1920s, more and more gas stations cropped up around the borough with the coming of the automobile. This station is on the corner of Mountain Avenue and Somerset Street.

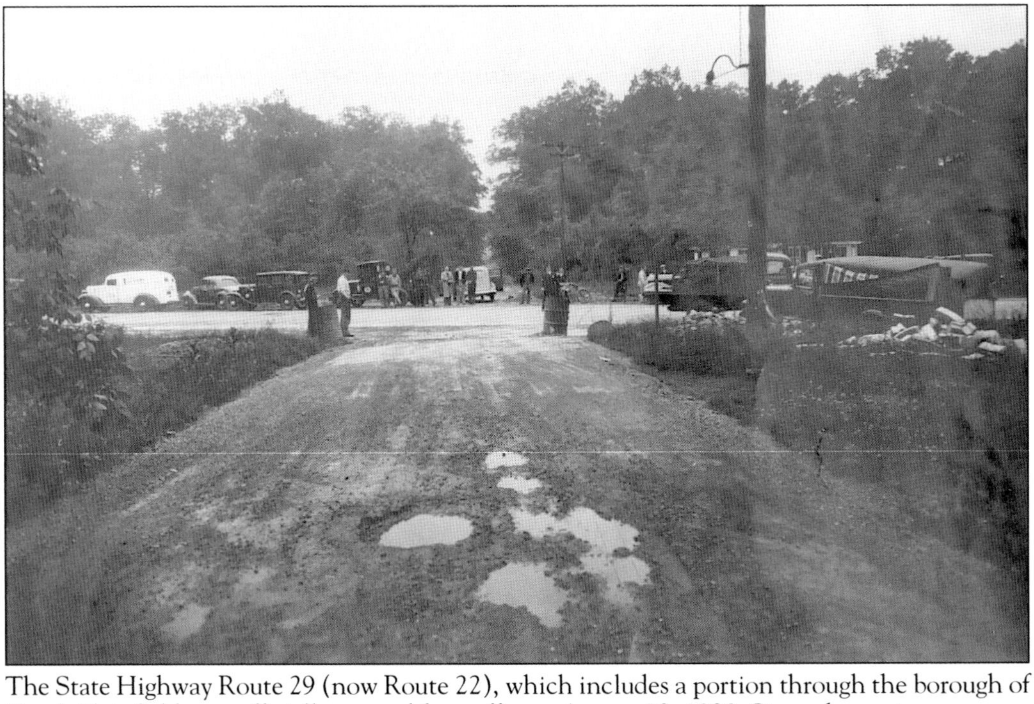

The State Highway Route 29 (now Route 22), which includes a portion through the borough of North Plainfield, was officially opened for traffic on August 13, 1930. Since the entire route was opened in November 1933, traffic has become very heavy and a source of danger at the cross streets. This picture was taken at the corner of Route 29 and North Drive.

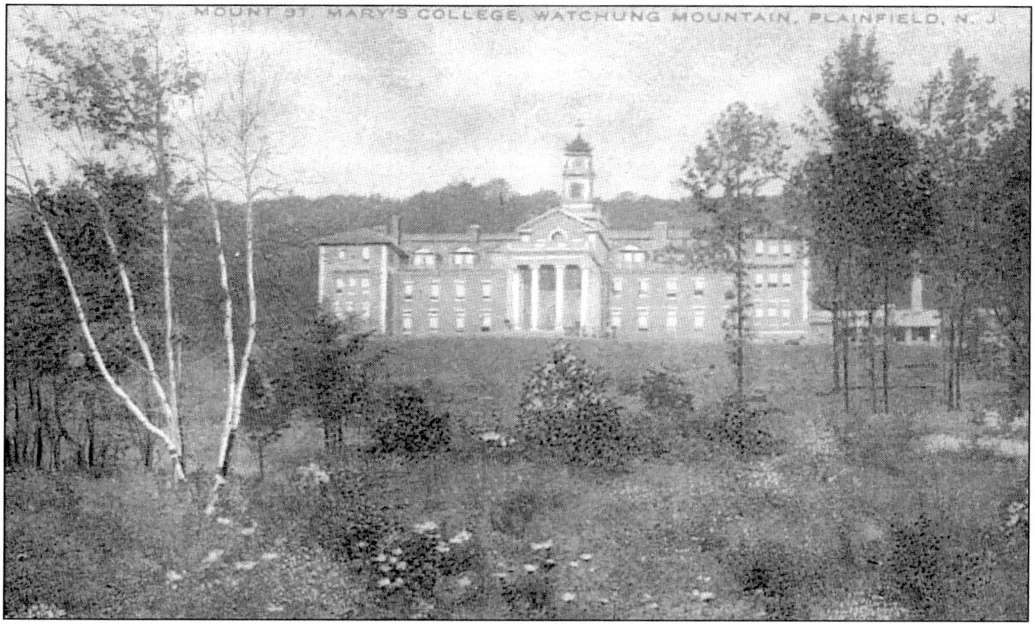

Mount Saint Mary's motherhouse originated in Bordentown, New Jersey. When they became overcrowded, the Sisters of Mercy searched for larger quarters. In 1908, they found their spot in the township of North Plainfield. David T. Kenney—the inventor of the vacuum cleaner—donated the land from Johnson's Drive to the Green Brook to them. His daughter Marie attended the academy; he asked the sisters to pray for his new invention.

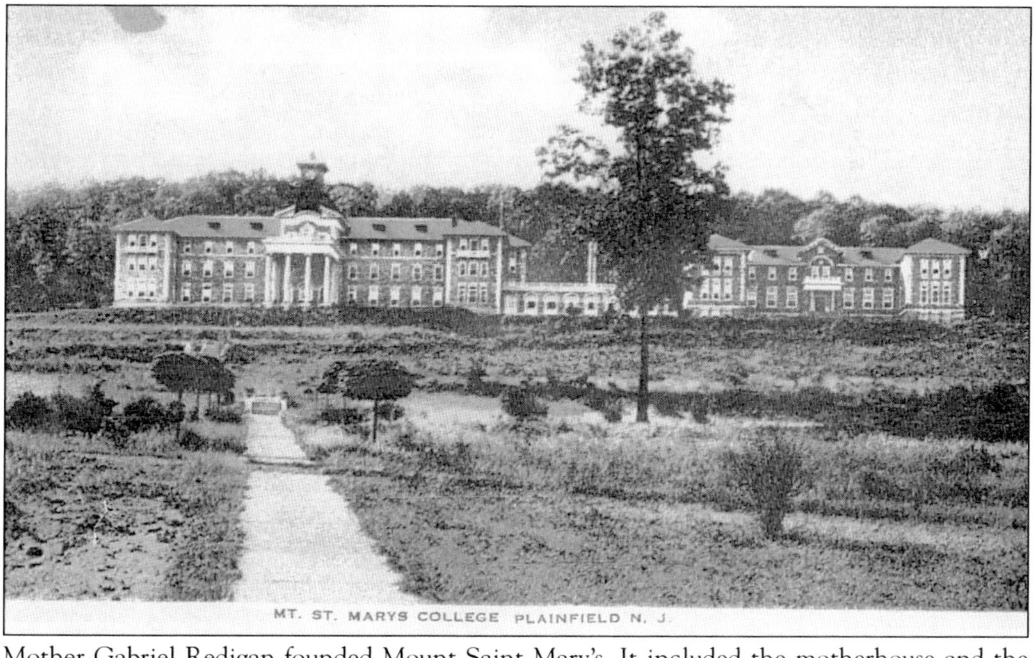

Mother Gabriel Redigan founded Mount Saint Mary's. It included the motherhouse and the schools Kindergarten through eighth grade, which included the boys and girls high school and college. In 1924, the college moved to Georgean Court in Lakewood. In the 1930s, the grammar school moved to St. Joseph's in North Plainfield. It is currently an academy for girls.

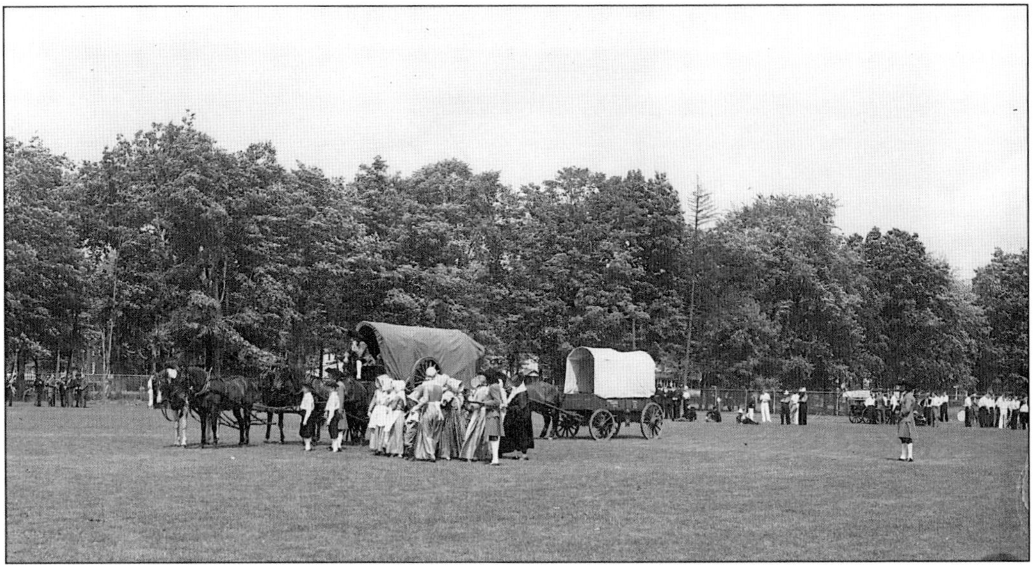

The history of the Borough of North Plainfield, revived in all the brilliance and splendor of pageantry, is shown above in the festivities of the 50th anniversary of the borough. A group of East End Civic Association members participate in the covered wagon episode.

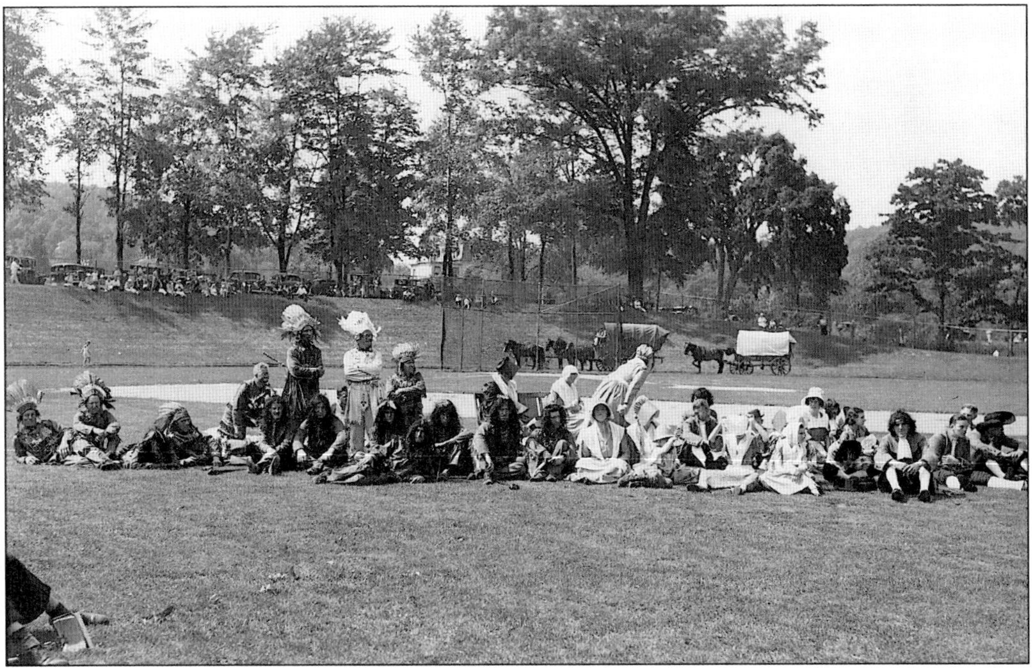

This scene from the early history of North Plainfield was performed at the 1935 celebration. Native Americans and early settlers were shown trading peacefully together. Members of the East End Civic Association portrayed the settlers; the Native Americans were played by members of the order of Red Men.

Ten

PEOPLE

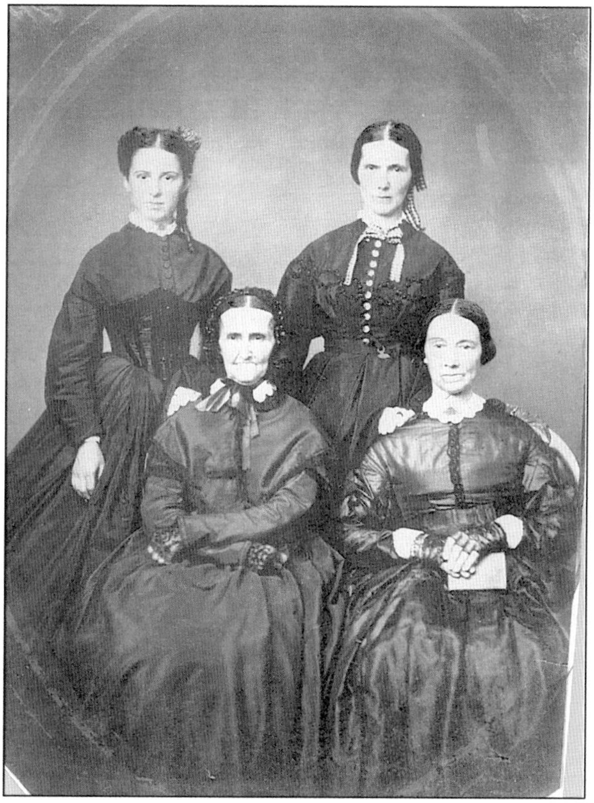

The history of any town is enhanced by the people who have lived and worked there to shape its current atmosphere. The picture above represents four generations of women from Somerset County. The first generation is represented by Sallie Line Wilcox, born 1791 in Watchung and died in 1882. The second is her daughter Caroline Wilcox Spencer, born 1808 and died in North Plainfield in 1895. The third generation is her daughter Elizabeth Spencer Allen, born 1829 and died in North Plainfield 1902. The last generation is Mary Schutt, born in North Plainfield Township and died in New York City.

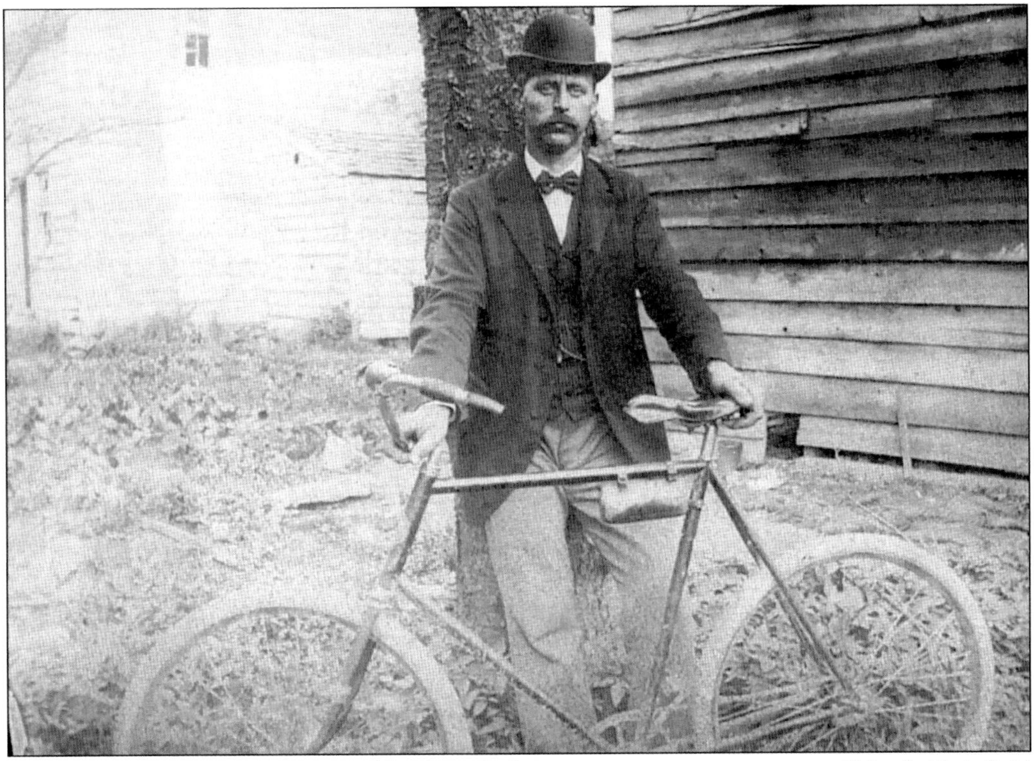

Local builder Charles L. Force used his bicycle for transportation to get around North Plainfield in 1903.

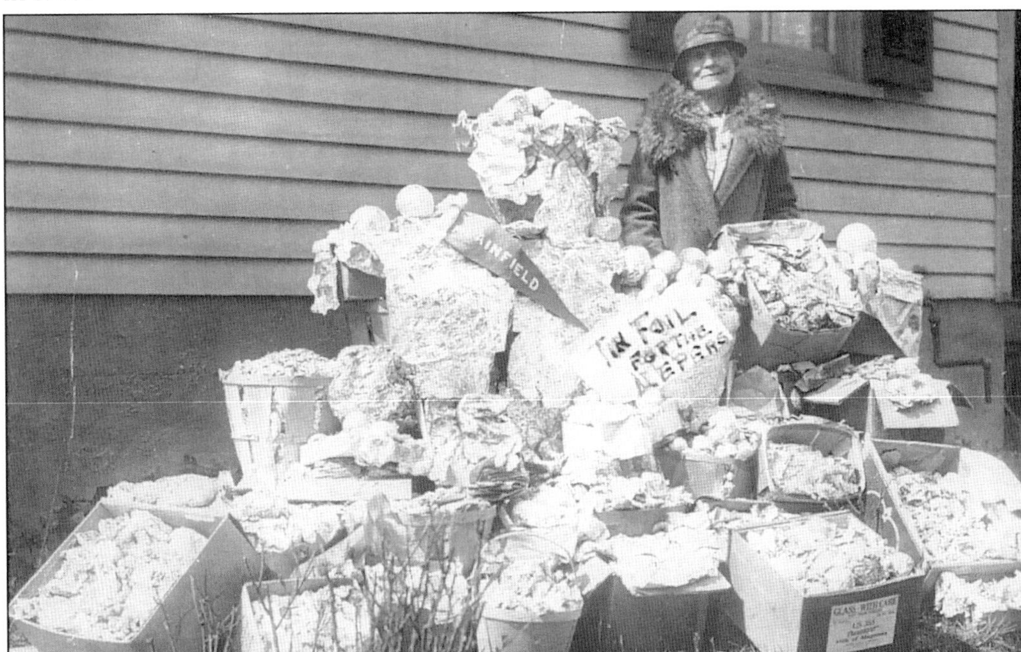

Nettie Beeching Love was known around the area as the "Tinfoil Lady." Mrs. Love collected tinfoil for the lepers.

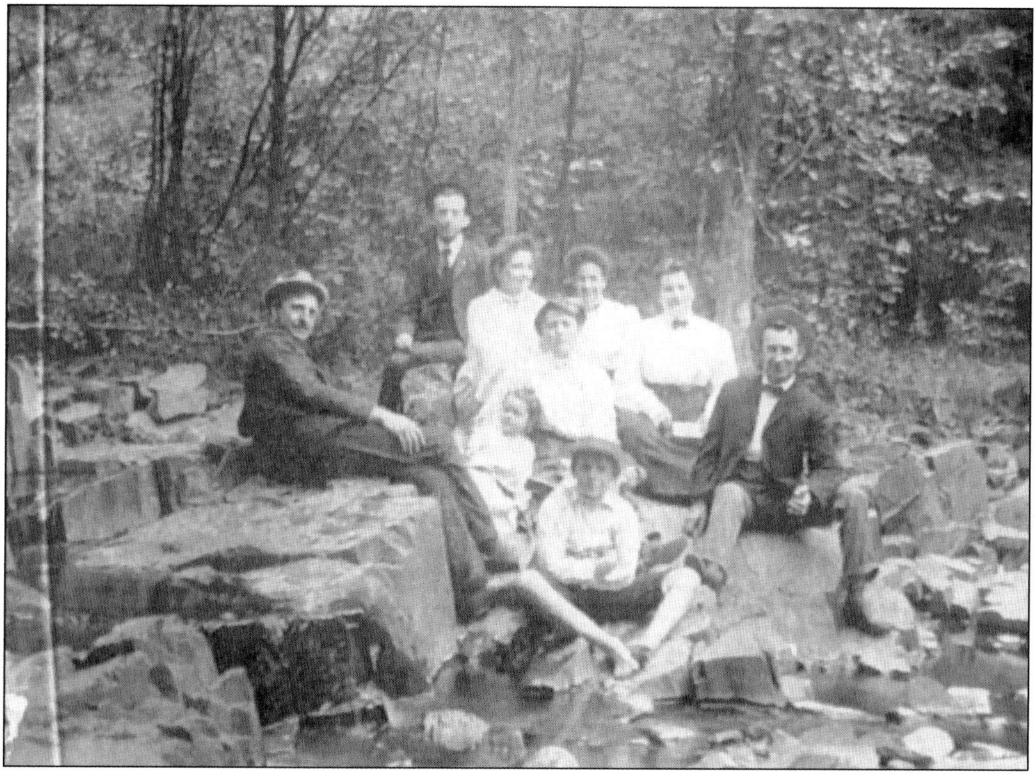

On a Sunday afternoon, one could always relax at the brook in Watchung. These members of the Beeching family are keeping cool on their outing in 1904.

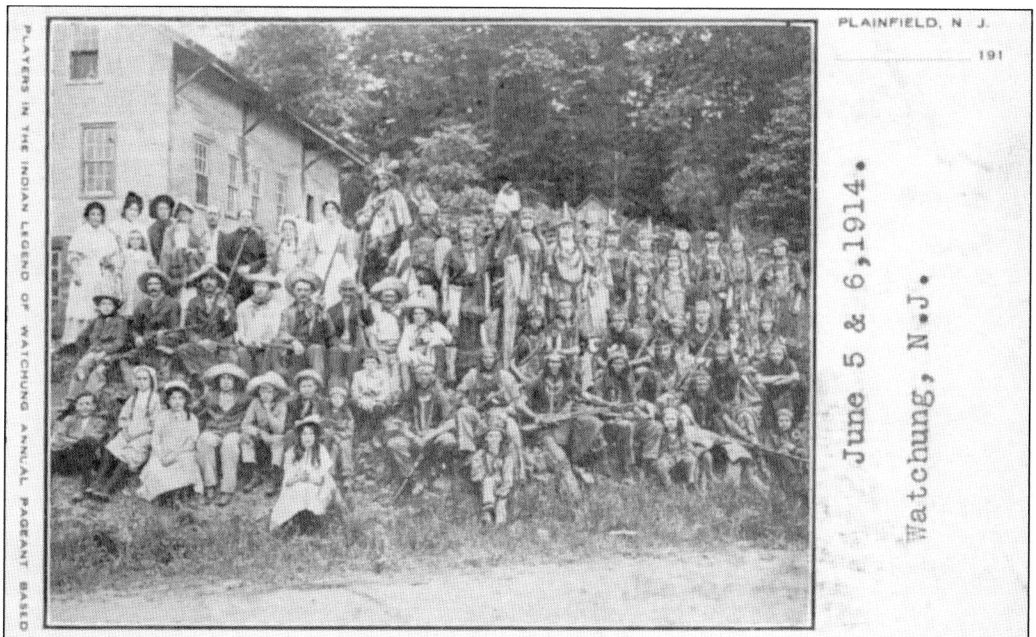

On June 5 and 6, 1914, Watchung's community members acted out its annual folklore pageant, "The Legend of Princess Wetumpka."

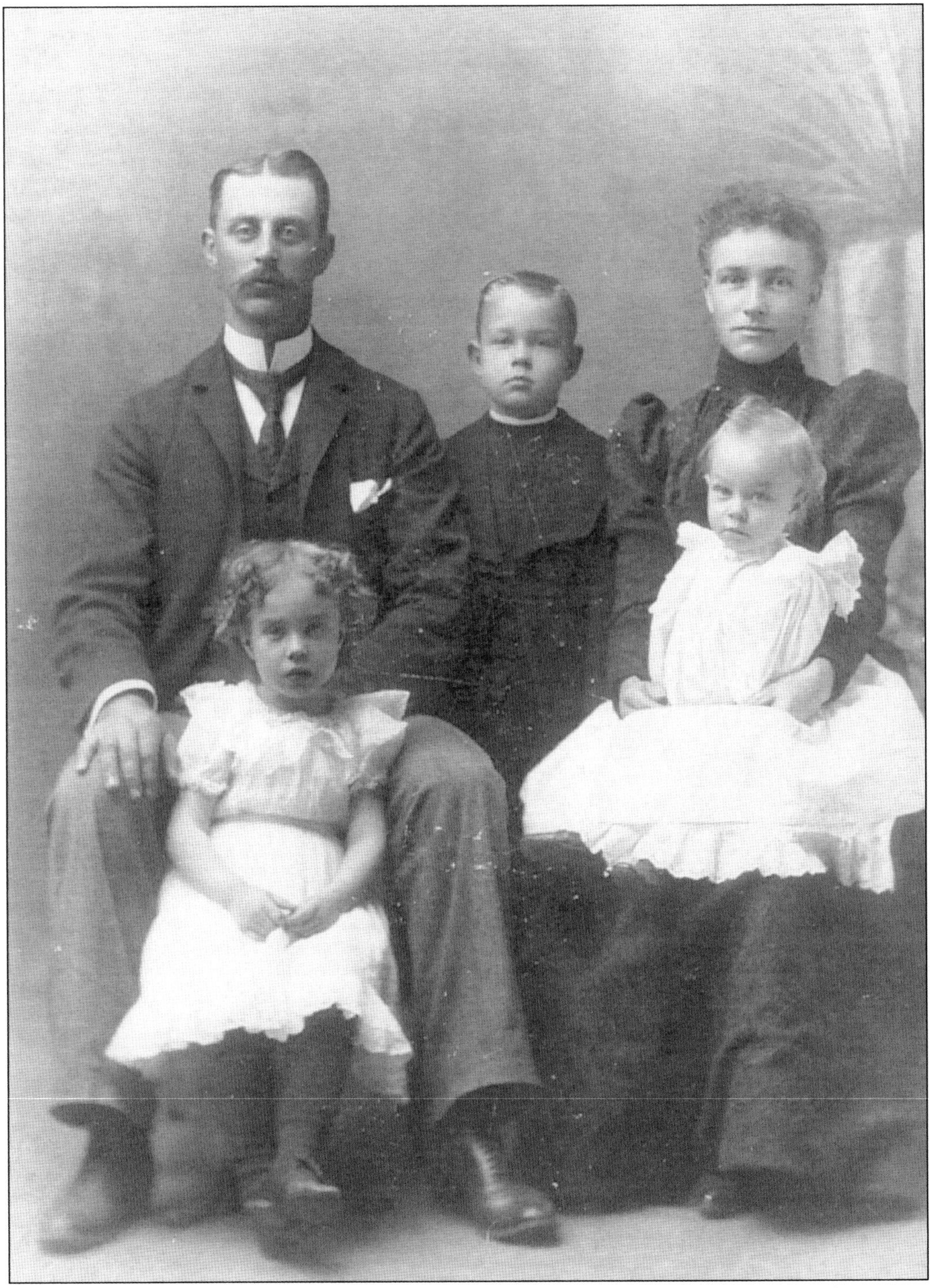

This photograph from the family album of Charles L. Force was taken in Plainfield in 1898. Shown in the photograph are, from left to right, Charles L. Force (father), son Raymond, Carrie A. Fenner Force (mother), Elva, and LeRoy (sitting on his mother's lap). At the time of the picture, the family lived at 23 Pearl Street.

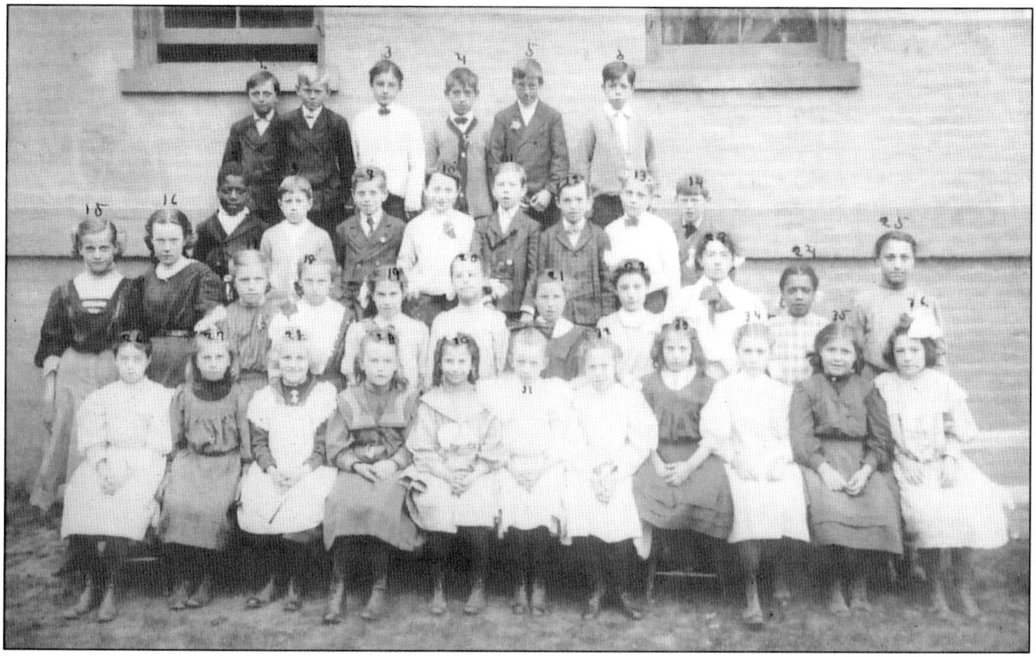

Students from a class at Somerset School took time out from classes to pose for the camera more than 50 years ago.

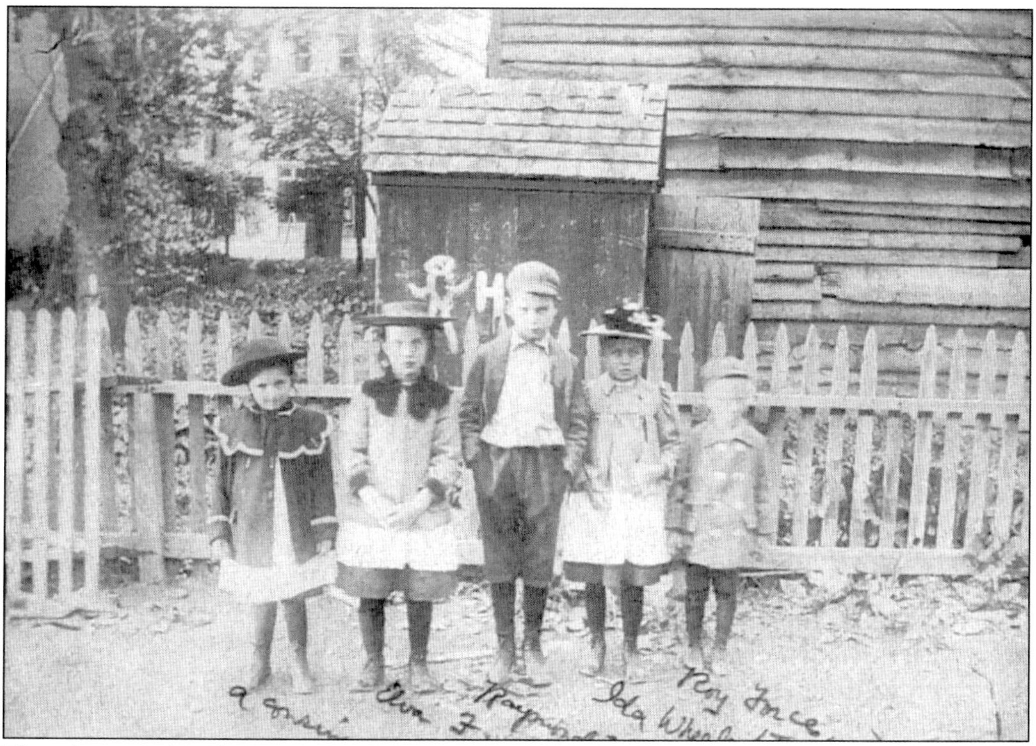

This photograph, taken c. 1903, shows the Force children lined up for this special picture. Seen here, from left to right, are a cousin, Elva Force, Raymond Force, Ida Wheeler (Taylor), and LeRoy Force.

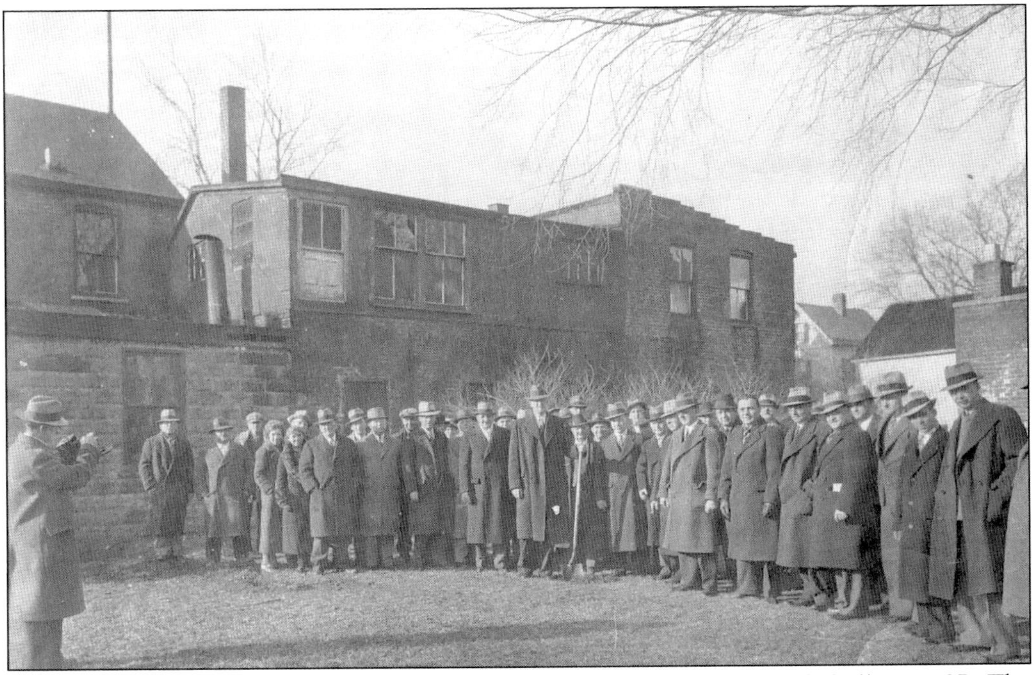

This groundbreaking ceremony was for the main section of the borough hall in 1937. The building is located at the corner of Somerset Street and Lincoln Place.

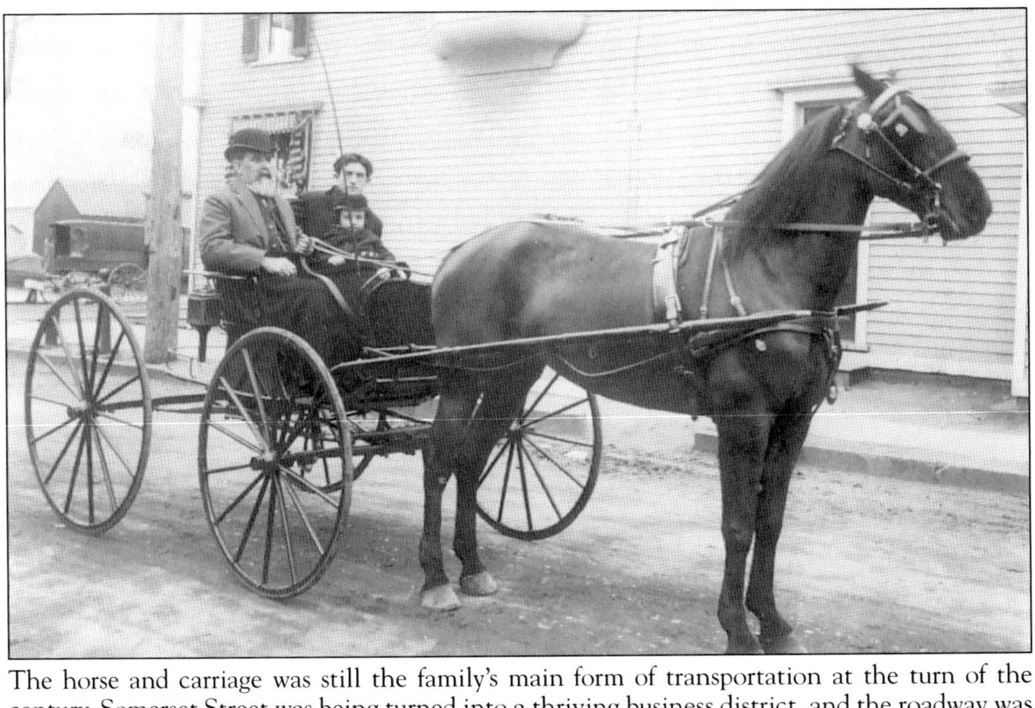

The horse and carriage was still the family's main form of transportation at the turn of the century. Somerset Street was being turned into a thriving business district, and the roadway was becoming very crowded.

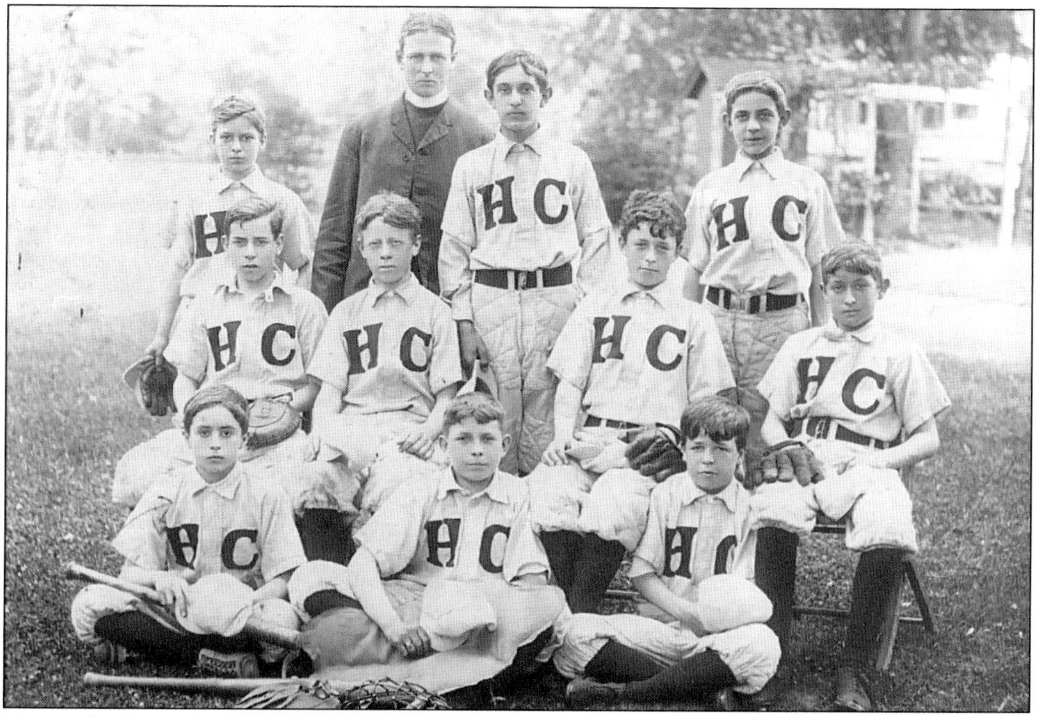

The Holy Cross choir baseball team can be seen in this *c.* 1906 photograph. Hub Stine, second row, second from the right, went on to become a well-known educator and football coach in the Plainfield area.

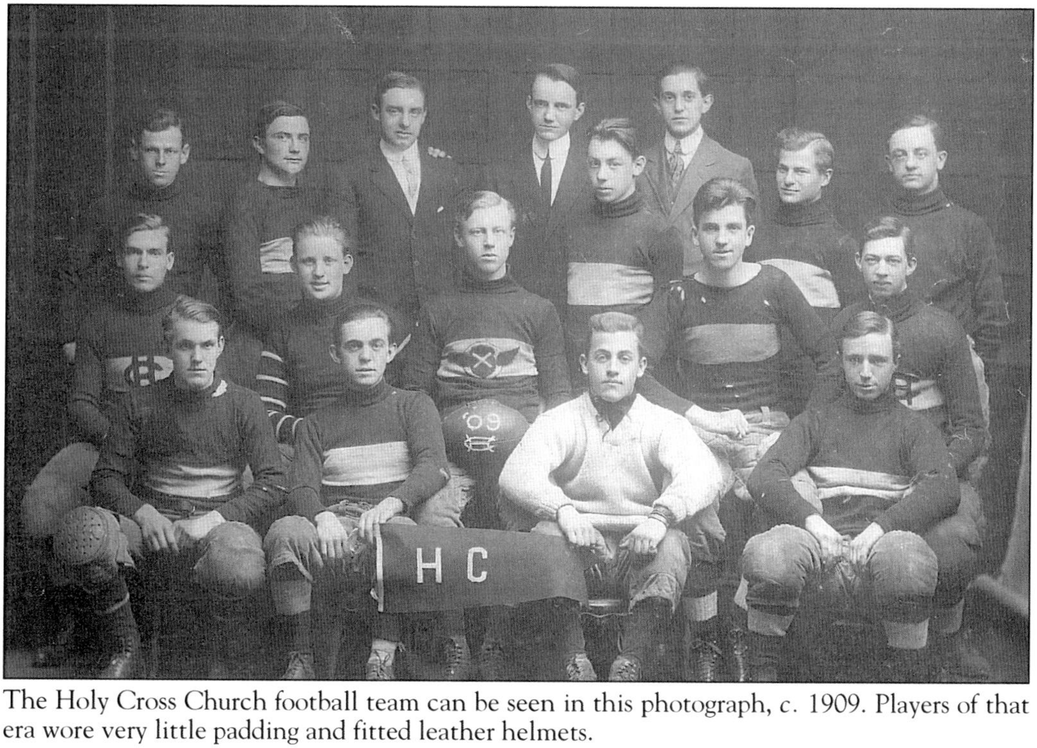

The Holy Cross Church football team can be seen in this photograph, *c.* 1909. Players of that era wore very little padding and fitted leather helmets.

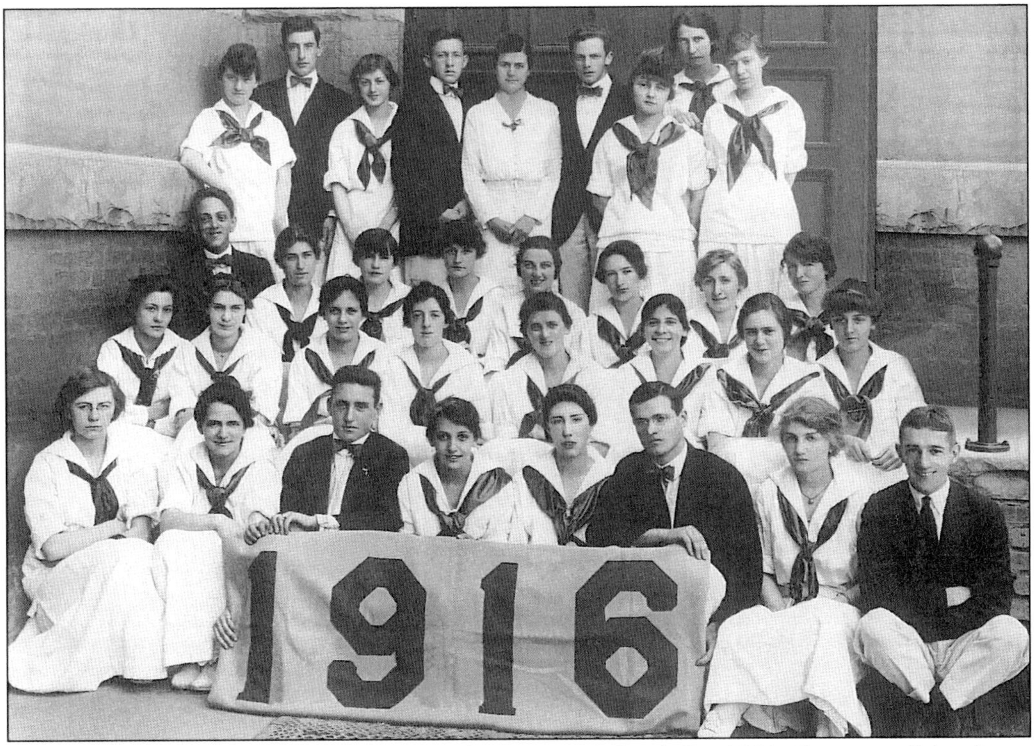

Seen here is the 1916 graduating class of Somerset School. By 1920, Somerset School was overcrowded, prompting the township to purchase land for a new high school.

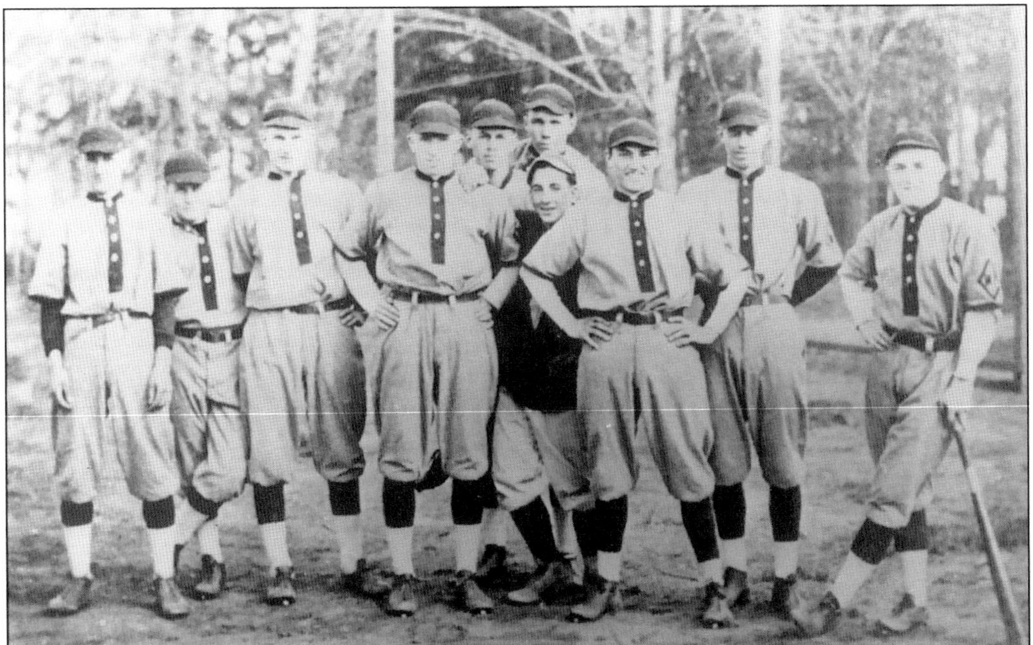

The young men in this 1917 baseball team were pleased to pose in their uniforms. Baseball was becoming a very popular sport to be played by the borough's young men.

The girls basketball team can be seen on the steps of Saenger Hall on Somerset Street, where they played all their games.

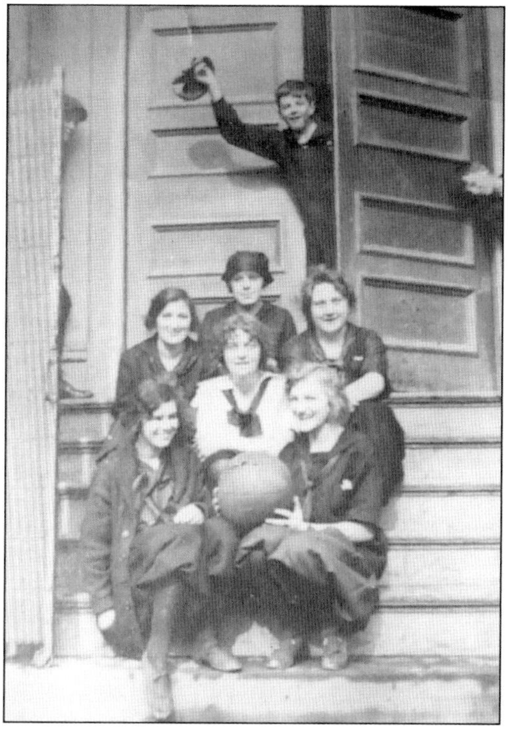

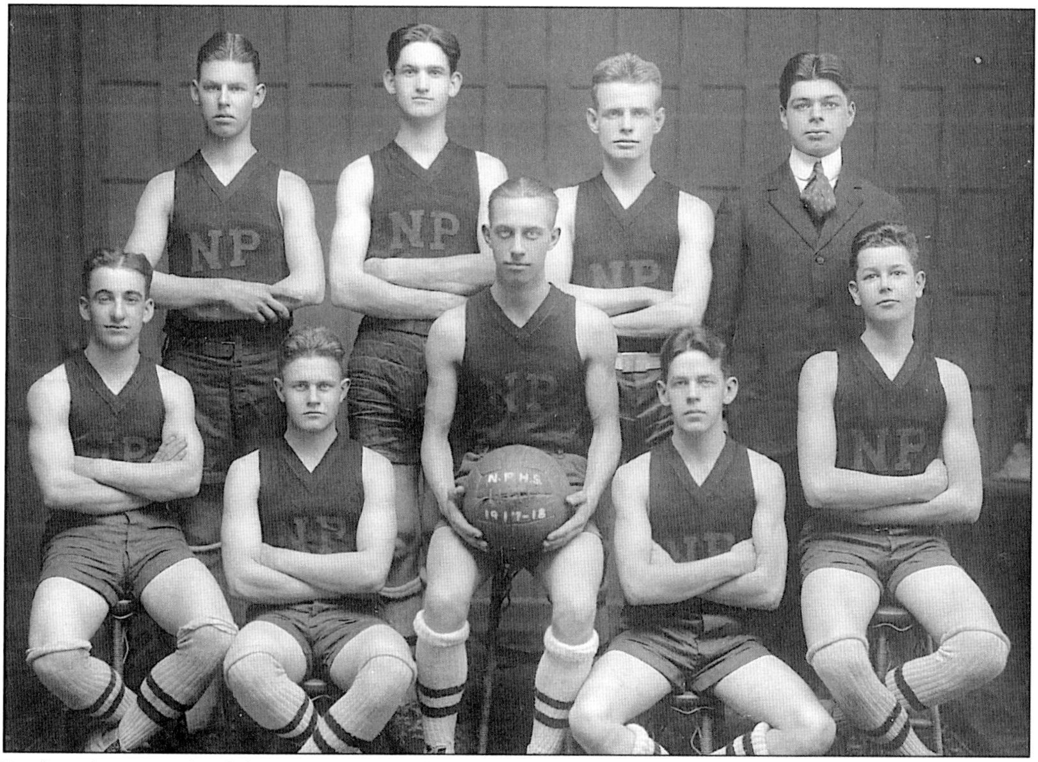

In this photograph of the 1918 North Plainfield High School Basketball team, the team captain, LeRoy Force (Dip), holds the ball.

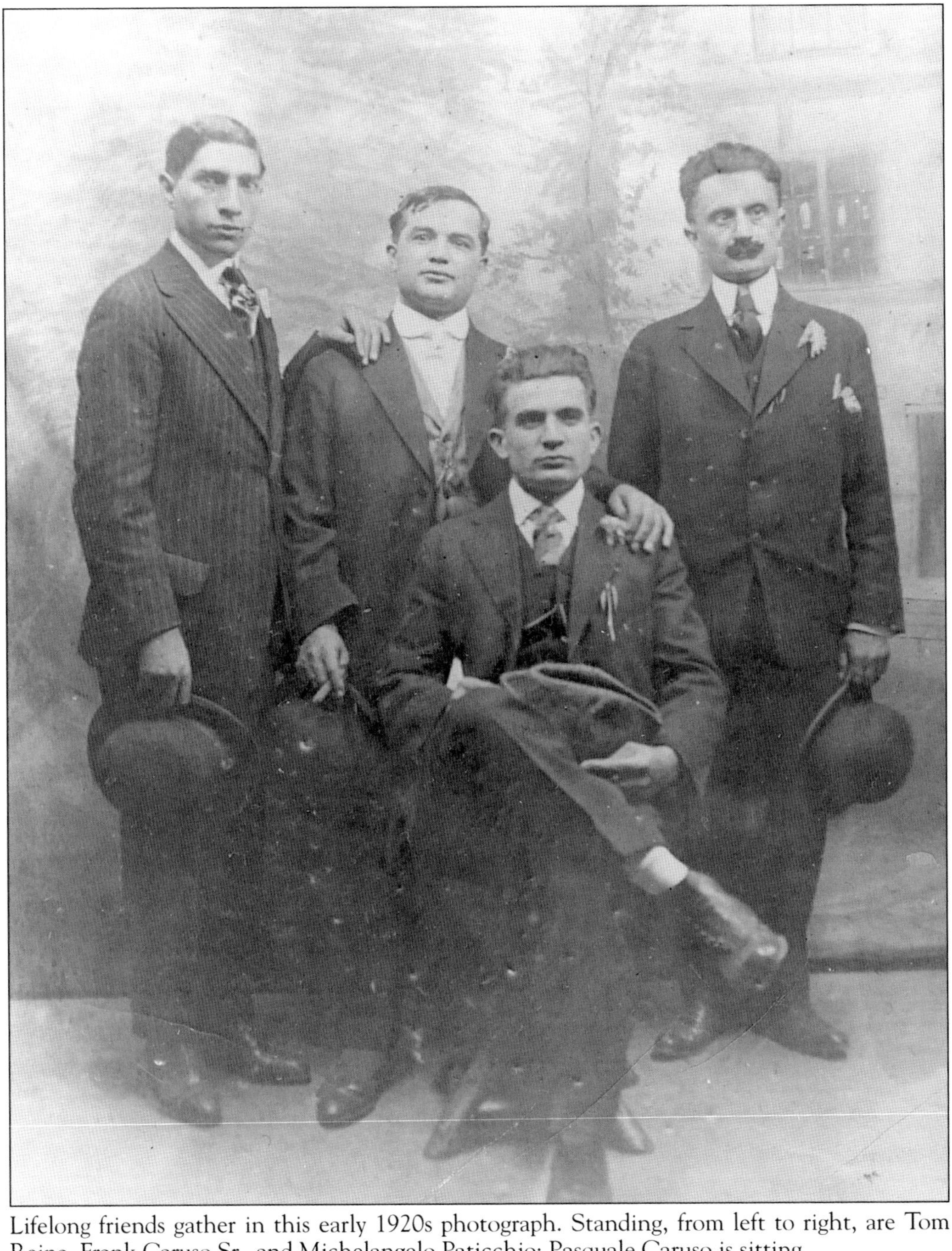

Lifelong friends gather in this early 1920s photograph. Standing, from left to right, are Tom Reina, Frank Caruso Sr., and Michelangelo Paticchio; Pasquale Caruso is sitting.

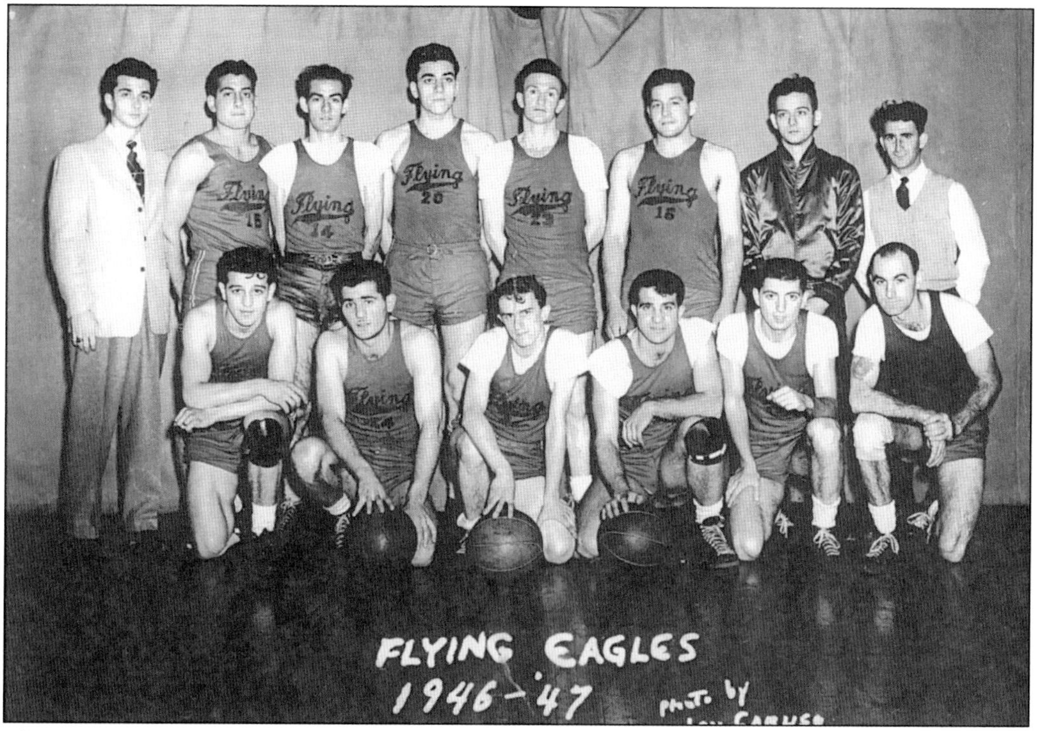

The 1946–47 Flying Eagles basketball team can be seen in this image. This Social Sports Club included all North Plainfield players and played against many other social clubs in the area.

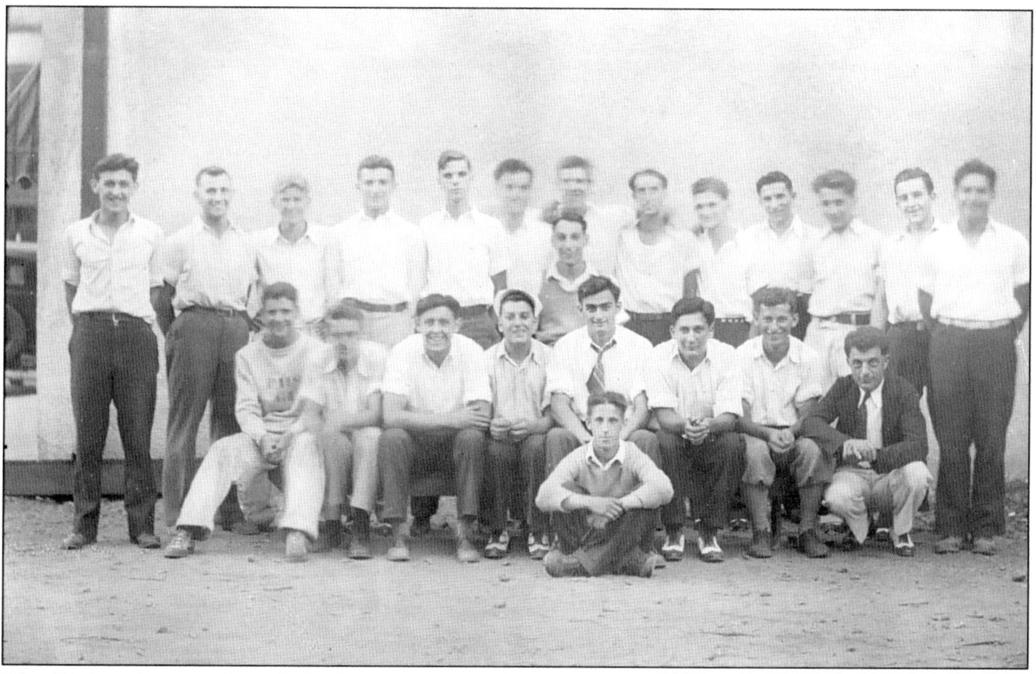

The Flying Arrows Social Club was organized as a sports club by a group of young men from North Plainfield in the late 1920s and early 1930s. World War II separated many of these men. This picture was taken on Somerset Street. It was one of many reunions held by the "Arrows."

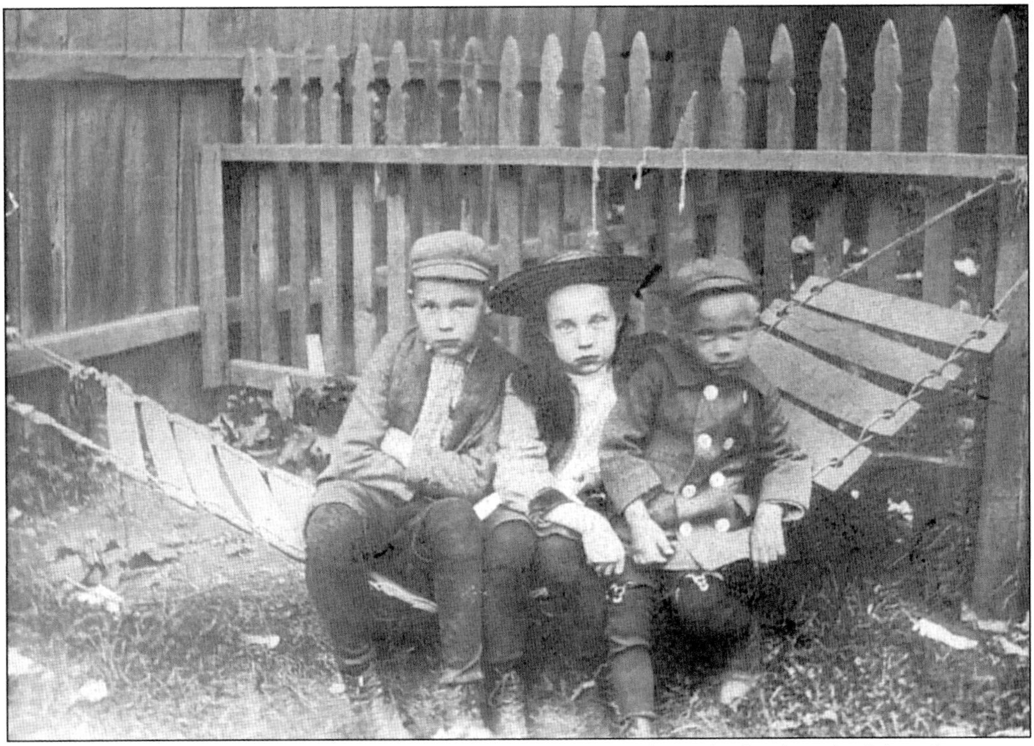

Raymond, Elva, and LeRoy Force sit on a wooden hammock in the backyard of their home on Somerset Place, *c.* 1903.

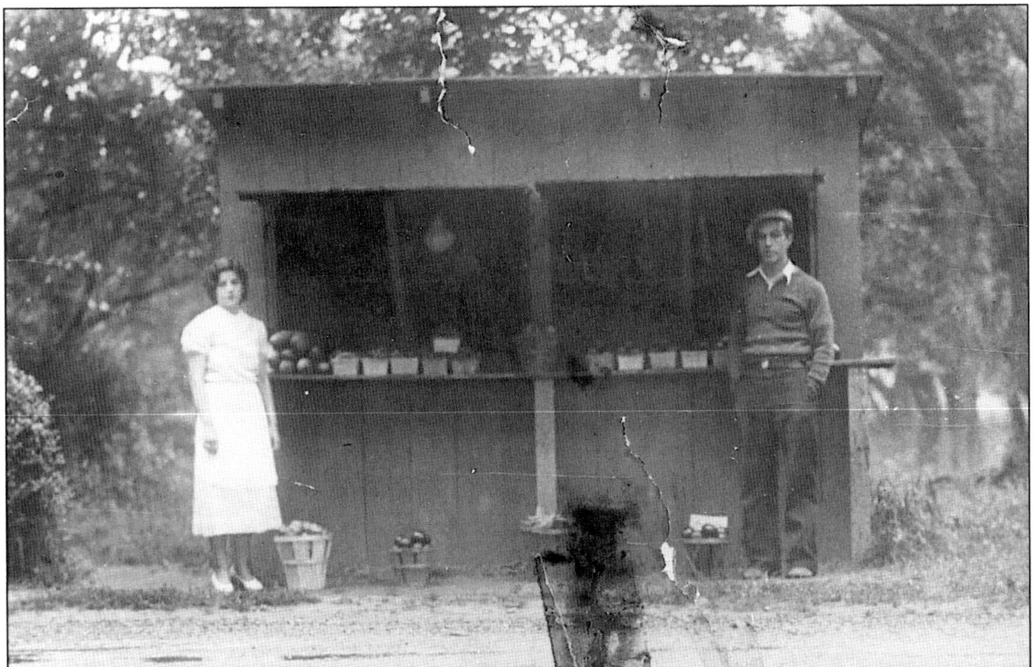

Norman and Frances Jennings stand beside Henry Jennings's road stand at the corner of Rock Avenue and Greenbrook Road, *c.* 1931–1932.

Frank Caruso and Frances Caruso can be seen here on their wedding day in 1913. All of their seven children were born in their home on 22 Warren Street.

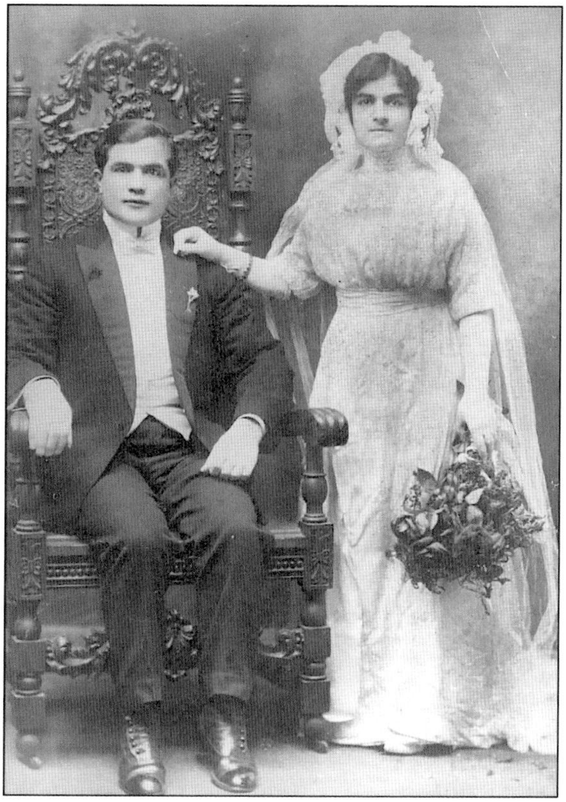

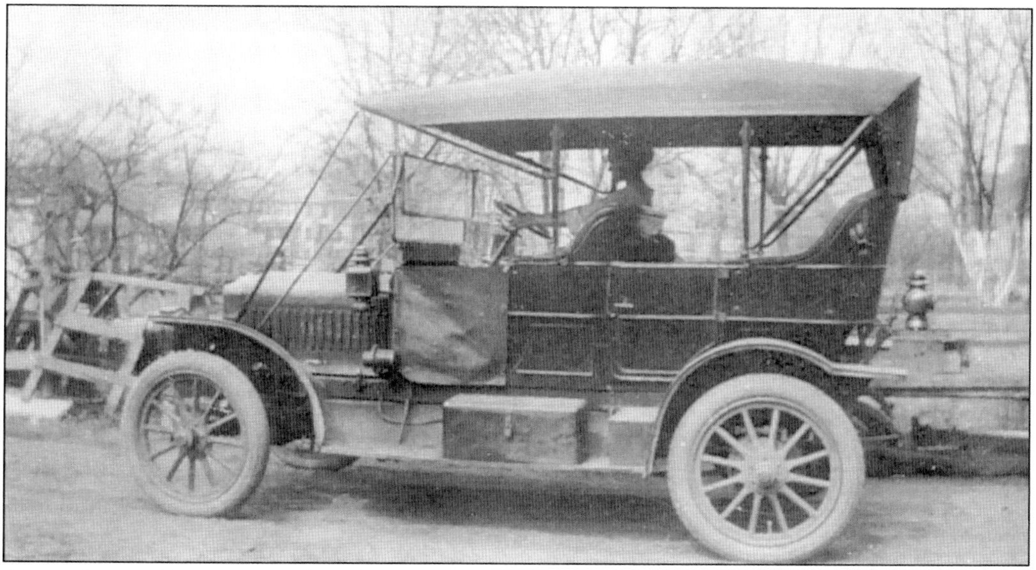

Carrie Fenner Force sits at the wheel of the family's new automobile. This picture was taken c. 1910 at the Force home at 43 Mountain Avenue, North Plainfield.

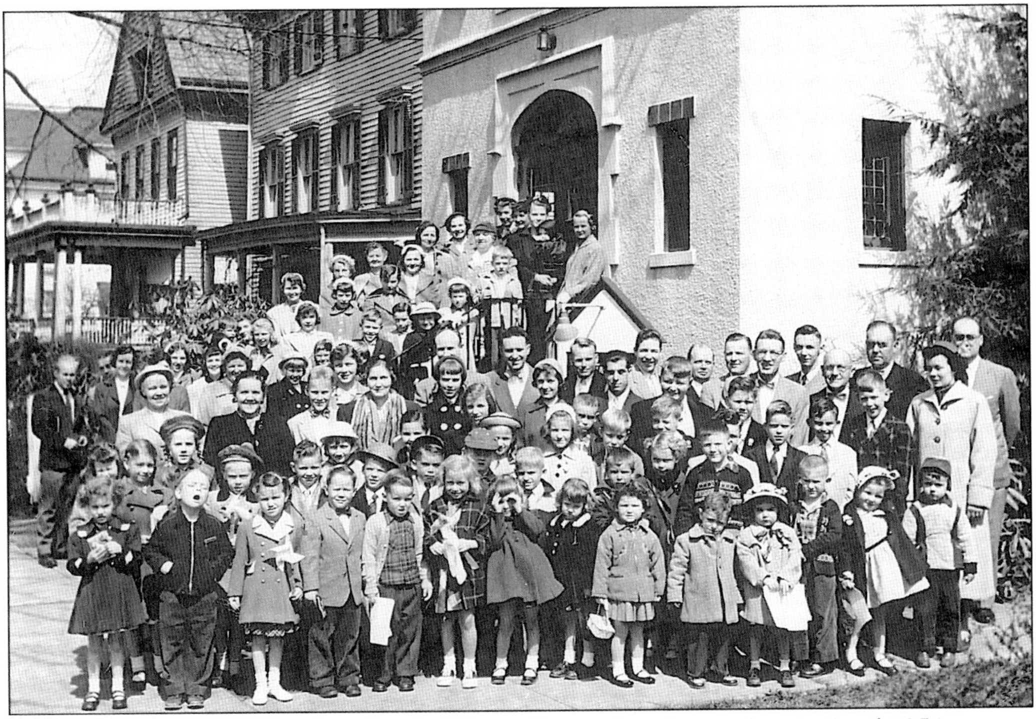

This photograph of the Sunday school of Grove Street chapel was taken in April 1954.

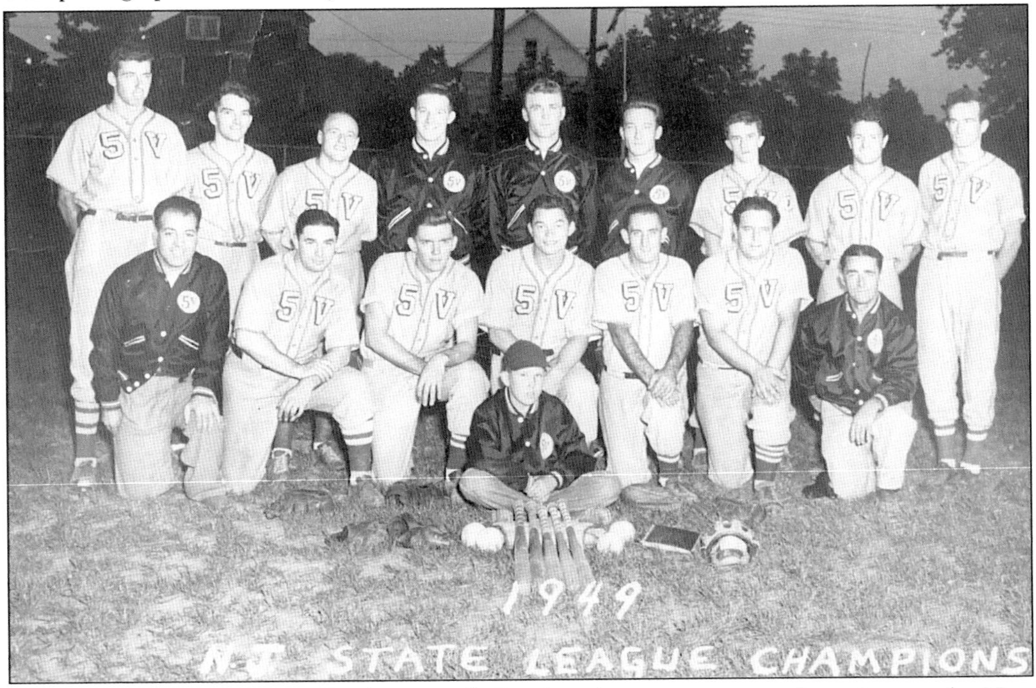

In 1949, the team sponsored by the 5 Vitelli Brothers liquor store were champions at the New Jersey State League. The 5 Vitelli Brothers liquor store was located on Greenbrook Road, just off Somerset Street. Buddy Gaub, second row, third from right, was named as an All-American Softball player.

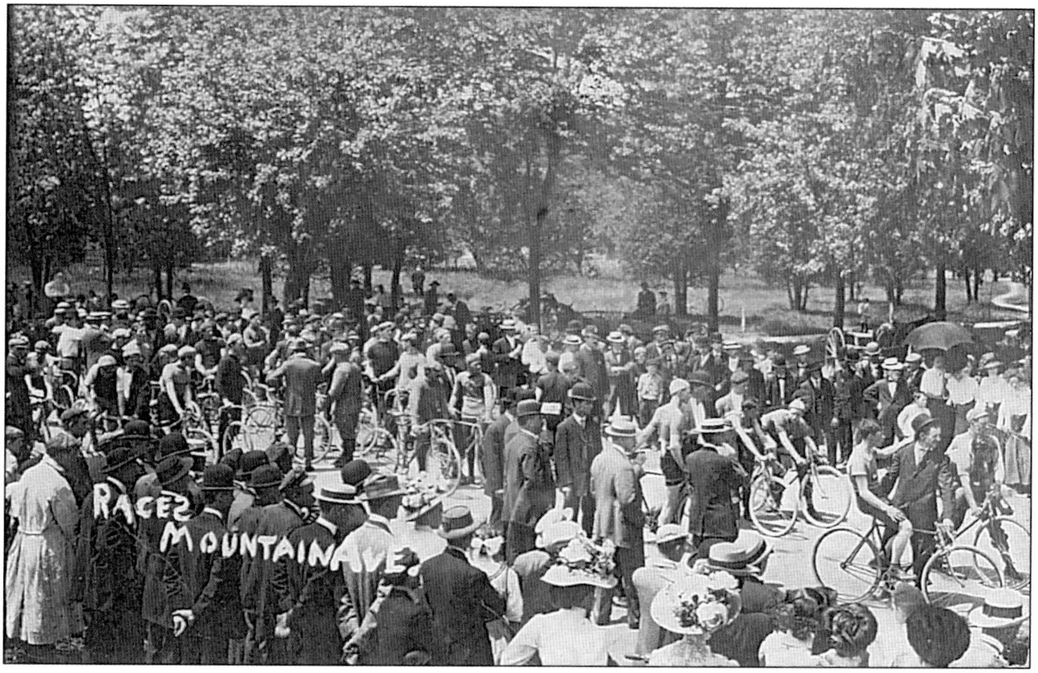

Bicycle races were very popular in the central New Jersey area in the 1920s and 1930s. This view of Mountain Avenue on Race Day shows how involved the families were in the sport.

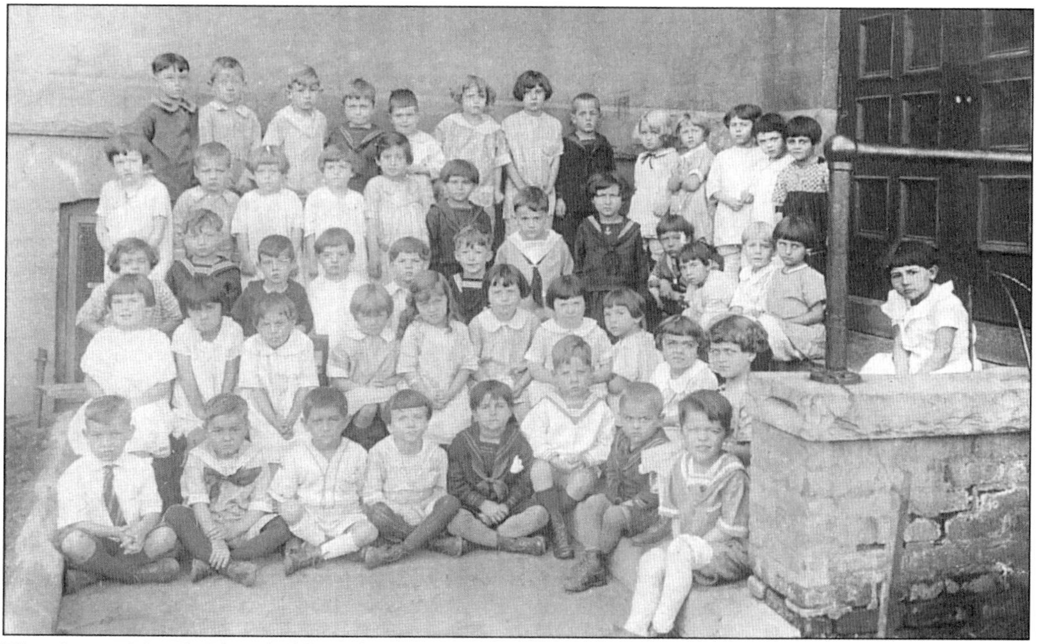
The future North Plainfield High School class of 1938 can be seen above. Taken in front of Somerset School, this is the 1925 kindergarten class.

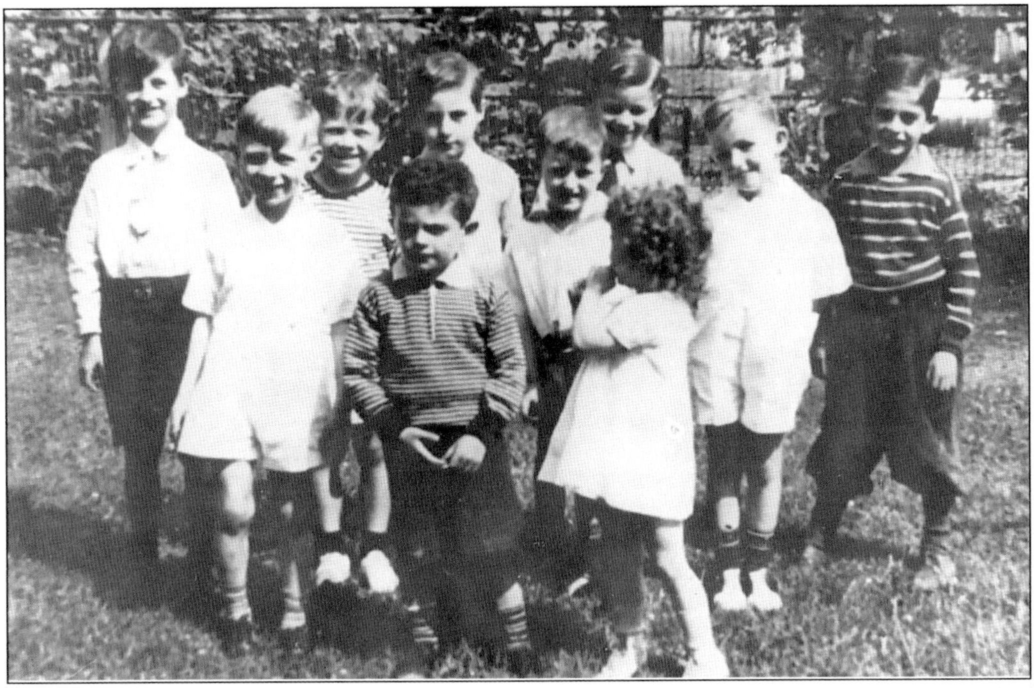

Above, Jack Richardson celebrates his tenth birthday party, *c.* 1940s. The group, comprised of East Enders and St. Joseph's Grammar School kids, included, Jack Richardson, George "Chippy" Mauro, Joe Stavish, Jim Zanowick, Fred Bohn, Charley Lubeck, Frank Caruso, Mario Caruso, and Mary Lou Mauro.

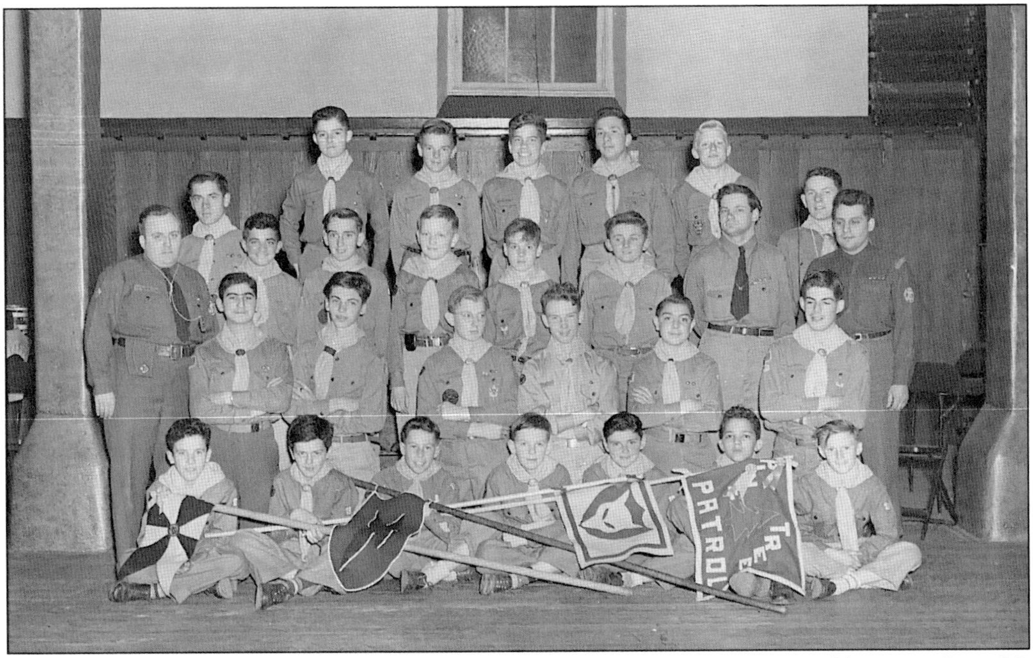

The Boy Scout Troop 19, led by Scoutmaster Al Pilon (left), was sponsored by Saint Joseph's Church. The picture was taken in the basement of the church where the troop meetings were held, *c.* April 1947.

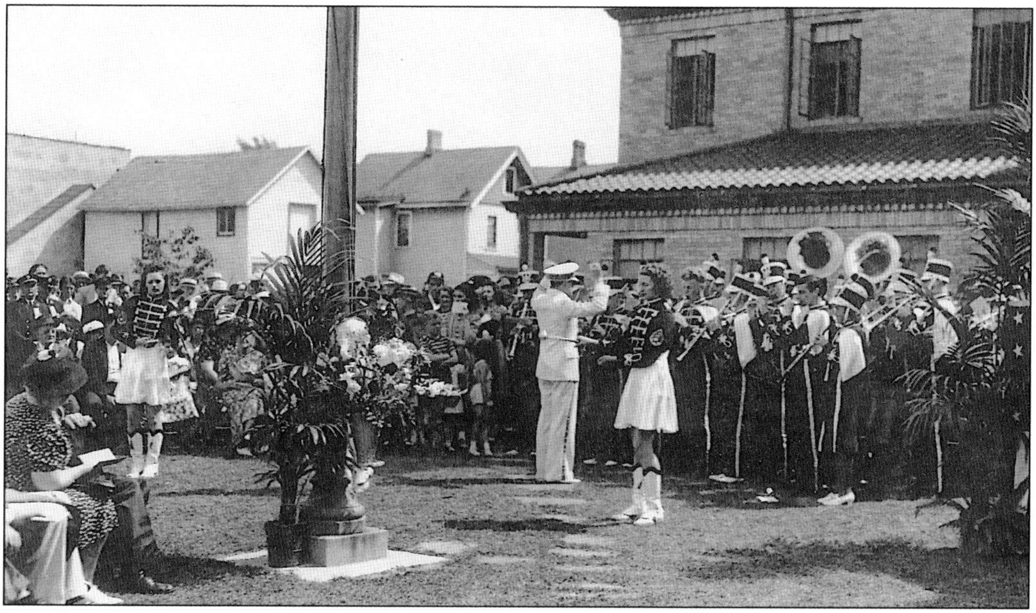

Joseph Schaedel conducts the North Plainfield High School band at a memorial ceremony in 1939. The site is the current municipal building on the corner of Somerset Street and Lincoln Place.

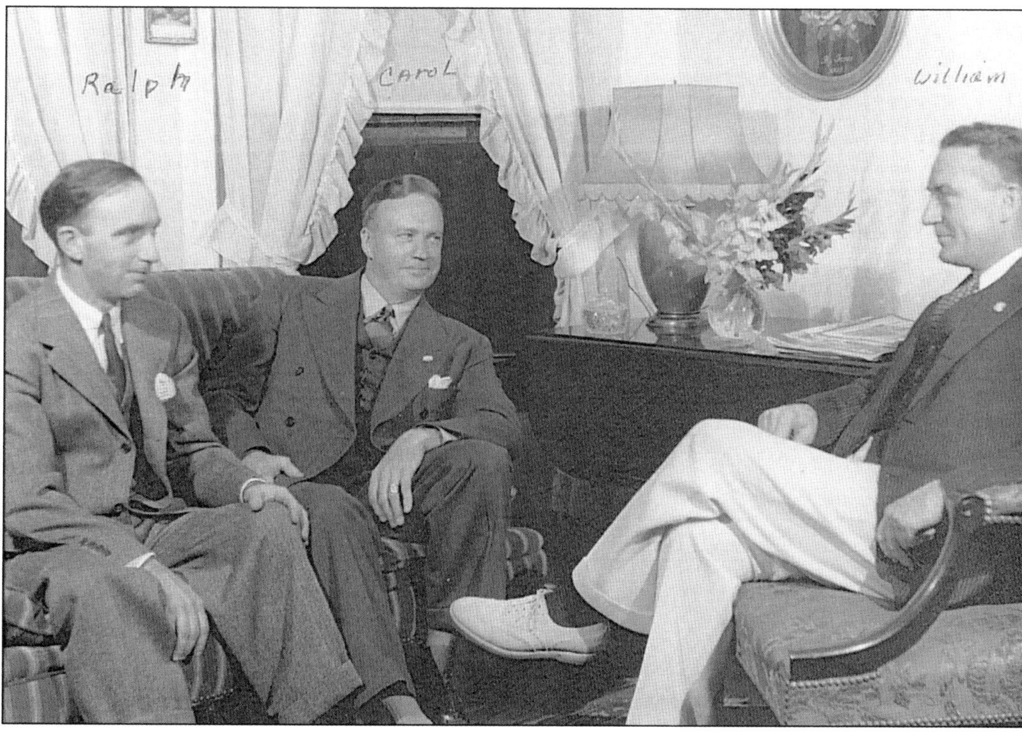

The three Taylor brothers reminisce in the Taylor family parlor at their home on the corner of Allen Place and Fairview Avenue in 1939. Of all graduates of North Plainfield High School, William and Carroll were the best scholar/athletes of that year (1912); both were nominated for the Yale Cup award.

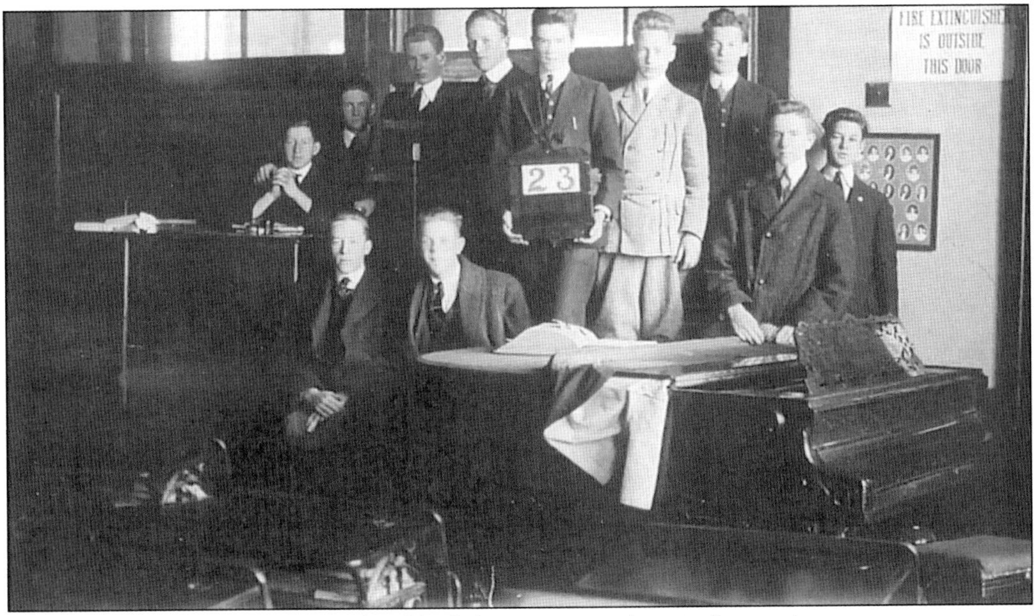

The men's chorus of Somerset School had their picture taken in the music room.

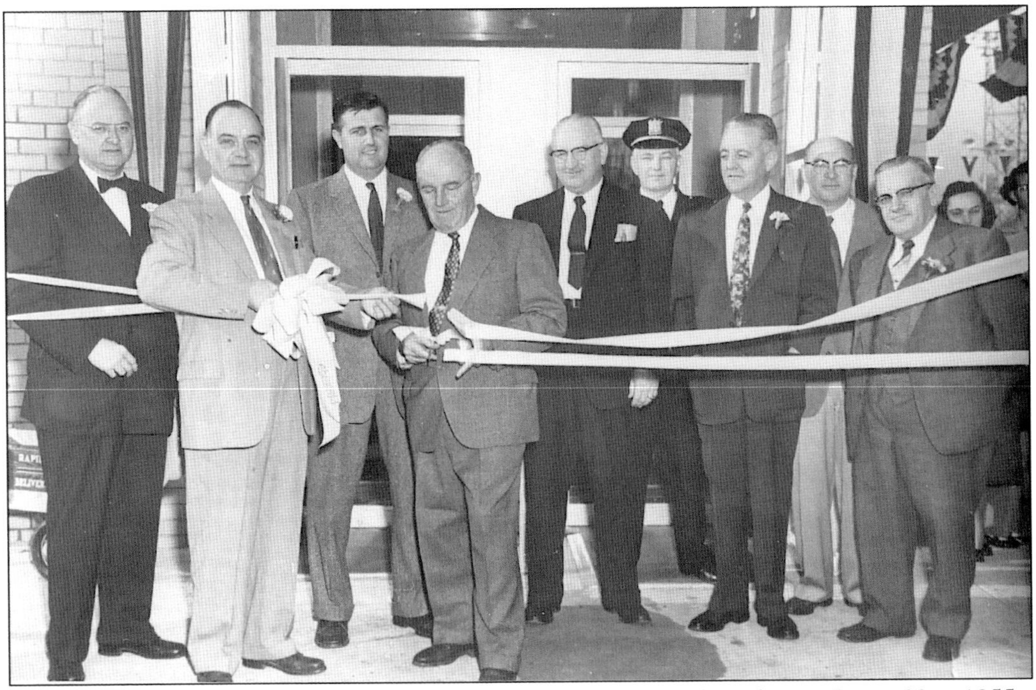

Local dignitaries cut the ribbon for the opening of the Acme Food Market on Route 22 in 1955.

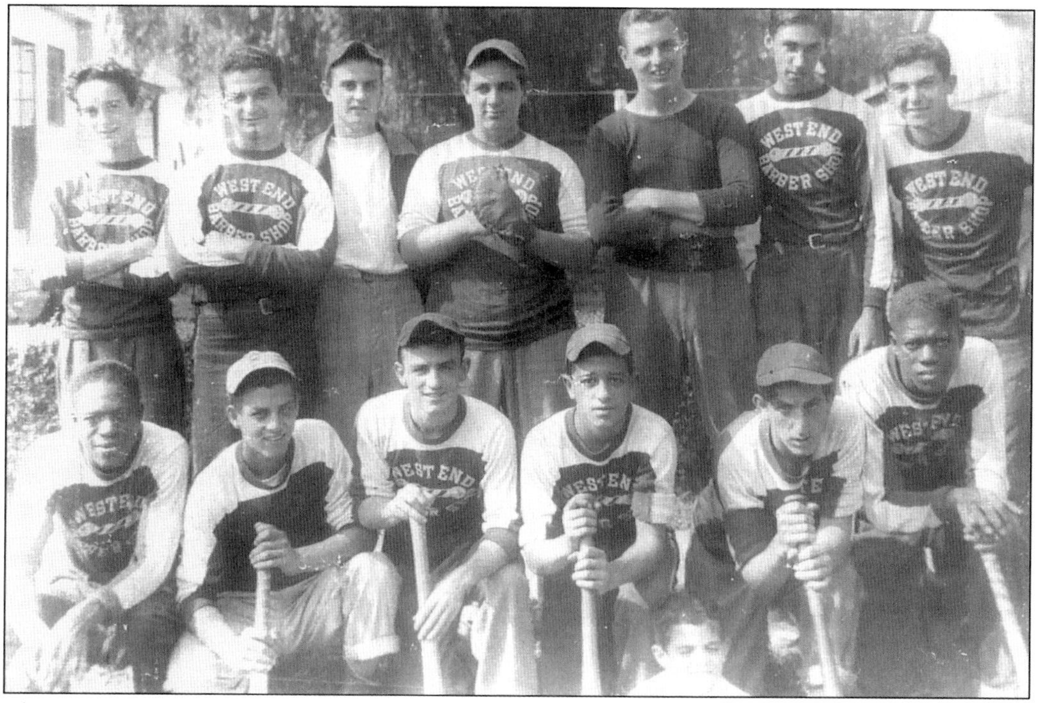

The Westend Barber Shop Softball team can be seen in this *c.* 1940 photograph. The team was made up of North Plainfielders and some employees of Kingston Conley on Brook Avenue. There were many softball leagues in the area at that time.

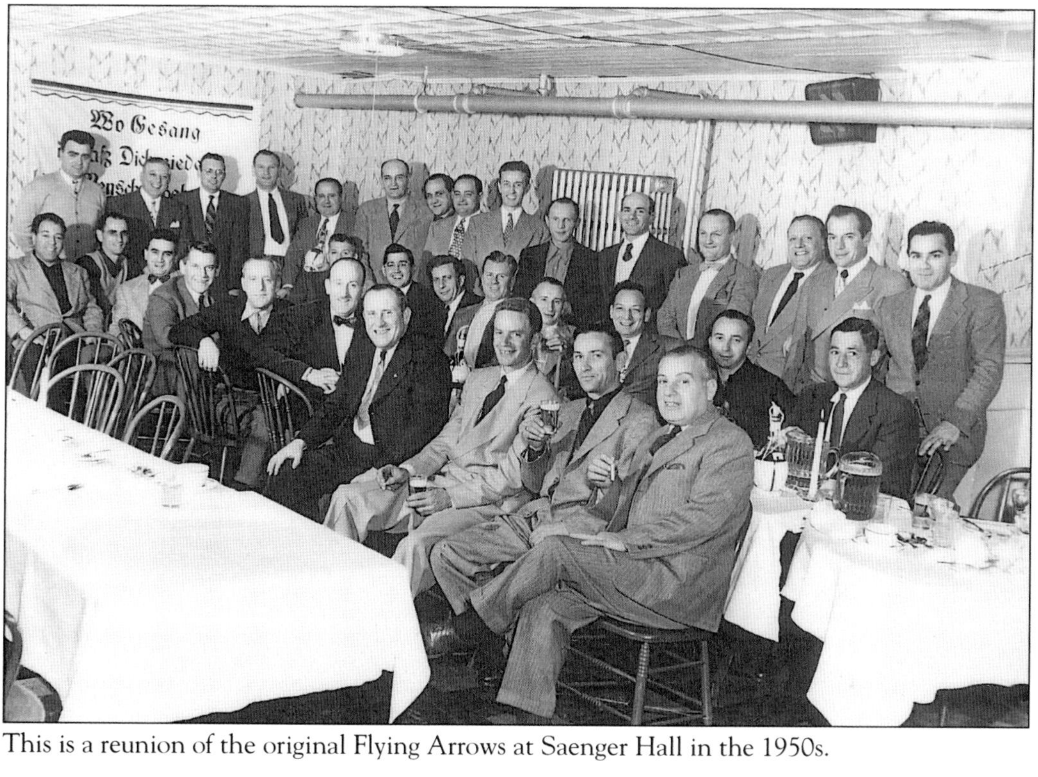

This is a reunion of the original Flying Arrows at Saenger Hall in the 1950s.

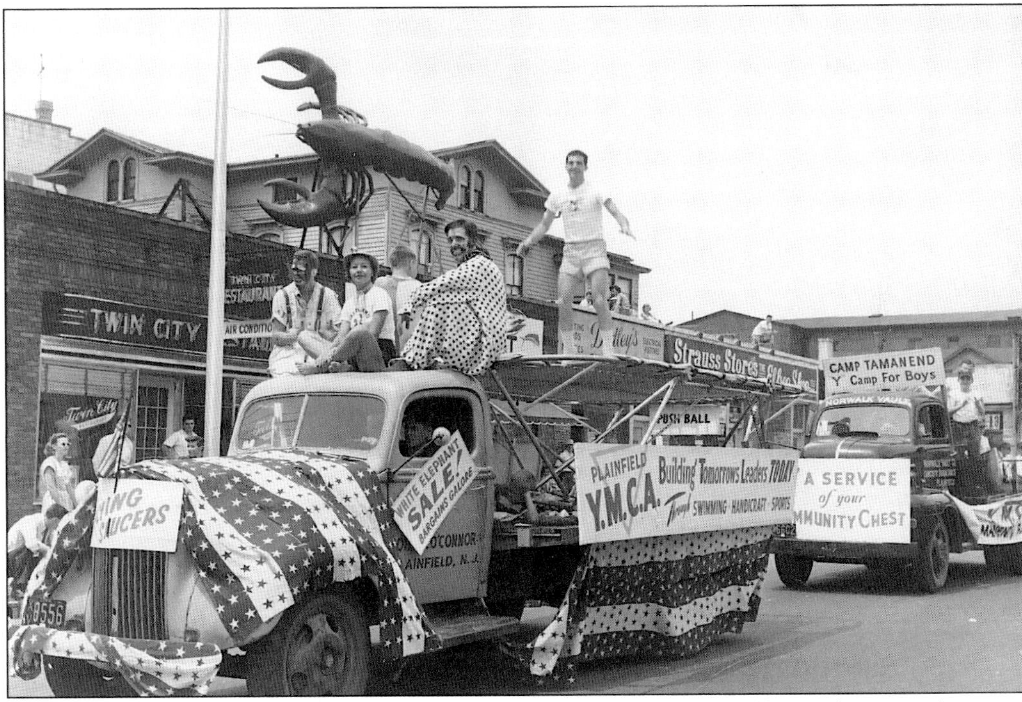

This Fourth of July parade, seen on Somerset Street, follows the old parade route that used to go from North Plainfield, through Plainfield, and end at Greenbrook Park for food, games, and fireworks. Notice the twin city diner on the corner of Craig Place and Somerset Street. The Giant Lobster was the trademark of Benny's Fish Market, which later became Somerset Seafoods.

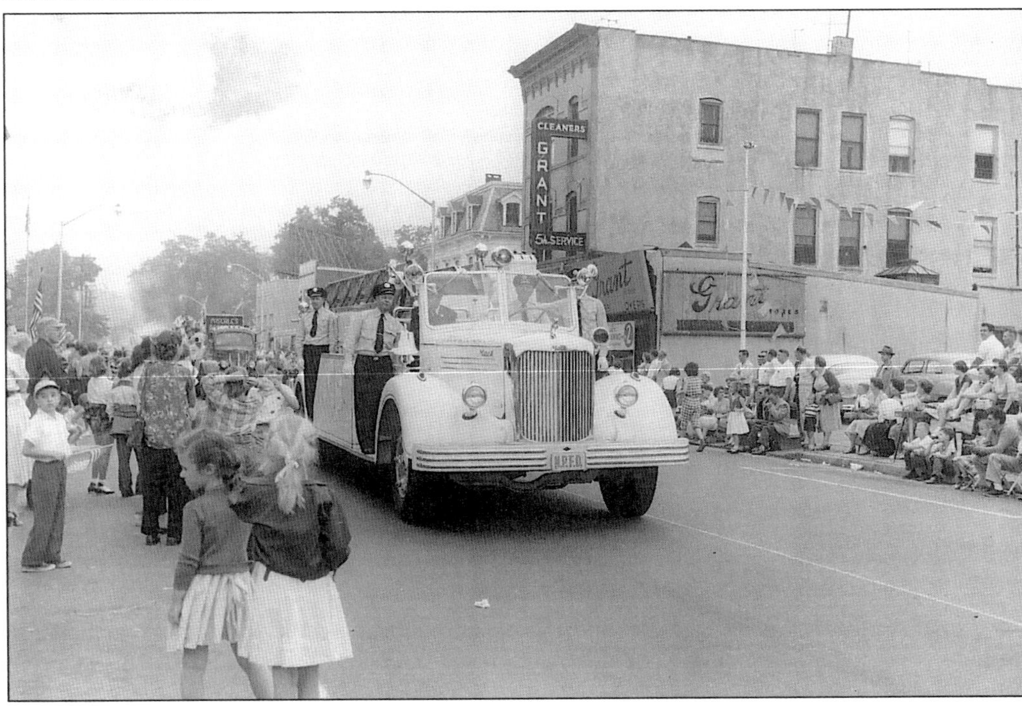

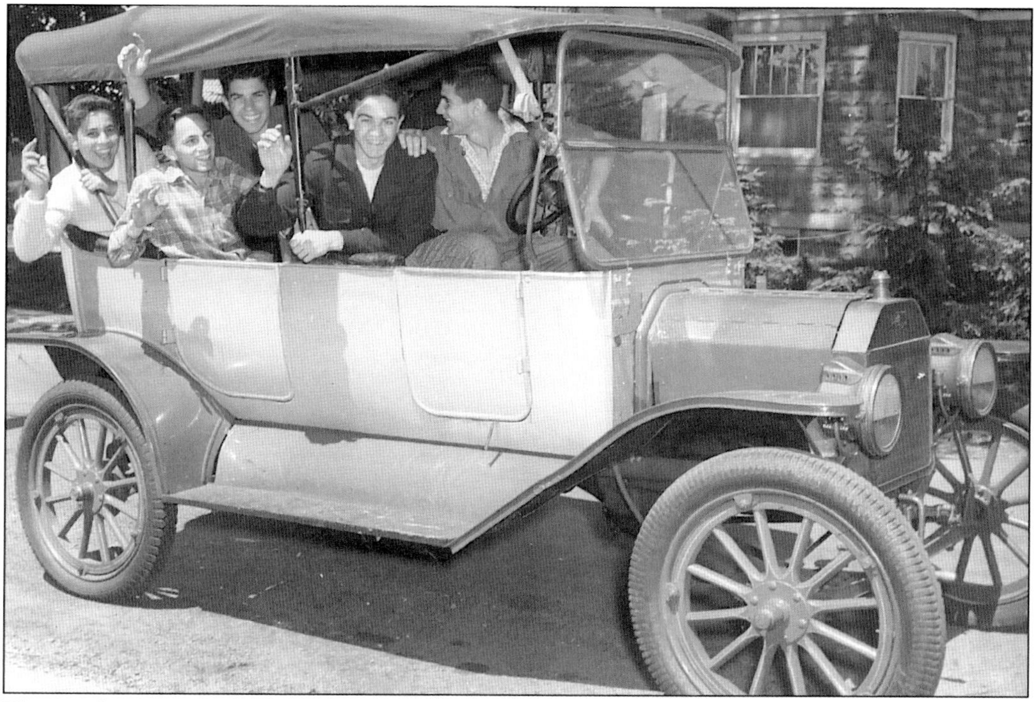

The "Hoboes A.C.," one of North Plainfield High School's many sports clubs, gets together on a Sunday afternoon on the corner of Watchung and Brook Avenues in the Model-T Ford.

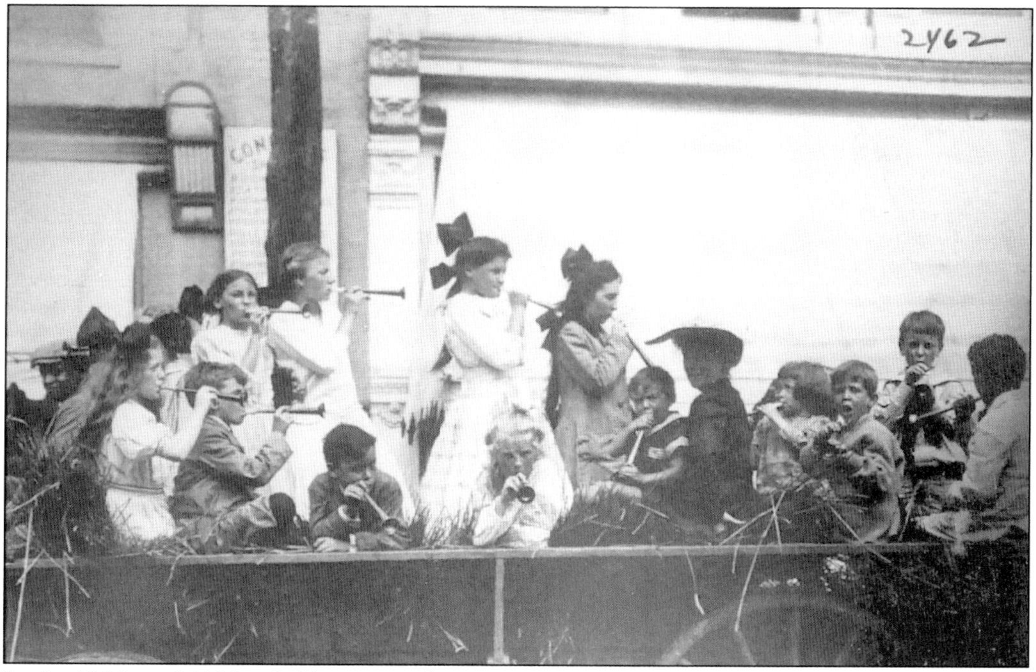

In the 1920s and 1930s, children's parades were very popular. These children riding on Somerset Street were celebrating Halloween.

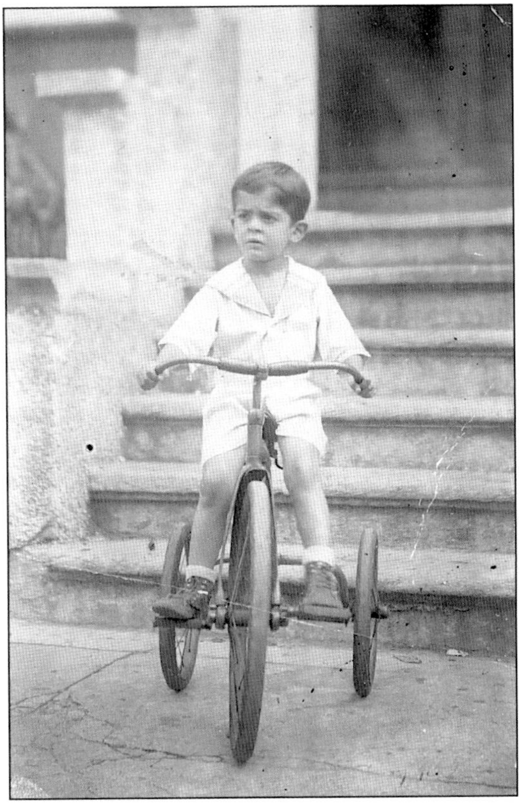

Frank Caruso rides his tricycle in the mid-1930s. Forty years later, he would ride a different high wheeler in the Fourth of July parade with his brother Mario. Notice the Mobil gas station, which is currently the municipal parking lot.

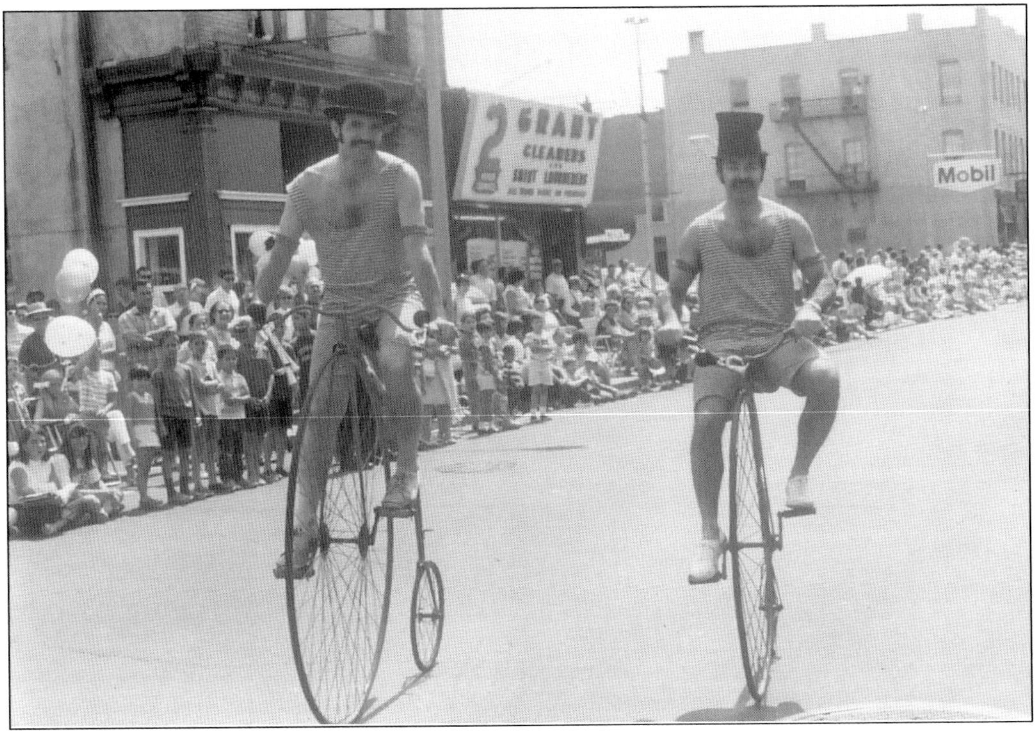

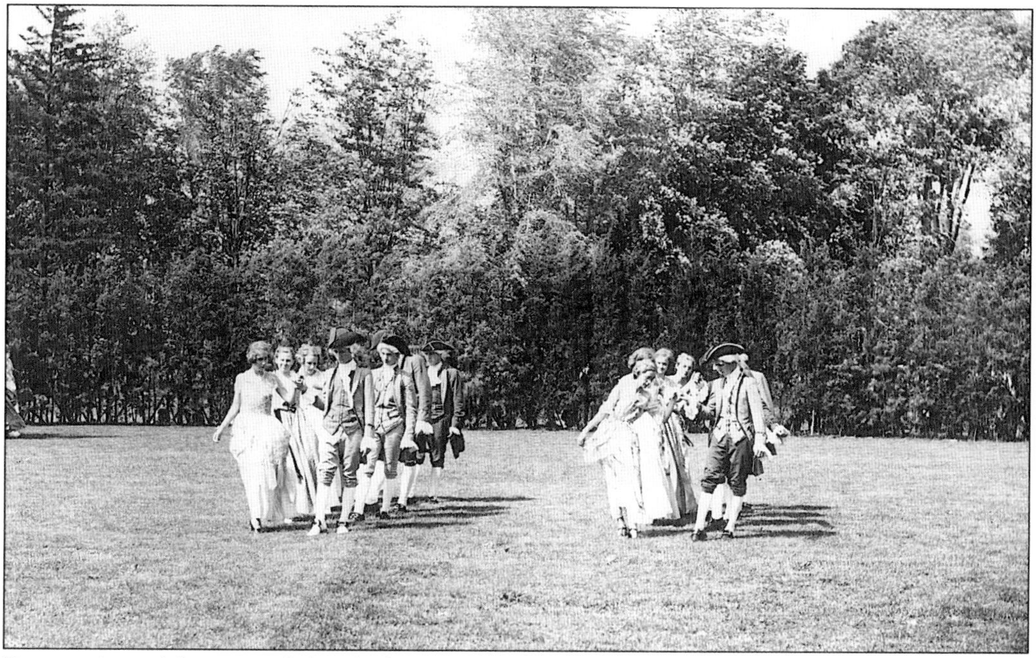

During the celebration of the 50th anniversary of North Plainfield, the Minuet dance was performed by members of the West End Civic Association.

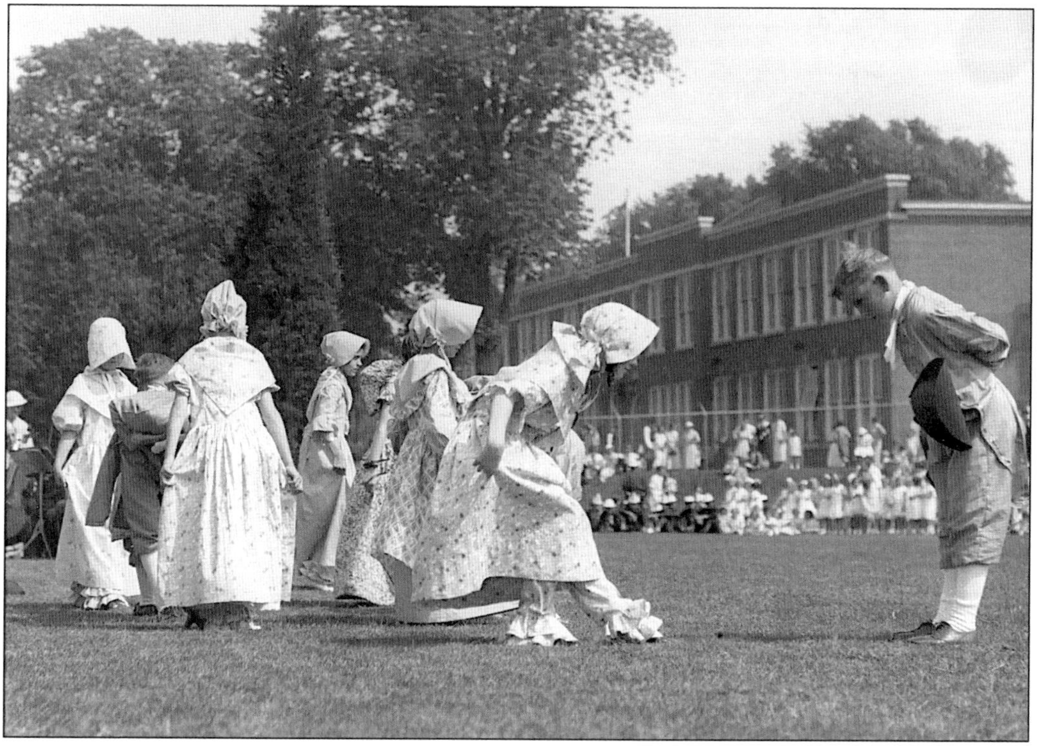

To celebrate the 50th anniversary of the borough, a short, historical play of the life of George Washington was portrayed by various town members. These young members are performing a dance Washington's children would have performed at Mount Vernon in Washington's time.

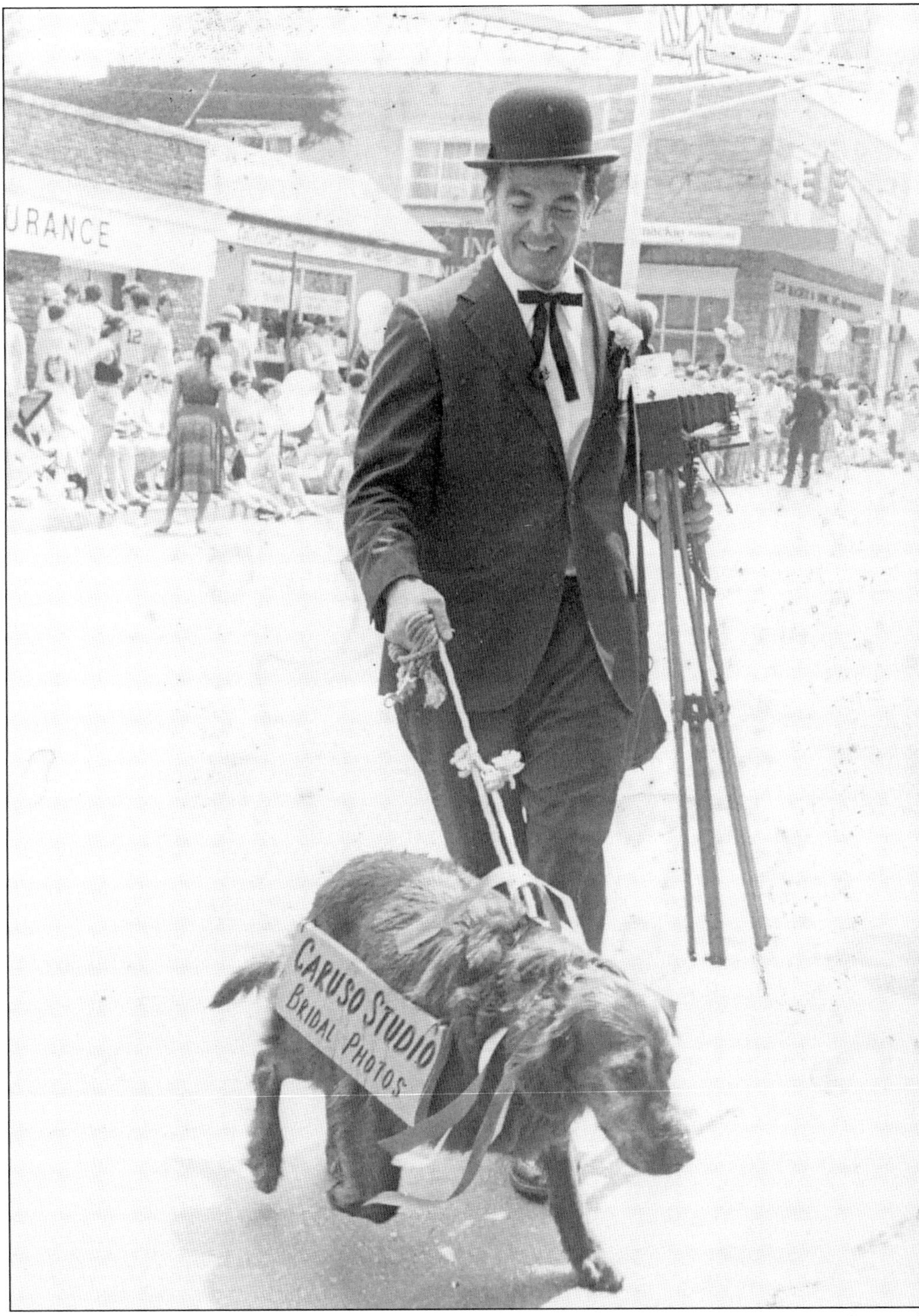

Local photographer Louis Caruso can be seen with his dog Shannon in the annual Fourth of July parade in 1985. This photograph was taken during the early years of his Charley Chaplin routine.

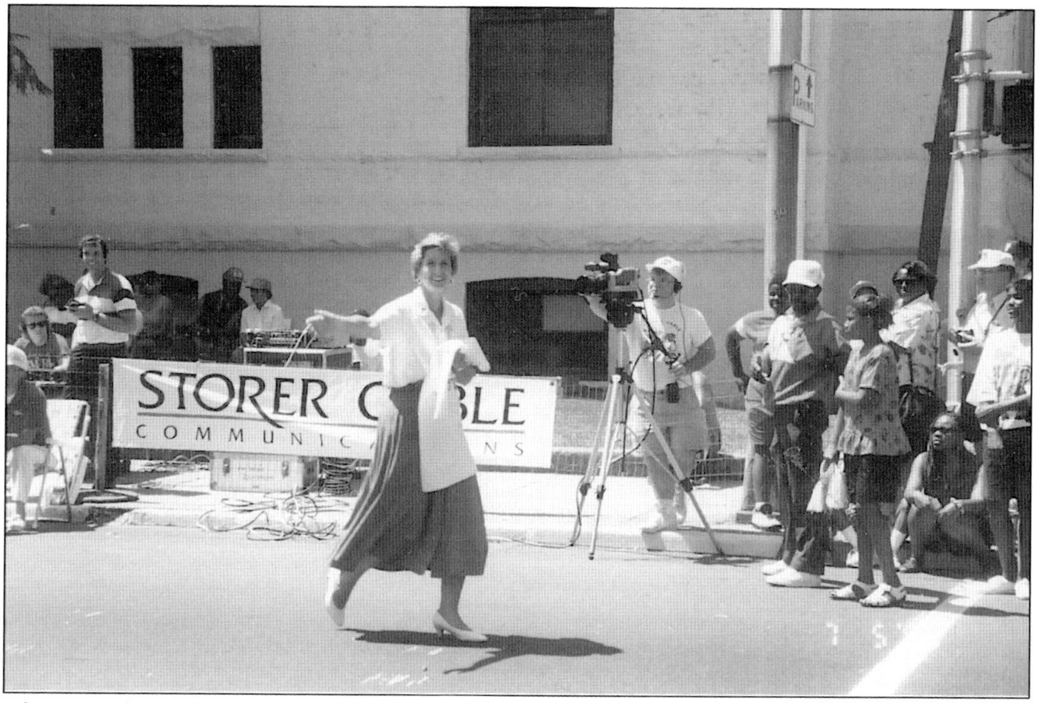

Christie Whitman helps celebrate the Fourth of July in front of Somerset School before she was elected governor.

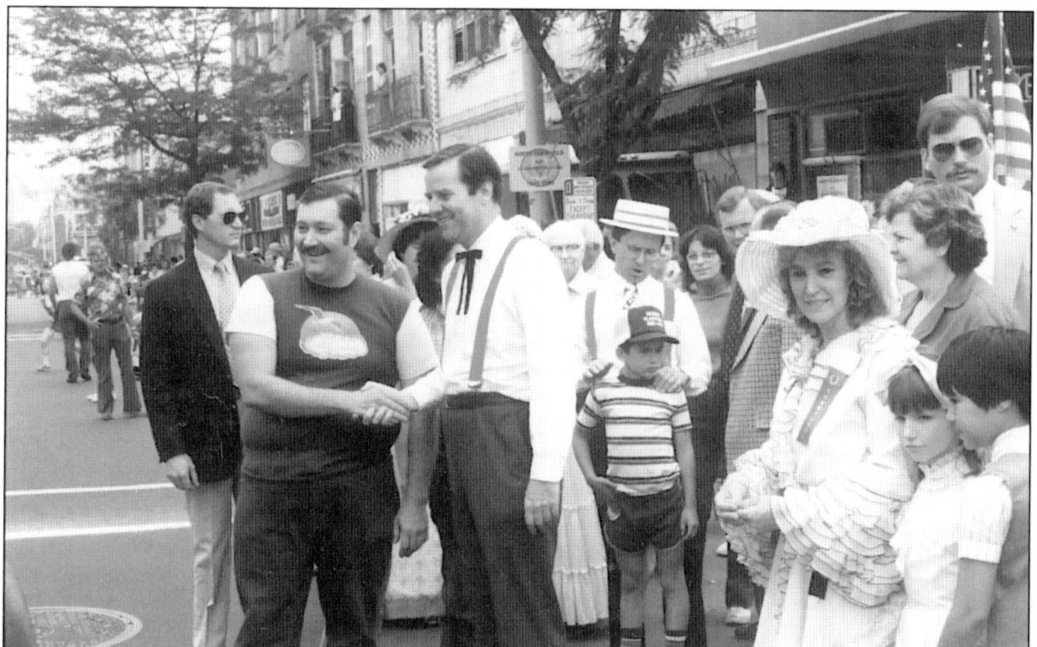

This photograph shows former governor Thomas Kean shaking hands with a local resident. Also pictured are Mayor Steven Novak (in straw hat) and parade chairperson Janice Allen.

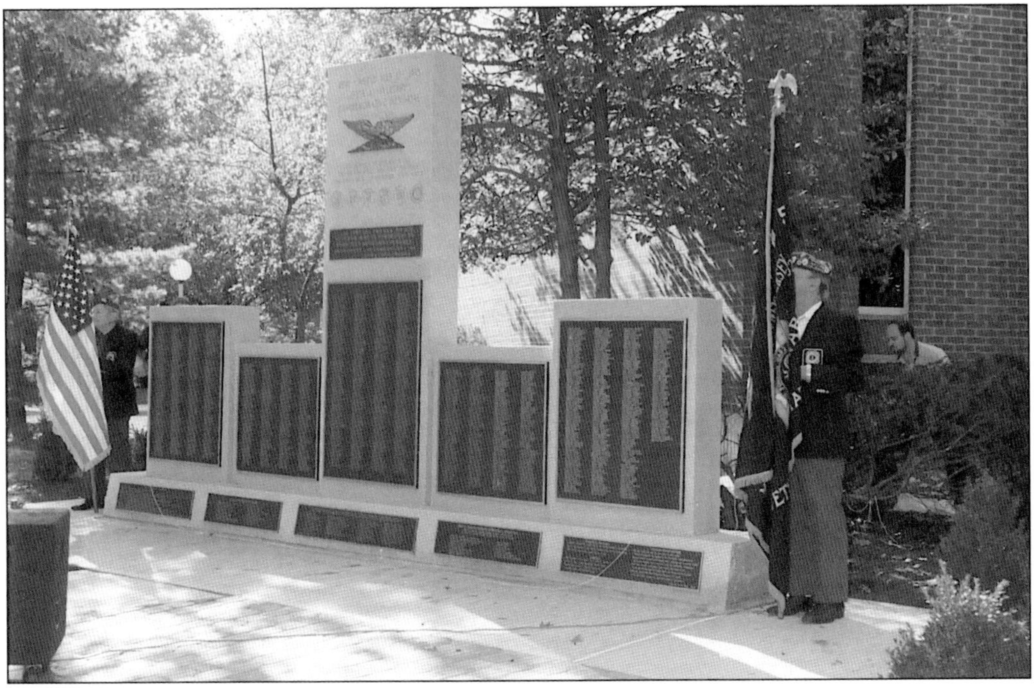

The North Plainfield Veterans World War II memorial was conceived in 1991 by Louis Caruso to honor the men and women of North Plainfield who served their country honorably. The North Plainfield High School Alumni Association adopted the project soon afterward. The monument contains approximately 1,600 names of borough veterans and is located at the North Plainfield Memorial Library. The project was dedicated on October 18, 1998.

Bibliography

The Honorable History and Standing of the Public Schools of North Plainfield 1856–1918. North Plainfield: North Plainfield Board of Education. 1918.

French, Edna, *The Autocrat*, North Plainfield Board of Education. 1897.

Hooker, Ralph Moreton and Rev. A.H. Lewis. *Plainfield, New Jersey Illustrated.* New York: Kittredge Company, 1895.

Kohler, Joann, Bruce Ryno, Norma Schneider, and Holly Jean Dunbar. *Looking Back, A History of North Plainfield.* Plainfield, New Jersey: 1985.

Mustin, M. *Somerset County New Jersey 1688–1930*. Camden, NJ: 1930.

Our Victorian Heritage. North Plainfield, New Jersey: North Plainfield Junior Woman's Club. North Plainfield. 1985.

Plainfield 300 Years 1684–1984. Jostens, Inc. 1987.

Victorian Treasures of North Plainfield. North Plainfield, New Jersey: Washington Park Historic Association. 1988.

Plainfield and Vicinity in Pictures. Plainfield, New Jersey: Courier-News Publishing, 1926.

1985 Celebration Borough of North Plainfield, New Jersey. Green Brook, New Jersey: Echoes-Sentinel. 1985.

Green Brook–North Plainfield Journal. Green Brook, NJ: Green Brook–North Plainfield Journal.

The Plainfield Courier-News, 1935.

The Plainfield Daily Press, Plainfield, NJ.

The Somerset Advocate, Golden Jubilee Edition, June 1935.